'WITH ANGELS AND ARCHANGELS'

'WITH ANGELS AND ARCHANGELS'

Sharing the Worship of Heaven

Bible, Poetry, Liturgy and Devotion
in the Middle Ages

John Blakesley

GRACEWING

First published in England in 2024
by
Gracewing
2 Southern Avenue
Leominster
Herefordshire HR6 0QF
United Kingdom
www.gracewing.co.uk

All rights reserved

No part of this publication may be reproduced,
stored in a retrieval system, or transmitted in any
form or by any means, electronic, mechanical,
photocopying, recording or otherwise,
without the written permission of the publisher.

© 2024, John Blakesley

The rights of John Blakesley to be identified as the author
of this work have been asserted in accordance
with the Copyright, Designs and Patents Act 1988.

ISBN 978 085244 719 2

Cover image: The Choirs of Angels, Rupertsburg Codex
illumination from St Hildegard of Bingen's *Liber Scivias*

Cover design by Bernardita Peña Hurtado

Typeset by Word and Page, Chester, UK

Contents

1. Prologue to the Ninth Century: Office Hymns   1
2. 'Damnable Novelties': Early Tropes and Sequences   9
3. Creativity and Conservatism: The New Poetry in Context   20
4. The Stammerer of St Gall: Notker's Sequences   35
5. English Exuberance: The Winchester Troper   65
6. Paris Fashions: The Regular Sequence   75
7. Poetry and Ecstasy in the Rhineland: Hildegard of Bingen and Elisabeth of Schönau   97
8. Poetry in Motion: Ceremony, Symbol, and Allegory   117
9. The Poetry of the Passion   138
10. 'With Angels and Archangels': Sharing the Worship of Heaven   152

    Notes   169
    Bibliography   181

✠ 1 ✠

Prologue to the Ninth Century: Office Hymns

Those who choose hymns and worship songs for church services in the twenty-first century are almost spoiled for choice. There is a huge and ever-growing number of items that could be selected, and many hymn books contain tables which group hymns according to the seasons of the Christian year. Some also relate hymns to particular passages of Scripture, thus giving poetic and musical reinforcement to the Gospel message.

The situation was very different, however, for Christians in Western Europe in the early ninth century. At that time hymns were confined to the Divine Office, the daily round of non-eucharistic services such as Lauds and Vespers (Morning and Evening Prayer), whose main content was psalms, readings, and prayers. St Augustine of Hippo (d. 430) tells us in his *Confessions* (ix.7) that it was his friend and mentor St Ambrose (d. 397) the Bishop of Milan who first introduced hymns into the Western Church. This happened at a time when Ambrose and his congregation were being persecuted by the soldiers of the boy-emperor Valentinian, whose mother Justina had embraced the heresy of the Arians. (They deny that Jesus is the eternal Son of God, saying 'There was a time when he was not'.) Ambrose strenuously opposed this doctrine, thus becoming the target of Justina's anger. He and his congregation, which included Augustine's mother Monica, were in real danger; they took refuge in the basilica and spent long nights of anxious vigil. Ambrose was clearly aware that communal singing raised people's spirits. Augustine tells us: 'Then it was that the custom arose of singing hymns and psalms, after the use of the Eastern provinces, to save the people from being utterly worn out by their long and sorrowful vigils.' Frederick Raby adds: 'The Basilica at

'With Angels and Archangels'

Milan, beset by the Gothic soldiery of Valentinian, heard the first strains of Catholic hymnody, in which with simplicity and beauty, Ambrose set forth the doctrines of the orthodox faith.'[1]

The simplicity and beauty of Ambrose's hymns meant that they soon became very popular. Their verse-form made them easily memorable: they stayed in the mind and could be remembered in times of particular need. The fact that they were sung had an emotional effect too, allowing those who used them to pray with the heart as well as the head. Augustine again bears witness to this:

> What tears did I shed over the hymns and canticles, when the sweet sound of the music of Thy Church thrilled my soul! As the music flowed into my ears, and Thy truth trickled into my heart, the tide of devotion swelled high within me, and the tears ran down, and there was gladness in those tears.[2]

Augustine goes on to quote the first two verses of Ambrose's evening hymn[3] to illustrate how sleep helped to alleviate his grief after his mother's death:

> O God, creator of us all
> and King of all the heavenly realms,
> You clothe the day with beauteous light,
> the night You grace with quiet sleep.
> May weary bodies find through rest
> the strength to take up work again,
> let minds worn down with grief and care
> obtain refreshment and relief.
> So, when the night's deep shadows fall
> and bring the daylight to a close,
> our faith may still shine on undimmed
> and turn the darkness into light.
> Christ and the Father we adore
> and You, blest Spirit, with them one,
> working through all things mightily:
> cherish us, Holy Trinity.[4]

Ambrose wrote this hymn for his congregation to sing at the lighting of the lamps when darkness was beginning to fall. He takes the simple natural fact that night follows day and sets it in the context of God's creative providence. He looks back in thanksgiving to the beauty of daylight, and looks forward to the night's blessings of rest and healing sleep. Then the kindling lamps become a metaphor of his people's faith, whose inner shining can turn darkness into light. No translation can hope to capture all the resonances of a poem's original words: in the last line the word 'cherish' is an attempt to render Ambrose's *fove*, whose literal meaning is 'keep warm'. It was used of a mother bird warming and protecting her chicks in the nest. Ambrose combines poetic boldness with theological insight in using that word to evoke the warm and tender love of God the Holy Trinity.

The Divine Office is also called the Liturgy of the Hours, and office hymns invited prayerful reflection on the passing hours of each day and night from cockcrow until late evening. They also celebrated the various seasons and festivals of the Christian Year. Here too Ambrose was a pioneer: he wrote a hymn for Christmas Eve which is still sung today in John Mason Neale's translation, 'Come, thou Redeemer of the earth'.[5] Ambrose however wrote an opening verse to this hymn which is missing from the translations in our hymn books:

> O Israel's Shepherd, bow Thine ear,
> enthroned above the Cherubim,
> and show Thyself to Ephraim,
> rouse up Thy mighty power and come.[6]

This is a quotation of the opening verses of Psalm 80 (79):

> Give ear, O Shepherd of Israel,
> Thou who leadest Joseph like a flock!
> Thou who art enthroned upon the cherubim,
> shine forth before Ephraim and Benjamin and Manasseh!
> Stir up Thy might, and come to save us!

Ambrose takes up that cry of the psalmist for God to come and save us with his own:

> Come, Thou Redeemer of the earth,
> And manifest Thy virgin birth ...

In rooting his hymn in the human longings and divine promises of the Old Testament Ambrose is continuing the practice of the Gospel writers. As they write their accounts of the birth of Jesus St Matthew and St Luke are both at pains to show that this saving act is the fulfilment of prophecy and promise: for example, St Matthew's quotation (1:23) of Isaiah 7:9: 'Behold, a virgin shall conceive ...' The human birth of His Son is part of God's loving plan for His people, and the Old Testament scriptures bear witness to its gradual unfolding.

'With Angels and Archangels'

Ambrose is following a traditional method of Christian writers and teachers in taking an Old Testament passage and applying it to Jesus, in order to bring out more of the full significance of Christ's life. Remembering this can help us to make sense of an otherwise puzzling verse later in this hymn:

> Forth from His chamber goeth He,
> that royal home of purity,
> a giant in twofold substance one,
> rejoicing now His course to run.

Though not quoting it directly Ambrose is here echoing Psalm 19 (18) 'The heavens are telling ...'. Verses 4b–6 of that psalm read:

> In them he has set a tent for the sun, which comes forth like a bridegroom leaving his chamber, and like a strong man runs its course with joy. Its rising is from the end of the heavens, and its circuit to the end of them; and there is nothing hid from its heat.

The psalmist is applying two poetic images to the sun: it emerges from the eastern horizon at dawn bringing joyful light to the earth, as a bridegroom emerges with joyful shining face from his wedding-canopy. The irresistible strength of its shining is like that of a mighty warrior, a giant (*gigas* in the Latin version) like the Philistines' champion Goliath. Ambrose sees this psalm-verse as pointing to the coming of Christ, who is the rising Sun of Righteousness promised by Malachi (4:2). Jesus is also the Church's bridegroom and the mighty conqueror of sin and death: He is 'a giant in twofold substance one' because He is both truly God and truly Man. Each of these poetic images sheds its own light on the mystery of Christ's Incarnation: in a few short lines Ambrose allows these Old Testament echoes to resonate in the minds of those who sing his hymn.

In using allusion as well as direct quotation Ambrose is also following a thoroughly biblical method of teaching. The Gospel writers sometimes quoted directly from the Old Testament but also referred to it in a more subtle and oblique fashion. The accounts of the baptism of Jesus (for example, Mark 1:9–11) portray the waters of the Jordan and the Spirit descending like a dove. In minds nurtured on the scriptures this would surely waken echoes of the Spirit moving over the face of the waters in Genesis 1:2 and Noah's dove heralding the renewal of life on earth in Genesis

Prologue to the Ninth Century: Office Hymns

8:8–12. Both echoes reinforce the message that the baptism of Christ marks the beginning of a New Creation.

In a university sermon at Oxford in 1951 Austin Farrer described this aspect of the New Testament writers' work:

> The disciples of Christ understood Christ by seeing his glory scattered in the Old Testament, and by gathering all those scattered lights into his divine splendour ... It was not, of course, the manhood of Christ that they collected from the Old Testament. The man stood before them; they took him in with their eyes and ears. It was the supernatural act and being of God in Christ that they sought in the ancient text, where all the images of divine action and divine indwelling were displayed.[7]

The popularity of Ambrose's hymns meant that other writers began to imitate them. In the following centuries a body of hymns grew up that was called 'Ambrosian' but, apart from those mentioned by Augustine, it is difficult to tell which ones were written by Ambrose himself. In the sixth century St Benedict of Nursia specified in his Rule that each canonical hour should include a hymn. He did not name particular hymns but merely referred to 'the hymn of that hour' or 'the *Ambrosianum*', which could mean 'the hymn by Ambrose' or simply 'the hymn in the style of Ambrose'.[8] The fact that office hymns were an integral part of the Rule of St Benedict meant that they not only survived but flourished and spread as Benedictine monasticism extended its influence throughout the medieval West.

By the ninth century a cycle of office hymns had developed which linked the ordinary Sundays and weekdays of the year with the seven days of creation in Genesis 1. Versions of these hymns by various translators appear in *English Hymnal*. Sunday was the first day of the week; in the Genesis narrative it was the day on which God created light, and it was also the day on which Jesus rose from the dead:

> This day the first of days was made,
> When God in light the world arrayed;
> Or when his Word arose again,
> And, conquering death, gave life to men.[9]

The weekday evening hymns invite prayerful reflection on the beauty and goodness of God's creation. Each day's theme corresponds to that day's creative work by God in the Genesis narrative. Monday, the second day of the week (*feria secunda*), saw the creation of the waters above and below the firmament (Genesis 1:6–8), and so that day's hymn focuses on the refreshing and life-giving character of water:

> E'en so on us who seek thy face
> Pour forth the waters of thy grace;
> Renew the fount of life within,
> And quench the wasting fires of sin.[10]

On the third day the earth is created with all the plants it brings forth (vv. 9–13); Tuesday's hymn is 'Earth's mighty Maker', which mentions 'flowers of golden hue,' 'fruit-trees bearing fruit,' and 'pleasant pasture of the field'.[11] On Wednesday the lights of heaven are created (vv. 14–19) and its hymn begins:

> Most holy Lord and God of heaven,
> Who to the glowing sky has given
> The fires that in the east are born
> With gradual splendours of the morn;
> Who, on the fourth day, didst reveal
> The sun's enkindled flaming wheel,
> Didst set the moon her ordered ways,
> And stars their ever-winding maze.

After rejoicing in the beauty of the created lights the poet then moves on to pray that the light of God's love may shine in the hearts of the singers, bringing cleansing, healing, and freedom:

> Illuminate our hearts within,
> And cleanse our minds from stain of sin;
> Unburdened of our guilty load
> May we unfettered serve our God.[12]

Before the making of human beings on the sixth day and the Sabbath rest there is the creation of birds and fish (vv. 20–3). For the author of Thursday's hymn these two types of creature represent two opposing spiritual dangers for the Christian:

> Be none submerged in sin's distress,
> None lifted up in boastfulness;
> That contrite hearts be not dismayed,
> Nor haughty souls in ruin laid.[13]

Here is sane and wise teaching in the best Benedictine tradition: we are not to get above ourselves, puffed up by spiritual pride, nor are we to be plunged into despair by our sins. Our place in the created order is to occupy the middle ground, aware of our limitations but confident in God's merciful love.

Another Benedictine feature of these hymns is the healthy balance they display between the objective outpouring of praise to the Creator and the inner subjective response of each singer to the love of God. St Benedict said in his Rule 'Let the heart and mind be in harmony with the voice' (*mens concordet voci*). Praising God in the Divine Office is an activity which involves the whole person: body, mind, and spirit. Human minds, of course, have a tendency to wander, and so these hymns ask God to pour out on His people the waters of His grace and to shed His light into their hearts. The worthy fulfilment of the 'work of God' (*opus Dei*), as St Benedict called the Divine Office, requires God's gracious help, and each office begins with a prayer for that help. Before the first outpouring of praise in the 'Glory be' there is the versicle and response taken from the beginning of Psalm 70 (69): 'O God, come to our aid; O Lord, make haste to help us.' Distractions in prayer still inevitably happen but, as Thursday's hymn teaches, no one need be submerged in distress by them. The wandering mind can always wander back again until it is once more in harmony with what the voice is singing or saying. Even when recited in solitude the Office is the prayer of the whole Church: like a thread in a tapestry the individual Christian is part of the mutually supportive fabric of the Body of Christ. Indeed Christ himself prays to the Father in the hearts and minds of his people through His indwelling Spirit.

In composing office hymns St Ambrose and his followers would often take themes and images from the Bible, for example, the Sun of Righteousness or the Days of Creation, and let them unfold into fresh poetic forms to enrich their churches' worship. Though their roots were often biblical, the hymns themselves, of course, were not. Bishops were understandably wary of allowing non-biblical compositions a place in the liturgy: hymns had been widely used by various heretical groups, especially the Gnostics and then the Arians, and it was feared that they could become a vehicle for importing unorthodox teaching. The Council of Braga in 563 forbade all non-biblical hymns but other councils allowed 'Ambrosian hymns' and others whose authorship was known.[14]

'With Angels and Archangels'

While the authority of St Ambrose and St Benedict ensured the survival of office hymns, the appearance in the ninth century of non-biblical compositions in the Eucharist was to arouse fierce episcopal displeasure.

✠ 2 ✠

'Damnable Novelties':
Early Tropes and Sequences

> Because of the altogether damnable wickedness of certain persons who, delighting in novelties, have dared to interpolate their own inventions into the purity of antiquity, it is decreed that no cleric and no monk should presume to add, insert, recite, mutter, or sing any compositions which they call proses (*prosae*), or anything they have made up (*fictiones*), in the Angelic Hymn, that is *Gloria in excelsis Deo* ('Glory to God in the highest'), and in the sequences (*sequentiae*) which are accustomed to be sung solemnly in the Alleluia. If this is done it should be discontinued.

These were the stern words of the bishops assembled at the Council of Meaux in northern France in the year 845. Other decrees of this council have long been known about but this one only came to light in the late twentieth century contained in a manuscript of the early tenth century in Wolfenbüttel's Herzog August Bibliothek.[1]

The two types of composition forbidden by the council are what came to be known as tropes and sequences. Both involved fitting words to the notes of chants sung at Mass. Those who attend eucharistic worship today are used to singing hymns at the beginning (Introit), before the Gospel (Gradual), and at the Offertory and Communion. In the Middle Ages the chants at these points were almost always taken from the Bible and most of them were verses from the psalms. Each Sunday or feast-day had its own proper set of these chants, but as well as the variable chants of the 'Proper' there were also the fixed ones of the 'Ordinary': *Kyrie* ('Lord have mercy'), *Gloria* ('Glory to God in the highest'), *Sanctus* ('Holy, holy, holy'), and *Agnus Dei* ('Lamb of God').

By the time of the Council of Meaux most of these chants were at least two hundred years old, allowing the bishops to refer to

'With Angels and Archangels'

them in terms of 'the purity of antiquity.' Some of their melodies contained long series of notes sung to a single syllable of text. For example, in the Kyrie-melody known from its trope as *Fons bonitatis* the 'e'-vowel of the first 'Kyrie' is sustained throughout a melody of twenty notes before 'eleison' is sung.[2] The author of this trope wrote a twenty-syllable line of text to fit each of these notes with one note per syllable:

> LORD, fountain of goodness, unbegotten Father, from whom all good things proceed, HAVE MERCY.

(Sadly, the English translation does not quite match the syllable-count of the Latin original.)

The Kyrie is a nine-fold chant with 'Lord have mercy', 'Christ have mercy', 'Lord have mercy' each being sung three times. This structure meant that it was natural to see the chant as a plea for mercy to God the Holy Trinity, with each group of petitions addressing in turn the Father, the Son, and the Holy Spirit. Accordingly, the *Fons bonitatis* trope continues:

> LORD, who sent Your Son to suffer for the sin of the world that He might save it, HAVE MERCY;
> LORD, through whose sevenfold Spirit You bestow gifts by which earth is filled with heaven, HAVE MERCY.
> CHRIST, only Son of the Father, whom the holy prophets foretold would be wonderfully born of a virgin into the world, HAVE MERCY;
> CHRIST, holy Lord of heaven's realm, in whose presence the highest of the angels ever sing of Your glorious might, HAVE MERCY;
> CHRIST, heavenly one, listen to our prayers as with humble hearts we devoutly worship You on earth, crying out to You, kind Jesus, HAVE MERCY.
> LORD, nourishing Spirit, close to the Father and the Son, being of one substance with them and breathed from them both, HAVE MERCY;
> LORD, who appeared in the shining form of a dove when Christ was baptized in the waters of Jordan, HAVE MERCY;
> LORD, divine fire, enkindle our hearts, that together we may ever be worthy to cry out HAVE MERCY.

In the manuscript transcribed by Hiley[3] the untroped melody is given after each verse and 'e'-vowels predominate in the Latin text of the trope. This suggests that the trope may have been performed by a soloist or small group of singers while the rest of the choir sang the untroped melody to the 'e' of 'Kyrie'.

'Damnable Novelties': Early Tropes and Sequences

By adding his words to this plea for God's mercy the trope-writer was presenting to its singers a range of theological ideas and biblical images which would make God's nature and attributes more vivid to their minds and so would enrich their devotion. The God whose mercy they seek is first of all the fountain of goodness and the giver of all good things. There is perhaps an allusion here to James 1:17: 'Every good endowment and every perfect gift is from above, coming down from the Father of lights.'

The second verse of the trope recalls God's love shown in the Incarnation and Passion of His Son; its words contain a strong echo of John 3:17: 'For God sent the Son into the world, not to condemn the world, but that the world might be saved through him.'

The sevenfold gifts of the Spirit in the trope's third verse are mentioned in the well-known ninth-century hymn *Veni, Creator Spiritus* ('Come, O Creator Spirit').[4] The phrase's biblical roots are in the seven spirits before God's throne in Revelation 1:4 and in the Spirit-filled branch from the root of Jesse in Isaiah 11:2. Only six varieties or characteristics of the Spirit are counted out in most English versions of this text (the 'fear of the Lord' appears twice) but in the Latin Vulgate, the version used in the Middle Ages, there are seven: 'wisdom and understanding, counsel and might, knowledge and piety, and the fear of the Lord.' There is probably also an allusion to Wisdom 1:7: 'The Spirit of the Lord has filled the world', a text used as the Introit chant on the Holy Spirit's great festival of Pentecost. The writer wakes these biblical echoes and then goes on to add his own delightful touch of poetic individuality: through the gifts of the Spirit 'earth is filled with heaven.'

This note of lyricism entitles the trope-writer, I would suggest, to be called a poet. His work brings together doctrine and devotion, the head and the heart, into a fruitful synthesis. He has already celebrated the work of all three Persons of the Trinity in the first three Kyrie-verses addressed to God the Father. He then goes on to portray God's goodness revealed in the Incarnation of His Son, wonderfully born into the world and yet the Lord of heaven, who in His kindness listens to our prayers. The verses addressed to the Holy Spirit contain several biblical images. The Spirit, one with the Father and the Son, is 'breathed from them both'; this recalls the scene in St John's Gospel where the risen Jesus stands in the midst of His disciples: 'He breathed on them, and said to them, "Receive the Holy Spirit ..."' (John 20:22).

'With Angels and Archangels'

The poet then refers to the descent of the Spirit in the form of a dove when Jesus was baptized (Mark 1:10). In the last verse of the trope the imagery changes to the tongues of divine fire which appeared above the apostles' heads at the first Christian Pentecost in Acts 2:3. The poet prays that the Spirit's flame may also burn in the hearts of the singers, so that they may worthily offer prayer and praise to God. His words echo one of the Pentecost Alleluia-verses sung before the Gospel at Mass: 'Come, Holy Spirit, fill the hearts of Your faithful people, and kindle in them the fire of Your love.'

This final verse of the trope perhaps offers a clue to the poet's motive in adding his words to the Kyrie-chant: he is trying to make more attainable the Benedictine ideal that in worship 'the heart and mind should be in harmony with the voice' – an ideal expressed by St Benedict but applicable to all Christian worship. The poet's balancing of doctrine and devotion is also both typically Benedictine and generally characteristic of a healthy Christian spirituality. It is part of the balanced Benedictine way of life, where Eucharist, Office, and individual prayer have their own important place. (Personal prayer and manual work can blend into each other through recollection of the presence of God.) Martin Thornton writes: 'The genius of St Benedict cannot be confined within the walls of Monte Cassino or any other monastery. The *Regula* [Rule] is not only a system of monastic order, it is a system of ascetical theology, the basis of which is as applicable to modern England as it was to sixth-century Italy.' This basis, says Thornton, is the three-fold Rule of prayer: 'The common Office (*opus Dei*) supporting private prayer (*orationes peculiares*) both of which are allied to, and consummated by, the Mass ... It provides a system of prayer which translates all the clauses of the Creed into practical terms and manifests a living faith in them.'[5]

Tropes to chants other than the Kyrie were usually shorter because these chants lacked the long melismas of the Kyrie, that is, series of notes sung to a single syllable of text. Gunilla Iversen[6] quotes this trope to the Agnus Dei found in manuscripts from Winchester, Cambrai, Le Mans, and St Evroult:

> LAMB OF GOD, WHO TAKE AWAY THE SINS OF THE WORLD, HAVE MERCY ON US.
> Who are true wisdom and the word and power of the Father,
> HAVE MERCY ON US.

'Damnable Novelties': Early Tropes and Sequences

Who sit at the right hand of God's majesty on high, HAVE MERCY ON US.

The Agnus Dei was one of the Eastern elements introduced into the Western liturgy by the Syrian Pope Sergius I in the late seventh century. During the second half of the eleventh century the third 'have mercy on us' came to be replaced by 'grant us peace'. It is, of course, a thoroughly biblical chant, being based on John the Baptist's prophetic witness to Christ in John 1:29: 'Behold, the Lamb of God, who takes away the sin of the world!' The Agnus Dei was sung while the Eucharistic bread was being broken, an action redolent of the sacrificial and saving death of Christ. To address Jesus at this point in the rite as the 'Lamb of God' is to underline the idea that the Eucharist is the Christian Passover: its echoes of Exodus suggest that God's redemptive acts culminated in the death and Resurrection of Christ, by which his people are led out of slavery and into freedom. St Paul applies Passover imagery to the death of Christ in 1 Corinthians 5:7: 'For Christ, our paschal lamb, has been sacrificed.'

The author of this trope allows further biblical images to cluster around the central one of Jesus the Lamb of God, and so illuminates further aspects of the mystery of the Cross: the man dying there, the slain Lamb, is the wisdom and power of God. There is a clear reference here to St Paul's theology of the Cross in 1 Corinthians 1:18 and 24: 'For the word of the cross is folly to those who are perishing, but to us who are being saved it is the power of God ... To those who are called, both Jews and Greeks, Christ the power of God and the wisdom of God.' The poet further develops the paradox of the crucifixion by calling Jesus the 'Word of the Father', echoing the opening verses of St John's Gospel. The crucified Jesus is the divine creative Word, the source of life and light, which even the darkness of Calvary cannot quench. The last line of the trope recalls another biblical text where Jesus is seen as the Word of God, Hebrews 1:3. Here he is enthroned in heaven, having achieved our redemption: 'He reflects the glory of God and bears the very stamp of his nature, upholding the universe by his word of power. When he had made purification for sins, he sat down at the right hand of the majesty on high.'

By his few well-chosen words the trope-writer has both widened the theological range of this Agnus Dei chant and also made the singing of it a richer devotional experience. He offers to its singers a cluster of biblical images to cast fresh light on the Person whose mercy they are seeking and to help their minds and hearts to be in tune with their voices. Perhaps his work also opened up further avenues of meditation which they could explore later in the day and which would help them recollect God's loving presence as they went about their daily tasks.

We know from the edict of the Council of Meaux, quoted at the beginning of this chapter, that tropes, at least to the Gloria, existed by the mid-840s. No actual texts, however, survive from this period. The earliest manuscripts to contain them date from about a century later; among the oldest is Paris, Bibliothèque Nationale lat. 1240, a troper (a book containing tropes and sequences) from Limoges in Aquitaine written about the year 936.[7]

The bishops at Meaux mentioned two points in the liturgy at which unauthorized texts were being inserted: the Gloria and the *'sequentiae* which are accustomed to be sung solemnly in the Alleluia.' The Alleluia chant was sung before the Gospel at Mass and is now often called the Gospel Acclamation. In the Gregorian chant-tradition it was customary to prolong its final a-vowel with a melody called the *jubilus*, which expressed the chant's character of joyful praise. There is evidence from the late eighth century that this wordless melody was sometimes prolonged still further, the extension being called a *sequentia* (a 'following-on' or 'sequence'). The manuscript Brussels, Bibliothèque Royale 10127-10144 was probably written in northern France but is known as the 'Blandiniensis' because it belonged to the Abbey of St Peter on Mont Blandin in Ghent. It contains a list of twenty-five Alleluia chants for the Sundays after Pentecost and beside six of them are the words CUM SEQUENTIA, 'with sequence'.[8]

Around the year 830, only fifteen years before the Council of Meaux, the sequence was still being described by Amalarius of Metz as a wordless melody:

> The Alleluia verse touches the cantor inwardly (*tangit cantorem interius*), so that he considers how he should praise the Lord, or how he should rejoice. This jubilation, which the cantors call the 'sequence', leads our minds and hearts into that state when the speaking of words is not necessary, but the mind will reveal what it holds within itself by thought alone (*sed sola cogitatione mens menti monstrabit quod retinet in se*).[9]

Amalarius allows us here to glimpse what he sees as the devotional effect of the words and music of the liturgy. The cantor, the leading solo singer, is 'inwardly touched' by the words of the Alleluia verse and expresses his joyful praise in a wordless melody which leads its hearers into a state of contemplative joy where words are no longer needed. This then was the earliest form of the sequence, a purely melodic piece which, at least for Amalarius and the cantors he knew, was conducive to contemplation.

Sequences with words clearly appeared soon after Amalarius was writing, and in sufficient numbers to merit the disapproving notice of the bishops at Meaux, but the old wordless variety survived in some places for several centuries. In his essay 'The Repertory of Sequences at Winchester',[10] David Hiley notes that the influential Order of Cluny operated a compromise: sequences were texted at the great festivals but purely melodic for most of the year. Durandus of Mende, writing *c.* 1280, says 'Certain churches mystically "pneumatize" the sequences without words, or at least do that to some of their verses.'[11]

Pneuma, the Greek word for 'breath' or 'spirit', could mean a single musical note but often meant a sung wordless melody. Durandus's use of the word 'mystically' (*mystice*) suggests that some churches still valued the contemplative qualities of the wordless sequence in evoking the transcendence of God's being, a mystery beyond words.

In the fourteenth century the choir of York Minster seem to have devised a way of combining both the wordless melody and the complete text of a sequence. One of the manuscripts of the York Missal[12] contains a rubric directing that the words of the sequence for the Fourth Sunday in Advent should be sung from the pulpitum by four Vicars Choral and that the choir should repeat the melody, sung to the vowel 'a', after each verse except the last.[13] The manuscript had been given to the parish church of Cuckney in Nottinghamshire, but its rubrics indicate that either it had been written for use in the Minster or it had been copied from a Cathedral book.

This sequence *Jubilemus omnes* was sung throughout England and France on the Fourth Sunday in Advent. It is an early sequence, being found in the oldest of the surviving tropers[14] and could well have been written in the ninth century. Like trope-writers, the authors of texted sequences generally followed the principle of fitting one syllable of text to one note of music, but the length

'With Angels and Archangels'

of the sequence-melodies gave them many more notes to play with. The poet of *Jubilemus omnes* had space to unfold the verse in Genesis 'And God saw everything that he had made, and behold, it was very good' (1:31) into a lyrical celebration of the beauties of Creation.

> Let us all rejoice in our God, who created all things
> and set the universe on its foundations:
> the sky, sparkling with the varied light of a myriad stars;
> the shining splendour of the sun, giving order to the world;
> the moon, adorning the night with her beauty;
> sea and land, mountains, plains, and deep rivers;
> the vast open spaces of the air,
> through which the birds and the winds fly, and the rains fall.
> All these things combine to serve You alone, O God our Father;
> now and through all the ages of eternity their praise resounds to Your glory.
> For our salvation You sent Your only Son to this earth;
> guiltless Himself, He suffered for our sins.
> O Trinity, we ask You to rule over our hearts and bodies,
> and grant to us sinners Your pardon and protection.

In the last four lines the theme and mood of the poem changes from joyful praise to a more sombre note as Christ's Incarnation and Passion are recalled. The melody also changes at this point; its pitch goes up a fifth before moving back for the last verse. The poet moves from Creation to Redemption, and ends with a prayer to the Trinity for guidance, protection, and pardon.

The melody was known as *Veni Domine*, from the Alleluia-verse for the Fourth Sunday in Advent: 'Come, Lord, and do not delay; release Your people from their sins.' Sequences for feasts of virgins were also written to this melody, hence its alternative title *Adducentur*, an allusion to Psalm 45:14 (Vulgate 44:15): 'The virgins that be her fellows shall be brought unto the king'.[15]

It seems strange at first sight that an Advent sequence should be so largely devoted to the theme of Creation. A possible explanation may be found in the biblical texts that were used in worship at that time of the Church's year. The poem's opening invitation to rejoice in God recalls the first of the proper Mass texts for the previous Sunday: 'Rejoice in the Lord always' (Philippians 4:4). The prophet Isaiah was read at Matins during Advent; in several passages God's promise of Redemption is set in the context of Creation. On the Tuesday before Advent IV the reading is Isaiah

'Damnable Novelties': Early Tropes and Sequences

42:1–12. The coming of the promised Saviour was seen to be prefigured in verses 1–4: 'Behold my servant, whom I uphold, my chosen in whom my soul delights; I have put my Spirit upon him ...' Then in verse 5 the theme of Creation appears: 'Thus says God, the Lord, who created the heavens and stretched them out, who spread forth the earth and what comes from it ...' It reappears in verses 10–12: 'Sing to the Lord a new song, his praise from the ends of the earth! ... Let the inhabitants of Sela sing for joy, let them shout from the top of the mountains. Let them give glory to the Lord, and declare his praise in the coastlands.' Perhaps the poet of *Jubilemus omnes* saw himself as providing this 'new song' of joyful praise, in which Creation gives glory to God who is both its Maker and its Redeemer.

Among the texted sequences in the early tropers are a few which are only partially texted, where words have been fitted to just two or three melodic phrases. This seems to be another form of compromise between the sequence as a purely wordless melody and one which is fully texted. There is no evidence to support the idea that partially texted sequences represent an early stage in the evolution of the *genre*, though that remains a possibility. This example, found in Spanish sources and at Cluny,[16] is a Christmas piece, *Ecce puerpera*:

> See, a mother's womb has brought forth Emmanuel,
>   King of the ages.
> The mighty God most high, promised in the oracles
>   of the prophets.
> May He grant us all the eternal rewards which are His
>   and His Father's.
> To Him be salvation and victory and grace throughout
>   endless ages.[17]

The word 'Emmanuel' recalls the quotation of Isaiah 7:14 in Matthew 1:23: 'Behold, a virgin shall conceive and bear a son, and his name shall be called Emmanuel (which means, God with us)'. This biblical echo helps the poet to express something of the mystery of the Incarnation in just a few words: Mary's new-born baby is 'the mighty God most high'. The first couplet is set to part of the fifth section of the melody and is followed by three more wordless sections. Perhaps this provided some contemplative space for minds and hearts to ponder the mystery expressed in the poet's words. Then comes the second couplet, in which the focus changes from contemplation of Emmanuel's birth to the hope of sharing in the blessings He brings. The phrase 'His and His Father's' may echo Jesus' words about the Spirit in John 16:15: 'All that the Father has is mine; therefore I said that he will take what is mine and declare it to you.'

After contemplating the generous love of God revealed in the Incarnation the poem fittingly ends with an ascription of praise, which goes on resounding wordlessly through the last three sections of the melody.

Although the text of *Ecce puerpera* consists merely of two couplets, its structure demonstrates the feature of 'progressive repetition', which is characteristic of most early sequences. Apart from the first and last phrases, which are 'singles', each section of the melody is repeated. When words are fitted to the music, this results in a series of paired verses or 'double-versicles'. Each half of a double-versicle has the same number of syllables as its twin because it is sung to the same melody. The next double-versicle has a different melody and therefore a different line-length. The translation above attempts to reproduce this feature: the first pair of lines has seventeen syllables each and the second pair has eighteen. In a fully texted sequence a subtle pattern thus emerges, which is a satisfying blend of repetition and variation.

Stans a longe displays this typical structure but is unusual in not being related to an Alleluia. Instead, its opening words and melody come from an antiphon at Lauds on the Tenth Sunday after Pentecost.[18] There are scriptural echoes in *Ecce puerpera* but *Stans a longe* is thoroughly biblical: it is a meditation on the parable of the Pharisee and the publican in Luke 18:9–14.

> Standing afar off
> was a man who had committed many crimes,
> and his troubled mind was dwelling on his sins.
> He would not raise his eyes towards the high starry heaven
> but, beating his breast, he said these words, his face full of tears:
> 'God, be merciful to me, a sinner,
> and in your goodness wipe out my misdeeds.'
> These words won for him pity and kindness
> and he went to his house a righteous man.
> Gladly following his example, let us say to God:
> 'Merciful God, be gentle with us and free us from sin,
> in Your kindness treat us as righteous.'[19]

'Damnable Novelties': Early Tropes and Sequences

The poet ignores the self-righteous Pharisee in the story and concentrates on the penitent tax-collector. His imagination brings this figure to vivid life by a skilful sketching-in of detail, such as the tears on the man's face. His penitence is an example which the singers of this sequence are encouraged to follow: the poem ends with a prayer which involves the singers in their own petition for forgiveness. The musical theorist Hucbald of St Amand, writing about the year 900, quotes this sequence to illustrate various musical intervals, so it must have been well-known at least in north-eastern France by that time.[20]

It was commonly sung throughout the Middle Ages all over Europe on that Sunday, known in England as the Eleventh after Trinity, when its theme was the Gospel of the day. In the fourteenth century the monks of Whitby Abbey were using it, appropriately enough, on the feast of the ex-publican St Matthew.[21]

The three early sequences quoted in this chapter have a common devotional pattern: objective meditation moves into subjective petition. Creation is the main subject of *Jubilemus omnes*, Incarnation that of *Ecce puerpera*, and the penitent publican is contemplated in *Stans a longe*. In all three the meditative section of the poem is followed by a prayer which seems to encourage the singers to enter more deeply into their own personal relationship with God and to seek for themselves the blessings of His merciful love. In their different ways the three poets seem to have in view the same Benedictine ideal, that minds and hearts should be in harmony with voices.

Tropes and sequences clearly enriched the devotions of medieval Christians; by the end of the Middle Ages there were over five thousand sequences in existence throughout Europe. In his essay 'Notker in Aquitaine'[22] Alejandro Planchart aptly compares the bishops at Meaux to King Canute on the sea-shore trying to halt the advancing waves: tropes and sequences were a rising and unstoppable poetic tide.

Notker's sequences deserve a chapter to themselves, but first it might be useful to explore something of the context of the new liturgical poetry and to ask why its use of poetic images, often derived from the Bible, was both opposed and defended.

✠ 3 ✠

Creativity and Conservatism: The New Poetry in Context

THE CULTURAL LEGACY OF TROPES AND SEQUENCES

The Anglican Benedictine scholar Anselm Hughes says that 'a grimace of friendly incredulity' was turned in his direction by a musical expert at the BBC when during a radio programme the sequence was described by Dom Anselm as 'the parent of oratorio and the grandparent of the modern drama'.[1] It does seem a large claim to make for these ninth-century innovations in the liturgy but the claim can be substantiated.

The *Quem quaeritis* ('Whom do you seek?') is a trope in dialogue form which preceded the Introit of the Mass on Easter Day. Its wide distribution in the tenth century suggests that it was composed in the ninth.[2] In the English version from Winchester (*c.* 970) the trope has become a miniature play with stage directions: a monk in a white alb holding a palm sits beside the Easter Sepulchre to represent the angel at the tomb, while three monks in copes carrying thuribles and incense are the women with spices seeking the body of Jesus.[3] Later in the Middle Ages the Easter sequence *Victimae paschali* ('Christians to the Paschal Victim')[4] was sometimes sung as part of this play.

Other liturgical and biblical plays joined *Quem quaeritis* in the monastic repertoire, including the Christmas story with shepherds and midwives, the Wise Men at Epiphany, and the story of Daniel in the lions' den.[5] The dramas also moved outside the church and into the streets: the whole history of salvation from Creation to Last Judgement was enacted in a series of pageants performed by the craft guilds in many towns and cities, usually at the festivals of Whitsuntide and Corpus Christi. A touch of humour was sometimes shown in the way plays were assigned to particular guilds:

in Chester the watermen of the River Dee were given the task of enacting Noah's Flood.[6] The fifteenth-century Resurrection play performed by the carpenters of York has come a long way from the *Quem quaeritis* trope; its cast includes, as well as the angel and the three women, Pilate, Annas, Caiaphas, a centurion, and four soldiers.[7] From these 'mystery' or 'miracle' plays grew moralities such as the fifteenth-century *Everyman*, and so the scene was set for Marlowe, Shakespeare, and secular drama.

The composers of early tropes and sequences unwittingly left a rich legacy to later European culture. Ninth-century creativity produced not only the seeds of drama but also the beginnings of polyphony. In the treatise *Musica enchiriadis* (c. 850) there are examples of a form of part-singing called 'organum', where one group of voices sings the main tune while another group sings the same melody at an interval of a fourth or a fifth. Later the subsidiary tune began to differ from the main melody and went its own way.[8]

Sequence-texts themselves have inspired some sublime music, including the spine-tingling settings of *Dies irae* ('Day of wrath')[9] in the Requiems of Mozart and Verdi, and the haunting beauty of Fauré's setting of *Pie Jesu*, that sequence's poignant final verse: 'Lord all-pitying, Jesu blest, grant them Thine eternal rest.'

The creativity which began to flower during the ninth century had its roots in that revival of learning and Christian culture known as the 'Carolingian Reform' (or 'Renaissance').

THE CAROLINGIAN REFORM

The adjective 'Carolingian' refers to Charlemagne (Charles the Great, d. 814), who was king of the Franks from 768 and was crowned as Holy Roman Emperor in 800. His empire at the time of his death included most of what is now France, Germany, and the northern two-thirds of Italy. Charlemagne was determined to improve the educational standards of the Frankish clergy and to further their spiritual formation. As Jean Leclercq says, 'The revival of studies was intended to teach the monks and the clerics the right way to live, and at the same time how to speak well and write well in order to pray well'.[10] Charlemagne managed to attract to his court at Aachen some of the best scholars of the age. Alcuin of York (d. 804) was master of the palace school, where the curriculum was based on the study of classical authors such as Virgil as well as Christian poets. Alcuin later took over the school at Tours, while the poet Theodulf (d. 821) became Bishop of Orléans. His Palm Sunday hymn *Gloria, laus, et honor* ('All glory, laud, and honour') is written in a classical verse-form, the elegiac couplet, and has proved to be a lasting fruit of Charlemagne's revival of learning. Classical metres remained popular for much of the Middle Ages: many tropes and some sequences were written in hexameters, as were Graces at meals and other Blessings.

It took time, of course, for the educational reforms to bear fruit in the lives of the clergy, and Charlemagne was impatient to see results. In his biography of the emperor Notker tells of an occasion when Charlemagne asked Alcuin why he should not have twelve clerics as learned and holy as Jerome and Augustine. Alcuin replied 'The Maker of heaven and earth Himself has very few scholars worth comparing with these men, and yet you expect to find a dozen!'[11]

Two documents give a glimpse of how the educational programme could be put into practice in pastoral situations, helping ordinary priests and laypeople towards a better understanding of their faith. In 802 Theodulf issued statutes for his diocese which directed priests to encourage laypeople to say their prayers each morning and evening, preferably in church, and he provided some specimen prayers for their use.[12] About the same time another court scholar, Angilbert, produced a document describing how the services should be conducted at his abbey of St Riquier near Abbeville on the Somme. The Rogation procession here was not confined to the monks but included people from all the surrounding villages. They brought crosses, relics, and banners from their churches as they processed through the fields singing litanies and other chants, and asking God's protection and blessing on the land. Everyone walked seven abreast as a reminder of the sevenfold gifts of the Spirit in Isaiah 11; those too infirm to walk rode on horseback. The literate encouraged the illiterate to join in the litany responses, the schoolboys and anyone else who could sang the Lord's Prayer and the three Creeds: Apostles', Nicene, and 'Athanasian'.[13] Here was a piece of inclusive communal liturgy and an example of learning by doing; everyone could join in this devotional act at their own level, and be encouraged to grow in their knowledge and practice of the Faith.

The New Poetry in Context

After Charlemagne died in 814 his educational policies were continued by his successor, Louis the Pious. By this time, thanks to these policies, there were more and more monks and priests who were literate enough to try their hand at poetic composition. The most likely impetus for the writing of the first tropes came from the monastic reforms of the Council of Aachen in 817. The driving force behind these was Benedict of Aniane, one of the liturgical experts at the imperial court, whose monastery of Kornelimünster near Aachen became a model for monastic life throughout the empire. This Benedict added considerable elaborations to the original Benedictine pattern of worship: before Matins the monks said the Our Father and the Apostles' Creed at each of the altars in the church, and these visits were repeated before Prime and after Compline. The fifteen Gradual Psalms (or Songs of Ascents, Psalms 120–34, Vulgate 119–33) were said each day as an act of intercession for the monastery's benefactors, living and departed, and the whole psalter was recited on weekdays in Lent. All this, of course, was in addition to the psalmody in the regular Offices.[14]

Processions before Mass were another of Benedict of Aniane's innovations, and it has been plausibly suggested by Paul Evans that tropes were composed in order to make the Introit chant long enough to cover these entrance-processions.[15] Support for this suggestion comes from Pierre-Marie Gy's researches into the diffusion of early tropes, which point to Lotharingia as their likely region of origin. This was the central part of the empire which included Aachen and Metz, renowned as a centre of musical excellence.[16]

Amalarius of Metz played a large part in producing the documents issued by the Council of Aachen. One of these gives instructions to cantors: they should not let their art make them forget humility; they should accommodate their chants to the needs of the church; psalms should have a more simple tone than hymns.[17] These instructions imply that cantors enjoyed a certain amount of freedom in the exercise of their art; one wonders if the freedom extended to the composition of new chants or merely to making selections from an existing repertoire. The passage from Amalarius's *Liber Officialis*, quoted in Chapter 2 to illustrate the wordless nature of the early sequence, also demonstrates the cantor's freedom. He is 'touched inwardly' by the Alleluia-verse 'so that he considers how he should praise the Lord, or how he should rejoice.' Again it is not clear whether the cantor then chooses an existing melody or whether he freely extemporizes one to express his inner joy.[18]

Although the earliest mention of tropes and sequence-texts is their condemnation at Meaux in 845, it is not unreasonable to imagine a cantor, perhaps sometime in the 830s, extending his freedom to add words to the melodies he was artfully chanting. The literary skills were available by then, and the Council of Aachen had provided a suitably elaborate liturgical setting.

THE EUCHARISTIC CONTEXT

Tropes and sequences added their own strands of poetic imagery to a rite that was already a richly symbolic tapestry of words and actions. At its heart is a mystery which is at once very simple and inexhaustibly profound. At one level it could be described as an enacted poetic image. A. N. Wilson writes

> This action – taking bread, breaking it, repeating the words of Jesus, 'This is My Body' – is something which Christians have been doing as long as there have been Christians ... People have felt in it that they knew the presence of Christ. It is the centre of Christian life, and of its tradition.[19]

In a lyrical passage in *The Shape of the Liturgy* Gregory Dix evokes the great variety of the circumstances in which Christians have fulfilled Jesus' command to 'do this' in remembrance of him:

> Was ever another command so obeyed? For century after century ... this action has been done, in every conceivable human circumstance, for every conceivable human need from infancy and before it to extreme old age and after it, from the pinnacles of earthly greatness to the refuge of fugitives in the caves and dens of the earth. Men have found no better thing than this to do for kings at their crowning and for criminals going to the scaffold; for armies in triumph or for a bride and bridegroom in a little country church.[20]

Millions of Christians still obey this command for a simple reason which was expressed by Austin Farrer in a sermon preached just a few days before he died: 'You know what is the special mercy of Christ to us in the Sacraments. It is, that he just puts himself there.'[21]

Christians find in the Eucharist the presence of Christ; he makes himself known 'in the breaking of the bread' as he did to the disciples at Emmaus (Luke 24:35). As he gives himself sacramentally to his people, he reaffirms that union with himself which they received in baptism. Christ's presence in the Eucharist brings with it all the blessings he achieved by his incarnate life, death, and Resurrection. As Farrer wrote in his essay 'The Body of Christ',

> The sacrifice of Christ is present on the altar in the same way as the body of Christ is present; that is, in being set amongst us and united with us ... Both sacrifice and body, the one heavenly body and the sacrifice once for all offered, extend themselves to embrace us in the sacrament.[22]

In the Old Testament the ideas of sacrifice and covenant are closely related. A covenant or agreement was often sealed by the sacrifice of animals, as in God's covenant with Abram in Genesis 15:9. The words of Jesus at the Supper bring sacrifice and covenant together in a new way: it is His own body that is to be offered; the New Covenant is in His own blood which will be shed for the remission of sins.

These two biblical ideas of sacrifice and covenant are dominant themes in the eucharistic liturgy used in the churches where tropes and sequences originated. This was the Roman Rite, and its promotion was an important part of Charlemagne's programme of reforms.[23] Its eucharistic prayer, known as the Canon of the Mass, contains intercessions for God's people and a reminder of the Communion of Saints, but these are in the context of prayer for the acceptance of the offerings.[24] In the heart of the Canon, the Institution Narrative, the prayer is answered when the offerings are identified with the one acceptable offering of Jesus himself.

Sacrifice and covenant are also dominant concepts in the Letter to the Hebrews, and the second half of the Canon contains several echoes of this New Testament book. The figure of Melchisedek is both the type of a sacrifice of bread and wine (Genesis 14:18) and the type of a covenant establishing an eternal priesthood. In Hebrews 7:21 the writer quotes Psalm 110 (109):4, 'You are a priest for ever after the order of Melchisedek', and sees this text as foreshadowing the eternal priesthood of Jesus. The same writer in verses 4 and 17 of Chapter 11 mentions Abel and Abraham as examples of those whose sacrifices were acceptable because they were offered in faith (Genesis 4:4; 22:9). In the section of the

Canon beginning *Supra quae* the celebrant asks God to accept the eucharistic offerings 'as You vouchsafed to accept the gifts of Your righteous servant Abel, and the sacrifice of our patriarch Abraham, and that which Your high priest Melchisedek offered to You, a holy sacrifice, an unblemished victim'.[25] These three figures appear in vivid colour in a sixth-century mosaic in the apse of the basilica of S. Apollinare in Classe near Ravenna. Melchisedek is in the centre, offering bread and wine on an altar, flanked by Abel with his lamb and Abraham with the boy Isaac.[26]

Christ the Eternal Priest has entered once for all into the heavenly sanctuary (Hebrews 9:24); in the Book of Revelation that sanctuary and its altar are served by ministering angels (Revelation 14:17–18). The next section of the Canon, *Supplices te*, combines these biblical images with the early Christian idea that every altar at its consecration receives a guardian angel.[27] Bowing low over the altar the priest prays that the gifts may be 'borne by the hands of Your angel to Your altar on high in the sight of Your divine majesty, that all of us who have received the most holy body and blood of Your Son by partaking at this altar may be filled with all heavenly blessing and grace'. St Ambrose, however, speaks of 'angels' in the plural when he quotes a version of the Canon in his instructions to baptism candidates.[28] This prayer vividly evokes the sense that earthly worshippers are participating in the eternal worship of God in heaven, an idea that would be prominent in many tropes and sequences. It is also present in the Preface and Sanctus ('Holy, holy, holy') which precede the Canon. Here human voices join with the angelic hosts of heaven in the song of the seraphim (Isaiah 6:3).

The Roman Rite, then, was steeped in biblical imagery and its language was sober and concise, with finely balanced phrases and legal precision in its use of words. 'Make this offering wholly blessed, approved, ratified, reasonable, and acceptable' the priest prays in the *Quam oblationem* section of the Canon.[29] In the *Te igitur* God is asked 'to accept and bless these gifts, these offerings, these holy and unblemished sacrifices.' This use of near-synonyms in pairs or triplets is also found in pagan prayer-texts from Rome. Christine Mohrmann quotes a prayer said by Cato to accompany a field-lustration: 'that you would avert, banish, and keep away diseases seen and unseen, widowhood and devastation, disasters and storms.[30]'

The New Poetry in Context

In the *Book of Common Prayer* Cranmer would continue this Roman habit of using pairs of near-synonyms in liturgical writing; the penitential introduction to Morning and Evening Prayer contains four examples in its first sentence: 'acknowledge and confess', 'sins and wickedness', 'dissemble nor cloke', 'goodness and mercy'.

In its thoroughly biblical content and carefully constructed prayer-style the Roman liturgy contrasts sharply with the form of worship which preceded it in Gaul, the Gallican Rite. Its language tended to be verbose, inflated, and rambling. This is an extract from a long eucharistic prayer for an ordinary Sunday:

> You snatched us from perpetual death and the last darkness of hell, and gave mortal matter, put together from the liquid mud, to Your Son and to eternity ... When You had overcome chaos and the confusion of the beginning and the darkness in which things swam, You gave wonderful form to the amazed elements; the tender world blushed at the fires of the sun, and the rude earth wondered at the dealings of the moon.[31]

This prayer breathes a different devotional atmosphere from the sober precision of the Roman Rite; its emotional tone is reminiscent of a Romantic poet contemplating the beauties of Creation: Wordsworth and his daffodils compared to the cool classicism of Milton. Gallican liturgical language is much more emotionally charged than Roman; for example, 'amazed' and 'blushed' in the extract quoted above. What sometimes appears to be a verbose and rambling prayer-style could be viewed in a more sympathetic light as simply a leisurely and expansive way of praying. Gallican prayers can sometimes contain both biblical imagery and pleasing turns of phrase, as in this *Immolatio* (Proper Preface) for the beginning of Lent in the *Missale Gothicum*:

> Holy Father, as we take up our Lenten discipline, Your only Son, who lives in Your glory, nourishes our faith, increases our hope, and strengthens our love. He is the true and living bread, which came down from heaven, and yet remains in heaven for ever. He is the very substance of eternity and the food of virtue. For Your Word, by whom all things were made, is both the bread of our human spirits and also the bread of angels.[32]

The conjunction of faith, hope, and love is a clear reference to 1 Corinthians 13:13, and that particular piece of seventh-century French liturgy has been incorporated into the Post-Communion

Prayer for the First Sunday of Lent in the Anglican *Common Worship*. The 'living bread which came down from heaven' comes from Jesus' discourse in John 6:51, and the phrase 'bread of angels' is an echo of Psalm 78 (77):25: 'Man ate of the bread of the angels; he sent them food in abundance.'

As well as the contrasting prayer-styles the Gallican Rite differed from the Roman in having a much greater proportion of variable texts. The Roman eucharistic prayer, apart from a short Proper Preface and a couple of extra clauses on major festivals, was fixed and invariable throughout the year. The Gallican Rite had only two fixed elements in its eucharistic prayer, the Sanctus and the Institution Narrative; everything else varied from one Mass to the next. W. S. Porter pointed out the theological dangers of this when he wrote: 'The vital reference to the sacrifice of Christ – apart from the Institution formula – may almost or entirely disappear in a welter of hagiology and rhetoric.'[33]

The Roman Rite as celebrated in the Carolingian Empire did acquire some elements of Gallican pedigree, for example, the priest's personal devotions at the Offertory and before the Communion, but there was no opportunity to indulge the Frankish taste for expansive emotional prayers proper to each Mass. This fact could explain to some extent why sequences became so popular in the second half of the ninth century despite being officially condemned. They provide space for discursive meditation on the theme of the day's liturgy; they are not afraid of emotionally charged language – the celebratory exclamation *Eia* occurs frequently; they often end in direct personal prayer. All these features would suit Frankish devotional tastes, and a Mass with troped chants and a sequence would have a rather more Gallican proportion of variable texts than one without those adornments.

As was noticed at the beginning of the previous chapter, the creativity which produced these new texts was met with fierce opposition from the forces of conservatism. Were the bishops at Meaux simply motivated by a natural resistance to liturgical innovation? The vehemence of their language ('altogether damnable wickedness') suggests that something deeper lay behind their condemnation of tropes and sequences. The next section explores what this might have been.

The New Poetry in Context

LITERALISTS OF LYON

There is a suspicious similarity between the language used at the Council of Meaux and some of the writings of Agobard, Archbishop of Lyon (d. 840), and his archdeacon Florus (d. 860). These two men firmly believed that only texts from the Bible should be sung in church. In the eighth century the Roman Office had acquired some non-biblical antiphons and responsories for certain major feasts and processions, most of these being translations from the Greek.[34] Agobard removed all this material from the Lyon service-books and described it in his work *On Correcting the Antiphonary* as 'either superfluous, or trivial, or lying, or blasphemous'.[35]

At the top of the list of texts to which he took exception is the antiphon to Magnificat at Vespers on Christmas Eve, *Dum* (or *Cum*) *ortus fuerit*: 'When the sun has risen in the heavens, you will see the King of kings proceeding from the Father, like a bridegroom from his chamber.' Agobard claims that this denies Christ's taking of humanity from the Virgin, and says that it shows 'notable temerity and is an evident lie'.[36]

It is hard to understand why Agobard should see this antiphon as a denial of Christ's humanity. Its author does not explicitly mention the Virgin Birth, but on Christmas Eve it would be natural to assume that this would be at the forefront of worshippers' minds in any case. He is content to take for granted the real humanity of the birth, and to place the emphasis on Christ's divinity. His antiphon would be sung shortly after St Ambrose's Office Hymn *Veni Redemptor*, quoted above in Chapter 1. Both poets make use of the same biblical image from Psalm 19 (18):4–6, that of the sun appearing in splendour, like a bridegroom coming from his chamber. For Ambrose the chamber is Mary's womb: 'Forth from His chamber goeth He, that royal home of purity', but the Son's divinity is stressed in the next verse: 'From God the Father He proceeds'.[37] The author of the antiphon begins with the thought that by the time the sun rises on Christmas morning the celebration of Christ's birth will have begun; the Mass Preface will have greeted the appearance of 'our God made visible'. The idea of the sunrise naturally leads the author's mind to the Psalmist's image of the sun as a bridegroom. An antiphon is a much shorter piece than an Ambrosian hymn, and so the author must move swiftly to the heart of the Incarnation: the child in the manger is the King of kings, and the bridegroom's chamber is the Father Himself.

In both the hymn and the antiphon a poetic image from an Old Testament text is given a Christian application, in order to draw out more of the true significance of Jesus. Comparing him to the rising sun opens up a number of meditative paths which the Christian mind could follow: He is the Sun of Righteousness with healing in its rays (Malachi 4:2), or He is the Light of the World which no darkness can quench (John 1:4–5; 8:12).

The New Testament writers often made use of types and images from the Old Testament to shed light on the person of Christ; an example, noted in the previous section, is the figure of Melchisedek, used in the Letter to the Hebrews to emphasize Christ's eternal priesthood. Scriptural typology such as this abounds in the writings of the Fathers and, again as noted above, is embedded in the Canon of the Mass. Yet, despite all this weighty tradition, Agobard can only see the application to Christ of the Psalmist's imagery as an 'evident lie'. He goes on to describe the non-biblical material in the antiphonary as 'things made up by just anyone' (*figmenta quorumlibet hominum*) – a phrase reminiscent of the 'things made up' (*fictiones*) which were condemned at the Council of Meaux.[38]

Agobard died five years before that council but his archdeacon Florus was a man of similar views. Their literalism was in sharp contrast to the symbolical approach to Scripture and the liturgy shown in the writings of Amalarius. He had produced a version of the antiphonary where the biblical chants were rearranged into the order in which the verses appear in the Bible. He retained, however, the non-biblical chants, and this earned the disapproval of Agobard and Florus.

Agobard's personal history probably intensified his disapproval of Amalarius, who, though ending his days at Metz, had served under Agobard at Lyon. When the archbishop was exiled for his part in the revolt against Louis the Pious, Amalarius was appointed in his stead. Soon after his appointment Amalarius summoned a council at Lyon at which he read from his book on church services, the *Liber Officialis*. The assembled churchmen approved of what they heard, with the notable exception of Florus, who denounced Amalarius to the Council of Thionville in 835. The deposition of Agobard was ratified at this council but there was no time to debate the case of Amalarius. This was postponed to the Council of Quierzy in 838, where, in a reversal of fortunes, Amalarius was condemned and Agobard reinstated.[39]

The passage from the *Liber Officialis* quoted in Chapter 2 has already shown that Amalarius was sensitive to the relationship between liturgy and personal devotion: the cantor praises God by singing the sequence-melody because he has been 'touched inwardly' by the Alleluia-verse. This concern for the inward disposition of the worshipper is evident throughout his book. In answer to the question why *Kyrie eleison* ('Lord, have mercy') is sung, he gives two possible reasons: either the cantors might have become puffed-up with pride after singing the Introit, or the chant could be seen as asking God's mercy for the priest in case he should pray the words of the Mass inattentively (*sine mente*).[40] Amalarius had probably been a pupil of Alcuin and was closely involved with the Council of Aachen; he was keen to further the ideals of the Carolingian Reform, especially St Benedict's precept that in worship the heart and mind should be in tune with the voice.

In pursuit of this ideal Amalarius offers a host of possible meditative pathways for the worshipper to follow, starting from the various elements in the liturgy. His allegory and symbolism will be looked at again in Chapter 8, but an example which particularly horrified Florus involves the Fraction. There is a point in the Canon of the Mass when the priest breaks the Host in two, and then breaks off a particle before placing it in the chalice. For this short time the Host is in three parts, and this suggests to Amalarius that Christ is present in three domains: that of the saints in heaven, the souls of the departed, and the Church on earth. Florus failed to grasp that this was one of a range of optional suggestions for meditation based on the liturgy; to him it was a literal statement that Christ had a three-fold nature. He described Amalarius's work as 'a tissue of vanities and damnable errors, overflowing with them like the swollen hump of a camel ... corrupting the Gospel into sensual fantasy'. He went on to class Amalarius with the worst heretics he could think of, from Sabellius and Arius to the Adamites, who called the church their paradise and worshipped naked, and the Artonites who celebrated Mass with bread and cheese.[41]

The views of Florus clearly prevailed at Quierzy in 838, given the condemnation of Amalarius and the reinstatement of Agobard. There is a strong possibility that they were also the driving force behind the prohibition of tropes and sequences at Meaux. Nevertheless, a strong defence of liturgical poetry came from the monastic island of Reichenau.

PENETRATING THE HEART: THE GRACE OF COMPUNCTION

Since 1838 Reichenau has been joined by a causeway to the German shore of Lake Constance, but before then it was a true island. Its fertile soil makes vegetables, fruit, and flowers grow in abundance. There are three monastic churches here, and behind the central one, Mittelzell, a garden has been created like the one delighted in by its ninth-century abbot Walafrid Strabo ('the Squinter', d. 849). He celebrated in verse the medicinal virtues of the plants here, and the beauty and symbolism of the flowers: the roses reminded him of the blood of the martyrs on earth, and the lilies pointed to the shining rewards of the saints in heaven.

Frederick Raby described Walafrid as 'a poet of genuine gifts, a lover of nature, and a man of tolerant sympathies and humane learning'.[42] He was educated at Reichenau as a boy, and then sent to Fulda to study under Rabanus Maurus, who, like Amalarius, had been a pupil of Alcuin. After a spell at the court at Aachen as tutor to the young prince Charles, Walafrid returned to Reichenau as abbot.

His defence of liturgical poetry is found in a remarkable work, 'The Origins and Growth of Church Services' (*Liber de exordiis et incrementis quarundam in observationibus ecclesiasticis rerum*). It is the first known attempt to write a history of the liturgy, and in it Walafrid is very critical of the Spanish councils such as Toledo, which tried to ban the use of non-biblical texts in worship. He says that if everything said or sung in church had to come from the Bible, 'services would cease.' He mentions the use of metrical and rhythmical hymns in the Offices and specifies several authors including Ambrose, Hilary, Bede, and Prudentius. 'But', he says, 'there are also other songs of praise (*laudationes*) which are composed with fitting words and sweet notes.' It is possible that Walafrid is referring here to texted sequences; how likely this is depends on the dating of the work, a subject on which scholars disagree. Giulio Cattin, for instance, places it between 825 and 830, a time when there is no evidence for the existence of texted sequences.[43] More recently, however, Karl Schmuki has suggested that Walafrid wrote it at the request of Reichenau's librarian Reginbert between 840 and 842 during his politically enforced exile in Speyer. Texted sequences almost certainly existed at this date, given their condemnation at Meaux in 845.[44]

Walafrid goes on to say:

> There are many newly composed things in the Church which should not be rejected if they are not at variance with the true faith. Moreover, metrical and rhythmical hymns are sung in the Ambrosian Offices; meanwhile some people have even taken to singing them at Mass because of the grace of compunction, which is increased by their lovely sweetness.[45]

One of those accustomed to sing hymns at Mass was Paulinus of Friuli, Patriarch of Aquileia (d. 802), who used his own compositions as well as hymns written by others. Walafrid says 'Such a great and knowledgeable man would not have done this without authority or the weight of reason.' Parts of a hymn by Paulinus are still sung today at the Washing of Feet on Maundy Thursday: *Congregavit nos*, 'The love of Christ has gathered us together' with its refrain *Ubi caritas*, 'Where charity and love are, there is God'.[46]

Walafrid's appeal to the authority of Paulinus was one element in his defence of hymns, but his main argument was that sung liturgical poetry increased devotion, or as he put it, 'the grace of compunction'. Like the word 'puncture', 'compunction' has at its root the idea of piercing; the English word normally denotes the pricking of one's conscience but the Christian-Latin *compunctio* had a wider meaning. It could include penitence but also had a more general sense of having one's heart touched and one's emotions stirred. Walafrid was by no means the first to notice that sung poetry had this effect: it was mentioned above in Chapter 1 that Augustine was moved to tears by one of Ambrose's hymns, and about the year 400 Nicetas of Remesiana, the probable author of the *Te Deum*, wrote that the sweetness of sung psalms 'penetrates the heart' and induces *compunctio*.[47]

Bede, in his *History of the English Church and People*,[48] tells the story of Cædmon, an unlettered servant at Whitby Abbey around the year 680. Cædmon had the remarkable gift of being able to turn whatever passage of Scripture was explained to him into English poetry. Bede says his songs were composed *maxima suavitate et compunctione* (literally 'with the greatest sweetness and compunction'), a phrase which Leo Sherley-Price accurately and elegantly renders as 'delightful and moving'. Cædmon's songs encouraged in their hearers 'an appetite for the life of heaven'.[49]

Walafrid, as a good Benedictine, is concerned to uphold the ideal that for the monk in choir the heart and mind should be in tune with the voice.[50] Paradoxically the reform following the Council of Aachen must have made this more difficult to achieve because of the large quantity of extra psalmody which it imposed: the recitation of whole psalters for founders and benefactors in addition to the psalms in the Offices. Liturgical exhaustion is not conducive to an attentive heart and mind; Josef Jungmann points to the danger that the recitation of the psalter 'could so easily sink to the level of a purely external performance'.[51]

Walafrid is clear that sung liturgical poetry can help the monk to avoid this danger. Hymns, and the other 'newly composed' items which he mentions – possibly tropes and sequences – have the power to penetrate the heart and stir feelings of devotion. Walafrid's influence was almost certainly one of the factors which helped the new poetry to survive the attacks of the monobiblicist Lyon party.

In the second half of the ninth century the sequence was taken to new heights by Notker, whose poetic imagination produced works of great beauty and lasting value.

✠ 4 ✠

The Stammerer of St Gall: Notker's Sequences

The Swiss city of St Gall (St Gallen) lies in the mountains to the south of Lake Constance. It owes its name to Gallus (d. 650), a disciple of the wandering Irish monk Columbanus (d. 615). In 612 Gallus was following his master on a journey up the Rhine valley towards Italy when he fell ill of a fever at Bregenz on the eastern shore of the lake. Columbanus continued on his way but Gallus, once he had recovered, decided to seek a wild and remote spot, as Celtic monks loved to do, where he could devote himself to solitary prayer. His wanderings took him into the rugged valley of the River Steinach; here he tripped and fell into a thicket of thorns. It was, he thought, a sign from God that this was the place where he should build his cell and oratory. He applied to himself God's words about Sion in Psalm 132 (131):14: 'This is my resting place for ever.'

Today the site of his hermitage is marked by a roadside cross where a busy street crosses the river a few yards from the terminus station of the Mühlegg funicular railway. Despite the modern bustle, a glance over the bridge's parapet reveals something of the wildness that Gallus knew: the waters of the Steinach still rush down their rocky gorge as they did in his day.

His cell became a place of pilgrimage; a monastery was established here by Otmar in 719, and the church Notker knew was built by Abbot Gozbert in the 830s. The monks of Reichenau had presented to Gozbert a plan for an ideal monastery comprising a huge double-apsed church and around fifty surrounding buildings, but archaeology has shown that the actual abbey bore no resemblance to the plan.[1]

St Gall's Celtic origins continued to resonate down the years, and Irish influence was still strong there in the time of Notker (d. 912). Monks from Ireland on their way to or from Rome would often deviate from their route up the Rhine valley to visit Gallus's shrine, such was the fame of his sanctity. Some of them, like Notker's teacher Marcellus, stayed on and became brethren of the monastery. A large collection of Irish manuscripts still exists in the abbey library, which, like its neighbour the cathedral, is a magnificent example of eighteenth-century Baroque architecture.[2]

In his gossipy biography of Charlemagne Notker describes himself with self-deprecating humour as 'the little toothless stammerer'. He is known as Notker Balbulus (the Stammerer) to distinguish him from other monks of St Gall who were also called Notker. His sense of humour made him a popular teacher in the abbey school, and his writings include a martyrology and a dramatized life of Gallus, partly in verse.[3]

Notker is best known, of course, as a composer of sequences, and we are lucky to have an account in his own words of how he came to write them, especially since the very identity of most sequence-authors is unknown. In 884 he dedicated his book of sequences, which he called a 'Book of Hymns' (*Liber Hymnorum*) to Liutward, Bishop of Vercelli and Imperial Chancellor. Notker says in his dedicatory preface that a certain priest from Gimedia (probably Jumièges near the Seine estuary) sought refuge at St Gall after his monastery had been destroyed by the Vikings. The refugee brought a chant-book with him containing what Notker called 'verses to the sequences' (*versus ad sequentias*). He liked the idea, as he had always found the long wordless melodies difficult to remember – there was, of course, no stable system of musical notation in those days. The actual texts, however, were not to his taste; he found them 'extremely poor' (*nimium vitiati*). He tried his hand at one himself and showed the result, *Laudes Deo concinat*, to his teacher Iso. The master was moderately pleased with his pupil's effort, but said that each note of the melody should be set to a single syllable of the text (Iso had clearly come across sequences before). Notker tried again, following this rule, and produced the sequence *Psallat ecclesia*.[4]

The Stammerer of St Gall: Notker's Sequences

LAUDES DEO CONCINAT

There were several Viking raids on Jumièges, a particularly destructive one being in 851. Notker's editor, Wolfram von den Steinen, therefore dates the composition of *Laudes Deo concinat* to around the year 860.[5] It is a poem which celebrates humanity's redemption through Christ; despite its failure to obey the one-note-per-syllable rule Notker retained it in his book of sequences, where it is assigned to the Friday in Easter Week:

1a Let the whole world sing praises to God, for it has been freed by grace
1b through the mercy of the most high Father. He, full of pity that the human race had long been laid low through the Fall,
2a sent His Son here to the earth, that with His own right hand
2b He might raise to the heights those who were lying in the mire, and restore them to their native land.
3a And so, begotten in the womb of a pure mother,
3b He lived as the only human being free from sin and without guile.
4a The serpent, who led Adam astray,
4b did not taint Him with its deceit.
5a Indeed, though eager to devour His flesh as food,
5b it was itself deceived by the hook of divinity and was conquered for ever.
6a Therefore all you on whom the prince of this world has inflicted the things that please him, and whom he has ruined,
6b cling to this man, in whom nothing belonging to that prince was found. For those who cling to Him can never be lost.
7   Let us sing our thanks now and for ever to the almighty Redeemer.[6]

Notker packs a good deal of theology into this poem, including the doctrines of the Fall, the Incarnation, and the redemptive work of Christ. He begins and ends with praise for the free gift of salvation; within this framework of joyful thanksgiving he portrays the work of redemption by using the biblical image of the serpent, seen as the personification of the spirit of evil.

Several scriptural allusions are compressed into verses 4 and 5. The first and obvious one is the beguiling of Eve by the serpent in Genesis 3 and the consequent enmity between that reptile and the human race. The identification of the serpent with the spirit of evil is made explicit in Revelation, where its defeat is portrayed:

'And the great dragon was thrown down, that ancient serpent, who is called the Devil and Satan, the deceiver of the whole world' (Revelation 12:9). The divine victory over the serpent was foretold by Isaiah: 'In that day the Lord ... will punish Leviathan the fleeing serpent, Leviathan the twisting serpent, and he will slay the dragon which is in the sea' (Isaiah 27:1).[7] Here the serpent is identified with Leviathan, and two further biblical references to this creature explain Notker's curious phrase in verse 5 'the hook of divinity' and his mention of food: 'Thou didst crush the heads of Leviathan, thou didst give him as food for the creatures of the wilderness' (Psalm 74 (73):14); 'Can you draw out Leviathan with a fishhook?' (Job 41:1; Vulgate 40:20). All these passages of Scripture imply that victory over the serpent is beyond the powers of sinful humanity; it belongs to God alone. Notker suggests that the incarnate Son of God achieves this victory by living a human life free from the taint of evil. There is no flaw in His humanity which could allow evil to enter and take hold; He is divinely human and humanly divine. Thus the deceiver of the whole world is itself deceived; what appeared to be another piece of its human prey turns out to be the one who conquers evil for ever.

In verses 1b and 5b there are echoes of *Pange lingua* ('Sing, my tongue'), the well-known hymn in honour of the Holy Cross by Venantius Fortunatus (d. 609): 'God in pity saw man fallen', and 'That the manifold deceiver's art by art might be outweighed'.[8]

In verse 6 the imagery changes; the spirit of evil is no longer the serpent but is 'the prince of this world', recalling the words of Jesus in John 14:30: 'The ruler of this world is coming. He has no power over me.' The Latin Bible, which Notker would have known, follows St John's Greek more literally, saying 'and has nothing in me'. There is another Johannine echo in this verse: 'This is the will of him who sent me, that I should lose nothing of all that he has given me, but raise it up at the last day' (John 6:39).

Before the final burst of praise in verse 7 Notker makes a simple direct appeal to the singers and hearers of his sequence: 'Cling to this man, stick close to Him' (*huic adhaerete*). His message of hope is that, however wounded and damaged by sin, human beings can never be lost if they cling to Christ in faith, attaching themselves to His perfect humanity.

Given that *Laudes Deo concinat* was Notker's first attempt at writing a sequence it is a remarkable achievement. It is clearly the product of a mind steeped in meditation on the Bible, and it fruitfully combines doctrine and devotion, helping the message of the Gospel to penetrate the heart.

It would be interesting to know what it was about the sequences from Jumièges that caused Notker to consider them 'extremely poor' and 'bitter to the taste'. One likely factor is the quality of their Latin; this, of course, is difficult to illustrate when the texts are translated. St Gall prided itself on its Latin scholarship, and there are tutorial links stretching back from Notker to the leading scholars of the Carolingian Renaissance: two of the abbots in Notker's time, Grimald and Hartmut, were illustrious pupils of Rabanus Maurus, who was himself a pupil of Alcuin.[9]

Scholars have been able to reconstruct the probable contents of the Jumièges antiphonary using the surviving tenth-century manuscripts from Aquitaine. Richard Crocker has made a detailed comparison of Notker's sequences with the French (West-Frankish) texts set to the same melodies. Notker's source for his first sequence turns out to be *Laudes Deo omnis sexus*; he kept the first two words but then went his own way. This is Crocker's translation of its opening verses: 'All flesh sings praises to God, sweet songs for the crucified one, with consonant voice, pouring out prayers, as is fitting, to the King ever glorious, thronging together in gratitude on this paschal feast, devoutly and joyfully.'[10] Even in translation the difference from Notker in literary quality is apparent. Notker weighs his words and uses them carefully to convey his message whereas the French piece is repetitious, using many words to say not very much. Like Notker's poem it is an Easter sequence celebrating the redemptive work of Christ; it does this by telling the story of the Harrowing of Hell. This legend relates how Christ, after his crucifixion, descended to the underworld and liberated those who had died before him; it is found in the apocryphal Acts of Pilate, also known as the Gospel of Nicodemus.[11]

The two sequences differ not just in literary style but also in theological depth. The French poem is an unsophisticated celebration of the Resurrection but Notker works out a theology of redemption by using the image of the serpent in its various biblical forms. He has clearly asked himself the question 'How did God overcome evil?' and his answer is that God's Son achieved a human life free from evil's taint. Notker goes on to apply this theology to the lives of his fellow-Christians, urging them to attach themselves in faith to Christ's perfect humanity.

The French sequence may lack Notker's theological depth and elegant Latin but its words have a pleasingly musical sound. Richard Crocker says of it:

> In terms of pure sound – vowels and consonants – the West-Frankish text flows along in a remarkably easy way. In fact, one of the things one might object to is the facility of sound compared to the loftiness of theme; the author manages to rattle through the Harrowing of Hell with almost unseemly ease, which is especially noticeable in singing the piece.[12]

The French poet seems more concerned with the sound of his words than with their sense; in the opening verses especially some of the words seem to be mere padding to make the text fit the notes of the melody. The priority of sound over sense remained characteristic of French sequences, just as careful attention to the meaning of the words would be a feature of the East Frankish (German) tradition started by Notker. Wolfram von den Steinen sums up the difference between the two traditions by saying that in Germany 'the sequence has something to say' whereas in France 'the sequence likes to sound well'. England, he says, steered a middle course whereby each line of its sequences ended in an 'a'-vowel as in France, but their texts had a clear grammatical structure as in Germany.[13]

Dag Norberg has suggested that the differences in style may reflect differing ways of singing sequences. In Germany antiphonal performance, with the verses divided between the two sides of the choir, would preserve the clarity of the words, whereas in France the recurring 'a' at the end of each line could mean that the text was sung by a soloist while the choir was singing the wordless melody to the final 'a' of the Alleluia.[14] Firm evidence for the way sequences were performed is extremely scanty; a rare piece of it is the York rubric noted above in Chapter 2, where four cantors sing the text of *Jubilemus omnes* while the choir vocalizes the melody to 'a' after each verse. Perhaps this is another example of the English 'middle way', ensuring that the words could be heard clearly but also preserving the wordless melody.[15]

The opening verses of *Laudes Deo omnis sexus* contain several references to the singers themselves; this too was a characteristic feature of French sequences. Notker, by contrast, usually avoids any such reference and gets straight down to the business of conveying his message.

PSALLAT ECCLESIA

1. Let the Church, pure mother and spotless virgin, sing in honour of this church.
2a. This house is shown to be in fellowship with the heav'nly hall
2b. in the praise and solemn worship of the great king of heaven.
3a. Its continually burning lights imitate the city where there is no darkness
3b. and it cherishes in its bosom the bodies of those whose souls live in heaven.
4a. Long may God's right hand
4b. shield it for His praise.
5a. Here grace, made fruitful by the Holy Spirit, brings to birth a new offspring;
5b. here angels visit their kindred, and the body of Jesus is received.
6a. All things that harm the body flee away;
6b. the sinful soul's transgressions are destroyed.
7a. Here the voice of joy rings out;
7b. here peace and gladness abound.
8. This house resounds always with the praise and glory of the Trinity.[16]

This is Notker's second sequence; in it he follows Iso's instruction to fit one syllable of text to each musical note. The first and last phrases of the melody are not repeated so verses 1 and 8 are singles, but the rest of the piece displays an exact syllabic parallelism between the two halves of each verse, a feature which the translation attempts to reflect.

The title of the melody is *Laetatus sum*, taken from the opening verse of Psalm 122 (121): 'I was glad when they said to me, "Let us go to the house of the Lord!"' This verse was part of the Alleluia-chant for the Second Sunday of Advent; in France it was usually followed by the sequence *Regnantem sempiterna*.[17] Perhaps it was the psalm's mention of 'the house of the Lord' that prompted Notker to use the melody for a sequence celebrating his church's Dedication Festival on 17 October.

In the opening words of the sequence Notker is already conveying his message that the church at St Gall forms part of the

'With Angels and Archangels'

Universal Church and is in close communion with the Church in heaven. From the very first line he begins to wake biblical echoes: in Ephesians 5:27 the Church is Christ's beloved bride, who is 'without spot or wrinkle or any such thing, that she might be holy and without blemish.' The bride of Christ is also the mother of Christians and is identified in Scripture with the heavenly Jerusalem: St Paul says in Galatians 4:26: 'The Jerusalem above is free, and she is our mother.' The images of the city and the bride are combined in the first reading at the Dedication Mass: 'I saw the holy city, new Jerusalem, coming down out of heaven from God, prepared as a bride adorned for her husband' (Revelation 21:2).

Notker uses these biblical images of the heavenly Church to bring out the symbolic significance of his own earthly church. In verse 3a the lamps burning before the altars point towards the brightness of eternity: 'And the city has no need of sun or moon to shine upon it, for the glory of God is its light, and its lamp is the Lamb' (Revelation 21:23). Verse 3b develops the image of the church as mother: the bodies of the departed brethren buried in her consecrated ground are cherished maternally in her bosom while their souls live in heaven. The deceased members of the monastic family are loved and prayed for as much as the living.

There is more maternal imagery in verse 5a, where the Church brings new offspring to birth in the sacrament of Baptism. The other Gospel sacrament, the Eucharist, is mentioned in 5b after a reference to angels visiting their kindred. This seems a strange juxtaposition at first; the probable explanation of it is that Notker is once again waking biblical echoes. The Introit-chant for the Feast of Dedication is Jacob's exclamation after his dream at Bethel: 'How awesome is this place! This is none other than the house of God, and this is the gate of heaven' (Genesis 28:17). The Introit goes on to add the clause 'and it shall be called the palace (or 'hall', *aula*) of God.' Notker's use of *aula* in verse 2a suggests that the Introit was one of the influences at work on him as he was composing this sequence. Jacob dreamt of a ladder stretching up from where he lay and reaching into heaven, with God's angels ascending and descending upon it. In St John's Gospel it is Jesus who is the true Jacob's Ladder; His human yet glorified body joins heaven and earth in one: 'You will see heaven opened, and the angels of God ascending and descending upon the Son of Man' (John 1:51). It is at least possible that these scriptural texts provide the link which Notker makes between angels and the body of Jesus.

Verses 6 to 8 celebrate the church as a place of healing, forgiveness, joy, and peace – blessings which all flow from the loving presence of God the Holy Trinity, whose praise resounds within its walls.

Psallat ecclesia was one of the few sequences from the German-speaking lands to penetrate Anglo-French territory: it was sung in several French and English dioceses and was still in some manuscripts of the Sarum (Salisbury) Use in the fourteenth century as an option for the Feast of Dedication alongside later sequences.[18]

CHRISTMAS: NATUS ANTE SAECULA

Because sequences are attached to the Alleluia-chant they are absent from the liturgy when the Alleluia is not sung. Throughout the Western Church the Alleluia disappeared at Septuagesima, the Third Sunday before Lent, and made its joyful return at Easter. In Germany the Alleluia was also laid aside during Advent;[19] for this reason Notker's book of sequences begins with his Christmas piece, *Natus ante saecula*:

1a Born before the worlds began, the Son of God, unbounded and invisible,
1b through whom was made the fabric of sky and earth, the sea and all that live in them,
2a through whom the days and hours sink down and once again renew themselves,
2b whom angels in heaven's citadel adore for ever in sweet song:
3a He took upon Himself frail human flesh without the stain of Adam's ancient sin from Mary's virgin body, so that He might cleanse the primal guilt passed on from wilful Eve.
3b This present day, though short its hours, is called 'Supremely Bright'; its length is now increased since the True Sun by His birth has scattered this world's ancient darkness with His bright gleaming rays.
4a The night too is filled with the light of a new star which astounded the trained eyes of the Wise Men.
4b The shepherds also were blinded by the brightness of the heavenly angel-hosts in their glory.

> 5a Rejoice, O Mother of God, for at His birth there stood around you not midwives, but angels singing praises to God.
> 5b Christ, the Father's only Son, who for our sake took on human form, revive and cherish us who humbly worship You.
> 6a As You deigned to share our humanity, deign also, Jesus, in Your graciousness to hear our prayers,
> 6b that we may share in Your divinity through Your great goodness, You who are our God, God's only Son.[20]

Here again Notker weaves his own distinctive patterns from strands taken from the Bible and the liturgy of the day. The title of this sequence's melody is *Dies sanctificatus*, a reference to the Alleluia-verse in the Third Mass of Christmas: 'A hallowed day has dawned upon us; come, you nations, and worship the Lord: for today a great light has come down upon the earth.'[21]

The Alleluia-verse portrays the Incarnation in terms of light, echoing the prologue to St John's Gospel: 'The true light that enlightens every man was coming into the world' (John 1:9). Notker will develop this imagery of light in the heart of his poem, verses 3b to 4b, but first, in a long opening sentence, he is concerned to show who Mary's child really is. He is the eternal Son of God, through whom the world with its times and seasons came into being, and on this particular hallowed day he took human flesh for our salvation.

In verse 3b Notker turns to the paradox that this short winter day is called 'Supremely Bright' (*praelucida*). Being just after the winter solstice Christmas Day does see a slight lengthening of the hours of daylight, but for Notker its essential brightness comes from the birth of Christ, the True Sun. There are probable echoes in this verse of the healing rays of the Sun of Righteousness in Malachi 4:2, and of Isaiah's oracle 'The people who walked in darkness have seen a great light' (9:2, quoted in Matthew 4:16). Perhaps Notker also had in mind Jesus' words 'I am the light of the world; he who follows me will not walk in darkness, but will have the light of life' (John 8:12), and Zechariah's prophecy of the Dayspring which gives light to those in darkness (Luke 1:78–9).

The biblical allusions are more explicit in verse 4, where the signs that accompany Christ's birth illuminate the night: the star seen by the Magi (Matthew 2:2), and the bright glory of the angelhosts which terrified the shepherds (Luke 2:9).

The Stammerer of St Gall: Notker's Sequences

Notker begins this poem with a theological meditation on the mystery of the Incarnation and then illustrates it by weaving together strands of biblical imagery on the theme of light. In verse 5 meditation becomes colloquy, and theology turns into prayer. First he addresses Mary, bidding her rejoice because in giving birth she was surrounded by angels rather than midwives, and then he turns to Christ, asking Him for new life and warm cherishing.

He continues his prayer in verse 6, where he asks that the purpose of the Incarnation may be accomplished, that Christ's sharing in our human nature may bring us into fellowship with God. The liturgy has clearly influenced Notker in this verse; it contains strong echoes of the prayer *Deus, qui humanae substantiae*: 'O God, who wonderfully created and yet more wonderfully renewed the dignity of human nature, grant that He who deigned to share our humanity may make us sharers in His divinity.' This appears as a Christmas collect in the seventh-century Verona Sacramentary (the so-called 'Leonine'), and after the ninth century it is found in northern Europe as an Offertory prayer at the mixing of the chalice. Here the phrase 'by this mystery of water and wine' was added after 'grant that', and in this form it passed into the Roman Rite and was used in every Mass.[22]

Notker was not alone in writing sequences which moved from meditation to direct prayer; a similar movement occurs in the three west-Frankish sequences discussed in Chapter 2: *Jubilemus, Ecce puerpera*, and *Stans a longe*. Notker would sometimes write a whole sequence in the form of a prayer in which his theological meditation was expressed in direct speech addressed to God or one of the saints. Like the best theologians he did his theology on his knees, and exemplified Austin Farrer's maxim that 'Prayer and dogma are inseparable'.[23]

ST JOHN (27 DECEMBER): JOHANNES JESU

There are sequences in Notker's book for each of the saints' days in Christmas week: Stephen, John, and the Holy Innocents. For 1 January there is a Marian piece, *Gaude Maria*, which mentions the Circumcision. The poem for St John, *Johannes Jesu*, is an example of a whole sequence written in the form of a prayer:

1. John, pure and beloved friend of Jesus Christ,

2a for love of Him you left behind
2b your earthly father in the boat.
3a You renounced the tender breast of a wife and followed the Messiah,
3b that, allowed to lean on His breast, you might drink from that sacred fountain.
4a You, while still on earth, beheld the glory of the Son of God,
4b on which the saints alone are thought to gaze in life eternal.
5a As Christ triumphed on the cross He gave His mother to your care,
5b that, in your purity, you might look after that pure virgin.
6a Racked by imprisonment and burning, you rejoiced to bear Christ witness;
6b you raised the dead and conquered poison in the mighty name of Jesus.
7a Hidden from others, the most high Father reveals to you His Word.
7b Commend us all to God for ever by your constant faithful prayers,
8   John, Christ's beloved.[24]

This sequence displays again the now familiar pattern of interwoven strands from the Bible and the liturgy. Notker naturally accepted the traditional assumption that St John the Apostle and the beloved disciple in the Fourth Gospel were the same person. Within the monastic culture in which he lived it also felt natural to assume that it was John's virginity which made him especially loved by the Lord. A literal translation of the first verse reads 'John, virgin greatly loved by Jesus Christ'.

This echoes the first antiphon to the psalms at Matins on St John's feast-day: 'John, the apostle and evangelist, was chosen by the Lord for his virginity, and was loved more than the others.'

It was love that prompted John to leave his father and his livelihood to follow Christ (Matthew 4:22), and that love is encapsulated in a memorable image as he leans on the Lord's breast at the Last Supper (John 13:23). In Notker's imagination this physical closeness enjoyed by John allows him to absorb spiritual insights into the true nature of Jesus. As the apostle writes in his First Letter, he has seen and touched the eternal Word of Life (1 John 1:1–2), and in his Gospel he says 'The Word became flesh and dwelt among us ... we have beheld his glory' (John 1:14).

These texts seem to resonate in the background of verses 3 and 4 of the sequence, and the Divine Office has played a part here too: 1 John 1 was the first reading at Matins, and the second psalm-antiphon was 'Leaning on the breast of the Lord Jesus, he drank the streams of the Gospel from that sacred fountain of the Lord's breast'. Verse 5 recalls the incident at the crucifixion when the beloved disciple is entrusted by Jesus to Mary's care, as she is to his (John 19:26). Notker's words contain a further echo of the day's Matins: the first responsory begins 'Greatly to be honoured is blessed John, who leaned on the Lord's breast at supper; to whom, as a virgin, Christ on the cross commended his virgin Mother.' Verse 6 refers to various legendary exploits of the apostle which are recounted in a second-century work, the apocryphal *Acts of John*. In one version of these the saint emerges unscathed from a cauldron of boiling oil into which he had been thrown at the orders of the Emperor Domitian. The incident is supposed to have happened outside the Latin Gate of Rome, that is, the gate leading south towards Latium. It was commemorated on 6 May in the feast of St John *ante Portam Latinam*. On another occasion he was made to drink from a poisoned cup but remained unharmed; he then raised to life two men who had drunk from the cup before him and had died. St John is often depicted holding a cup from which the venom is departing in the form of a snake.[25]

Johannes Jesu was one of the most widely used of all Notker's sequences: it was sung all over Europe throughout the Middle Ages.[26]

EPIPHANY (6 JANUARY): FESTA CHRISTI

The Epiphany sequence begins with the visit of the Wise Men (Matthew 2:1–12). Notker makes a vivid contrast between the splendour of Herod's palace and the humble setting of Christ's birth: 'Passing by the golden couch of the proud prince, they seek out Christ's manger.' After a pair of verses on the slaughter of the Innocents (Matthew 2:16–18) the last section of the sequence is devoted to Christ's baptism (Matthew 3:13–17), an Epiphany theme usually celebrated on the octave-day, 13 January:

6a In the thirtieth year of His human life God bent down beneath the hands of His renowned servant, and so consecrated baptism to us for the forgiveness of our sins.

6b The Spirit, in the form of an innocent dove, came to Him, anointed Him as foremost of all the holy ones, and was happy to dwell for ever within His heart.

7a The Father's kindly voice resounded over the water; forgotten were His former words: 'It grieves me that I made mankind';

7b now He says: 'Truly you are my Son, most dear to me, in whom I am well-pleased. Today, my Son, I have begotten you.'[27]

The sequence for St John contained a vivid image of the saint leaning on the Lord's breast and drinking in precious insights into the divine Word. In this piece Notker presents another striking picture in order to illustrate the divine humility which characterized the Incarnation: God bending low beneath the hands of his servant as he was being baptized. Christ's baptism has happy consequences for all Christian people: He 'consecrated baptism *to us* for the forgiveness of our sins'. Notker is making clear, as he often does, that he and all who sing his sequences are personally involved in the saving events which his poems celebrate; the poet and the singers are themselves embraced by the divine love revealed in the Incarnation.

The anointing by the Holy Spirit in verse 6b recalls Isaiah 61:1: 'The Spirit of the Lord God is upon me, because the Lord has anointed me ...' In Luke 4:16–21 Jesus explicitly applied this text to himself in the synagogue at Nazareth. Notker is also sensitive to the other Old Testament echoes which resonate in the Gospel accounts of Christ's baptism: the Spirit moving over the face of the waters at the beginning of Creation (Genesis 1:2), and the dove doing the same after the Flood (Genesis 8:8). Since New Testament times Noah's Ark had been seen as a prefiguration of baptism, being an image of salvation through water, and Notker makes a striking contrast between God's angry voice at the time of the Flood (Genesis 6:6–7) and His loving words to Jesus in the Jordan, which echo Psalm 2:7 ('You are my son, today I have begotten you') and Isaiah 42. 1 ('Behold ... my chosen in whom my souls delights; I have put my Spirit upon him'). The cumulative effect of all these echoes is to suggest that baptism is both New Creation and Redemption; the Incarnation has made it possible for all to enjoy the glorious liberty of the children of God.

CANDLEMAS (2 FEBRUARY): CONCENTU PARILI

This feast on the fortieth day after Christmas celebrates the Purification of Mary and the Presentation of Christ in the temple as described in Luke 2:22–40. It was observed at Jerusalem in the fourth century and introduced into the Western Church in the late seventh century by Pope Sergius I, whose ancestry was Syrian.[28]

Notker's sequence *Concentu parili* draws on two Old Testament images to illustrate Mary's fruitful virginity: Aaron's rod, which blossomed and bore almonds (Numbers 17:8), and the closed eastern gate of the temple, only entered by God Himself (Ezekiel 44:2). Notker marvels at the humility of Mary in fulfilling the Law's rites of purification for women after childbirth (Leviticus 12:2–8) despite being the mother of God's Son:

> 4a But since you desired to commend to us an example of motherly virtues, you submitted to the remedy prescribed for mothers ritually unclean.
>
> 4b Virgin Mother, you brought with you to the temple for purification Him who gave you in abundance integrity's glory: God, born as a human child.
>
> 5a Rejoice, holy Mary! He who searches our hearts and our inmost being found you alone a worthy dwelling for Himself.
>
> 5b O Mary, be joyful, because your little one, who then smiled up at you, has made us all secure and happy in His love.
>
> 6a As we keep this feast of Christ, made a small child for our sake, and of His holy Mother Mary,
>
> 6b though we, slow-hearted, cannot match God's great humility, let us take His Mother as our guide.
>
> 7a Praise to the Father of glory who, in revealing His Son to Israel and the nations, unites us with the company of His people.
>
> 7b Praise also to His only Son who, in reconciling us to the Father by His own blood, has united us with the citizens on high.
>
> 8 Praise also to the Holy Spirit throughout all ages.[29]

In verse 5b Notker presents a delightful picture of the child smiling up at Mary as she holds him in her arms and, no doubt, smiles down at him. Perhaps the poet was reminded of the child at rest in its mother's arms in Psalm 131 (130):2. As he often does, Notker goes on to expand and apply the image: because Mary's child embodies all the love of God, the warm embrace of that love is offered to everyone.

Candlemas is the last feast of the Christmas cycle; it is soon followed by Septuagesima and then Lent, when alleluias and sequences are absent from the liturgy. This change of mood in the Church's Year is reflected in Notker's book by a clear break between its two sections after *Concentu parili*. The poet marks

'With Angels and Archangels'

this division with a verse in classical hexameters addressed to the book's dedicatee, Bishop Liutward:

> The first part, Liutward, ends on a narrow path. After the earthquake and the abyss of misery sing in joyful melodies of the Holy One's fair dwelling, and fix your eyes and your mind on the King of Heaven, until you are found worthy to reach the heavenly Jerusalem, where you will laugh at the sore lashes you once endured and will rejoice with your King, who here was crucified. The second part gleams with flowers in broad meadows.[30]

Notker the monk is not afraid to remind this prince of the Church of what really matters: seeking God, and preferring absolutely nothing to the love of Christ, as St Benedict taught. The poet seems to picture the path he is tracing through the Christian year as entering a narrow steep-sided valley as it approaches Lent and Passiontide. Then come the earthquake and the abyss, which mark the crucifixion and the descent into the realm of the dead (Matthew 27:51ff). The Resurrection, however, brings deliverance from the valley of the shadow of death; the flowery meadows, bright with the promise of new life, point to the glorious mysteries of Eastertide with which the second part of the book begins.

EASTER: LAUDES SALVATORI

1. Let us humbly sing praises to our Saviour,
2a. and with songs of devotion rejoice in our heavenly Lord, the Messiah,
2b. who emptied Himself for us, that He might give freedom to lost humanity.
3a. Veiling in flesh the glory of His Godhead, He is wrapped in swaddling-clothes in the manger, out of pity for the one who broke the commandment and was driven naked from his homeland of paradise.
3b. He is subject to Joseph, Mary, and Simeon; He is circumcised, and He whose nature is to forgive our sins is purified by the offering required by the Law, as if He were a sinner.
4a. He stoops beneath a servant's hand to be baptized and withstands the deceits of the tempter; He flees from those who pursue Him with stones.
4b. He suffers hunger, sleeps, and knows sadness; He who is God made man washes the feet of His disciples in supreme humility.

The Stammerer of St Gall: Notker's Sequences

5a Yet in this humble bodily life His divinity could not stay always hidden but showed itself in teachings and in many varied signs.

5b He gives to water wine's rich taste at the wedding, blind eyes He clothes with bright and shining light, lurid leprosy is banished by His gentle touch.

6a He cures weak limbs and raises up the dead from their decay. He stemmed a flow of blood, and satisfied five thousand with five loaves.

6b He walks the lake's rough waves as on dry land, and stills the storm. He heals dumb tongues and ears deprived of sound; fevers He drives away.

7a After so many of these wonderful miracles He even accepted crucifixion;

7b He is willingly arrested and condemned, but the sun could not bear to look upon His death.

8a Brightly shines the day which was made by the Lord; the Conqueror, destroying death, shows Himself alive to those who love Him:

8b first to Mary, then to the apostles; teaching the scriptures, opening their hearts, revealing hidden truths about Himself.

9a At his rising all created things greet Christ with joy. Flowers and cornfields flourish with new fruitfulness; birds sing their sweet delight, now the sad season of frost is past.

9b Darkened at His death, the sun and moon now shine more brightly; the risen Christ is welcomed by the green earth, which at His crucifixion trembled as if about to fall.

10a So let us too be glad today, for Jesus, in His rising, has opened up to us the path of life.

10b Let stars and earth and sea rejoice, and all the choirs of blessed spirits in the heavens thank the Trinity.[31]

Notker's sequence for the Queen of Festivals is his longest and most ambitious. It is certainly unusual for an Easter sequence only to deal with the Resurrection in its last three verses, but Notker is trying to give as much theological depth as he can to his depiction of the Risen Jesus. He used a similar approach in his Christmas sequence, *Natus ante saecula*, where his treatment of Christ's birth is preceded by a meditation on the Eternal Son by whom all things were made. The Easter poem places the Resurrection in its context as the climax of God's whole saving purpose for humanity. That purpose was revealed in the incarnate life of His Son, which Notker skilfully sums up in these verses, including an extraordinary number of incidents from the Gospels. His emphasis is on the divine humility of the Incarnation, and his language in verse 2b recalls Philippians 2:7, where Christ 'emptied himself, taking the form of a servant'.

In verse 3a Notker plays with images of clothing and nakedness. In God's saving plan of Incarnation naked Deity, too much for humans to bear, is clothed in flesh, and so the naked new-born Child is wrapped in swaddling-clothes as He begins his incarnate life. This is done out of divine pity for lost humanity, whose primal representative was driven naked from Paradise (Genesis 3:24). Notker plays with words here as well as images; he rarely uses assonance and alliteration, but this half-verse contains *praesepi, praecepti, pulsum patria paradysi*. The idea of Godhead being hidden beneath a veil of flesh prompts Richard Crocker to ask 'Is there a hint of Docetism here?'[32] Surely Notker can justly be acquitted of any heresy charge because a Docetic Christ only appears to be human whereas this poem makes clear, especially in verse 4b, that his humanity is absolutely real.

Notker continues the theme of Christ's humility throughout verses 3 and 4, referring to His Presentation and Baptism in language reminiscent of the Candlemas and Epiphany sequences. His humility is shown especially in His washing of the disciples' feet (John 13:5), and in verse 7 it culminates in His acceptance of death on a cross.

The signs which reveal his divinity are celebrated in verses 5 and 6. Most of the verbs here are in the present tense; perhaps Notker is suggesting that the healing and life-giving power of Christ is still a present reality in the life of the Church.

In verse 7b the poet's interpretation of the darkness at the crucifixion (Matthew 27:45) skilfully evokes the horrific nature of that death – even the sun could not bear to look upon it. The Resurrection, by contrast, is a time of shining brightness; Notker alludes in verses 8a and 10a to Psalm 118 (117):24: 'This is the day which the Lord has made; let us rejoice and be glad in it'. The appearances of the Risen Jesus in 8b come from John 20:11–23 (Mary Magdalen and the apostles) and Luke 24:27 (opening hearts and minds on the road to Emmaus).

In verse 9 all Creation shares in the joyful new life of the Resurrection, as the fresh green growth of the earth's spring-time follows the deadness of winter. There is a probable echo here of the great Easter hymn of Venantius Fortunatus (d. 609), *Salve, festa dies* ('Hail thee, festival day'), with its verse:

Lo, the fair beauty of earth, from the death of the winter arising, Every good gift of the year, now with its Master returns.[33]

Processional hymns like this one were very popular at St Gall, where they were known as *Versus*. Processions before Mass had been promoted by Benedict of Aniane at the Council of Aachen (see Chapter 3 II); they were clearly taken up enthusiastically at St Gall since Notker's friend Hartmann wrote a processional hymn for ordinary Sundays which consisted of eighty verses! *Salve, festa dies* would have been well-known to Notker as it was sung during the procession on all the Sundays of Eastertide.[34]

As the sequence ends, the joy of Easter has spread through the whole Creation; it unites the Church on earth with all created things and with the whole company of heaven in one great thanksgiving.

Laudes salvatori was widely sung not just in Germanic territory but also in England. The canons of York Minster sang it on Easter Monday, but most churches, including the Benedictines of St Mary's, York, followed the Sarum custom of singing it on Low Sunday. It is just possible that the name of this Sunday is derived from the first word of the sequence.[35]

EASTER WEEK

Notker provided shorter sequences for the days of Easter Week; in some of them the melody of each verse was not repeated and so they lack the usual pattern of double verses. In all he produced eight of these repetitionless sequences as opposed to twenty-five of the double-versed type.[36]

An example of the 'aparallel' sort is the piece for Easter Tuesday, *Christe, domine*:

> Lord Christ, make Your bride the Church glad in these festal days, by which, O Christ, You have betrothed her to Yourself, and have brought her bridal gifts of wonderful worth.
>
> Once by Your Resurrection You consoled the holy women and men who were grieving at Your death. Now seated at the right hand of the Father, protect us, O Christ, from all assaults of death.[37]

Easter joy is Notker's main theme in this sequence; its last line contains a strong echo of the verse which preceded the doxology in the Office Hymns of Eastertide: 'Maker of all, to thee we pray, fulfil in us thy joy today; when death assails, grant, Lord, that we may share thy Paschal victory.'[38] The hymn's text is *Ab omni mortis impetu*, and Notker wrote *Omni mortis ab incursu*.

The nuptial imagery at the beginning of the sequence was probably inspired by the first words of the hymn *Ad cenam Agni*: 'The Lamb's high banquet we await in snow-white robes of royal state.'[39]

Its scriptural source is the heavenly song of joy in Revelation 19:7–9:

> The marriage of the Lamb has come, and his Bride has made herself ready; it was granted her to be clothed with fine linen, bright and pure ... Blessed are those who are invited to the marriage supper of the Lamb.

The next day's sequence, *Agni paschalis*, continues the theme of the Lamb's banquet, but here the imagery has changed from a marriage supper to the feast of Passover:

> Let all Christian souls show themselves worthy, by a sincere way of life, to eat and drink of the Paschal Lamb;
> He, the supreme High Priest, offered Himself as a sacrifice to God on their behalf.[40]

There are further echoes here of the Office Hymn ('Now Christ our Passover is slain'), and of another of its biblical sources, 1 Corinthians 5:7–8: 'Christ, our paschal lamb, has been sacrificed. Let us, therefore, celebrate the festival ... with the unleavened bread of sincerity and truth.' The feast of Passover is, of course, embedded in the narrative of the Exodus, with all its Easter overtones of liberation from slavery and deliverance from death. This is the ultimate source of the typology in both the hymn and the sequence. Notker continues:

> Their foreheads are marked with His most holy blood, as the door-posts were of old.
> They are safe from the disastrous fate of the Egyptians; their cruel enemies were overwhelmed in the Red Sea.
> Let them gird their loins with modesty; let their feet be protected from vipers; let them always carry in their hand a spiritual staff against dogs, so that they may be worthy to follow the Passover of Jesus, by which He returned victorious from hell.

> See, the world, rising with Christ and alive again with beauty,
> shows the faithful that after death they will live a better life
> with Him.

The Exodus typology in the hymn includes the Passover sacrifice, ensuring protection from the angel of death, and the crossing of the Red Sea. Notker, however, delves more deeply into the detail of the Passover ritual: in Exodus 12:7 the people are told to mark the door-posts and lintels of their houses with the blood of the lamb, and for Notker this mark is now on the foreheads of Christians. Perhaps he had in mind the servants of God in Revelation, who were sealed on their foreheads (7:3), had 'washed their robes and made them white in the blood of the Lamb (7:14), and whose seal was in the form of the Lamb's Name (22:4). Austin Farrer points out that 'Sealing with the Name is surely the imparting of Christian status in Baptism'.[41] The baptismal liturgy was almost certainly in Notker's mind too, as the newly baptized Christian was anointed on the head with the Oil of Chrism in a ceremony known later as Confirmation but anciently called 'Sealing', for example, by St Ambrose.[42] Christian foreheads may not be marked literally by the blood of the Lamb, but they bear his sacramental seal; all the baptized belong to him and share in his victory over death.

In Exodus 12:11 the people were told to eat the Passover with 'your loins girded, your sandals on your feet, and your staff in your hand' so that they might be ready for a speedy departure. Notker brings his own allegorical twist to this text in applying it to Christians: the girded loins represent modesty, and the sandals and staff symbolize the need to guard against the assaults of evil. He had biblical precedent for being disparaging about snakes and dogs: there is the serpent who bruises the heel in Genesis 3:15, the fiery serpents of Numbers 21:6, and dogs are equated with evil-doers in Psalm 22:16 (21:17).

In this verse Notker sees the Passover as Christ's victorious passing from death to life, bringing his people with him. There is a further echo here of the Office Hymn: 'For Christ, arising from the dead, from conquered hell victorious sped ...'

Both hymn and sequence use the rather unusual word *barathrum* for 'hell'.

The last verse again recalls *Salve, festa dies* in seeing the new life of the natural world in spring as an image of Resurrection.

Nuptial imagery returns in the piece for Easter Saturday, *Carmen suo dilecto*:

1. Let Christ's Church sing a love-song for her Beloved; for her sake God clothed himself in our nature, leaving father and mother, and renouncing the synagogue.
2. Her sacraments flowed from Your sacred side, O Christ; by the help of Your cross may she be kept safe in the flowing tides of time.
3. For love of this bride You were confined in Gaza, but would break open its gates; to rescue her from her enemies You fought the tyrant Goliath, felling him with a single pebble.
4. Beneath Your pleasant vine, O Christ, the whole Church plays in peace. You rose from the dead in a garden, O Christ, and You open up to your people the flowery garden of Paradise which had long been closed to them, Lord and King of kings.[43]

The typology in *Agni paschalis* was firmly focused on the Passover, but here Notker's biblical allusions are more diffuse. The opening line recalls Isaiah 5:1: 'Let me sing for my beloved a love-song concerning his vineyard', and love-songs and vineyards are features of the Song of Solomon (1:14; 7:12), a book widely seen as reflecting the love between Christ and his Church. Notker draws the parallel between married love and the love which prompted the Incarnation: God's Son left His heavenly home to take human nature as 'a man leaves his father and his mother and cleaves to his wife' (Genesis 2:24).

In verses 2 and 3 Christ's love for His bride has led Him to the cross and His victory over death. The primal bride, Eve, drew her life and being from the wounded side of Adam (Genesis 2:21–2). Christ, the New Adam, gave His very life for the Church; the water and blood flowing from His wounded side symbolize the sacraments of Baptism and Eucharist which nourish the life of the Church (John 19:34). Christ's triumph over death is seen as foreshadowed in Samson's breaking open of the gates of Gaza (Judges 16:3), and in David's slaying of Goliath (1 Samuel 17:49).

The image of a vineyard, which had been hinted at in the first line, becomes explicit in verse 4. In John 15:1 Christ is the true vine; Notker sees him as offering protection which allows the Church to 'play in peace' and safety. The scene is reminiscent of Micah's vision in 4:4: 'They shall sit every man under his vine and under his fig tree, and none shall make them afraid.'

The Stammerer of St Gall: Notker's Sequences

The imagery moves from a vineyard to the Easter Garden and then to the Garden of Paradise, which the Risen Christ has once more opened to humanity. Notker again echoes the Office Hymn in using the same word *resera(n)s* for opening Paradise.

EASTERTIDE

The sequences for the Sundays of Eastertide are also short and largely repetitionless. Several of their biblical allusions come from the Psalms, as is the case with *Laus tibi sit*, set for the Second Sunday after the Easter Octave, now called the Fourth Sunday of Easter:

> Praise be to You, O faithful God; You never put to shame those who trust in You, but instead You make them glorious.
> You are our defence against the assaults and ambushes of the enemy.
> Our shepherd, breaker of the snare, You keep safe those who revere You,
> granting them very great sweetness, O God.[44]

The title of this sequence's melody is *In te, Domine, speravi*, the first verse of Psalm 71 (70), which also forms the last verse of the Matins canticle *Te Deum laudamus*. The Revised Standard Version of the Bible has 'In thee, O Lord, do I take refuge; let me never be put to shame!' but the Authorized Version's 'In thee, O Lord, do I put my trust' is closer to the Latin Notker knew. He has taken several elements from the psalm: there is the near-quotation of the first verse, God is described as a 'strong fortress' in its third verse, and His faithfulness is praised in verse 22. But Notker subtly transforms the psalm's opening into something that expresses the joy of Eastertide: because of the Resurrection those who trust in God are not only spared being put to shame, they are actually glorified.

This Sunday's Gospel begins with Jesus' words 'I am the good shepherd' (John 10:11). Notker calls God 'our shepherd' and in his next phrase, 'breaker of the snare', he alludes to Psalm 124 (123):7: 'the snare is broken, and we have escaped!' This is another reference to the Resurrection: Christ has broken the snare of death and has given life and freedom to his people.

In the last line of the sequence God is described as giving 'very great sweetness' to those who revere Him. The idea of sweetness as an element in the Christian's relationship with God is more commonly associated with the spiritual Romanticism of St Bernard (d. 1153) and the Cistercians. An example of it is the so-called 'Rosy Sequence' *Dulcis Jesu memoria* ('Jesu! – the very thought is sweet!') in honour of the Holy Name.[45] Walafrid, echoing Nicetas and Bede, had written of the sweetness of hymns, which allowed the grace of compunction to penetrate the heart (see Chapter 3.V), but Notker seems to be ahead of his time in seeing sweetness as a direct gift from God to the praying Christian.

Sweetness appears again in the sequence for the Sixth Sunday of Easter, *Laeta mente*:

> With joyful hearts let us praise our God, who always renews His Church when she falls short through her sins.
>
> When she is weak and pale, He brightens and warms her with the rays of the true sun.
>
> He has led her out of the land of slavery with its fiery furnaces; when she cries to Him in any kind of distress, He hears her.
>
> He nourishes her with bread from heaven, and teaches her to love and worship Him. With sweet honey from the rock He satisfies her.[46]

The sequences for the Sundays of Eastertide all have melody-titles taken from the psalms. *Laeta mente* has *Exultate Deo*, the beginning of Psalm 81 (80). The general theme of both psalm and sequence is the loving care of God for His people, which endures despite their sins. Verses 7, 10, and 16 of the psalm are clearly echoed in the sequence: 'In distress you called, and I delivered you'; 'I am the Lord your God, who brought you up out of the land of Egypt'; 'I would feed you with the finest of the wheat, and with honey from the rock I would satisfy you'.

ASCENSION: CHRISTUS HUNC DIEM

1   May Christ grant this day to be a happy one for all Christians who love Him.

2a   Christ Jesus, Son of God, joining Your divine nature to ours: as eternal God You visited the earth, as new man You seek the skies.

2b   Angels and clouds attend You as You return to the Father. And no wonder, since, while still a tiny child, a star and angels served You.

3a Today, O Lord, You have given to those who dwell on earth a new and sweet thing: the hope of heaven.
3b You are raised up, not as an apparition but as man, above the starry regions, Lord of kings.
4a What great gladness filled Your apostles,
4b as You let them watch Your ascension!
5a How joyfully the nine-fold angel hosts rush to meet You in the heavens,
5b as You bear on Your shoulders the one flock that had long been scattered by wolves!
6   Graciously guard that flock, O Christ, Good Shepherd.[47]

The happy combination of Notker's theological mind and his poetic imagination is especially evident in this sequence. The Incarnation joined Christ's divine nature to our humanity; now at his Ascension he takes our human nature with him, giving us 'a new and sweet thing: the hope of heaven.' In verse 2b the poet draws together the beginning and end of Christ's earthly life in an unusual but effective way: angels appear both at the Ascension and at the Nativity (Acts 1:10; Luke 2:13) and so do the 'heavenly' phenomena of a cloud (Acts 1:9) and a star (Matthew 2:2).

There is another boldly original touch in verse 5: Notker links the joy in heaven at Christ's Ascension with the joy over a repentant sinner in the parable of the lost sheep (Luke 15:3–7). The sheep on the shepherd's shoulders represents the whole flock of fallen and redeemed humanity, for whom the Good Shepherd is preparing an eternal home.

The simple petition in the last verse is a reminder to the singers that they too are part of that flock, and are personally involved in the mysteries of which they sing.

PENTECOST: SANCTI SPIRITUS ASSIT

1   May the grace of the Holy Spirit be with us,
2a and make our hearts a dwelling for Himself,
2b driving out from them all that harms the soul.
3a O loving Spirit, light of humankind,
3b dispel the fearsome darkness of our minds.
4a Holy One, always looking with love on our thoughts and feelings,
4b anoint our senses, pouring upon us Your tender mercy.

'With Angels and Archangels'

5a O Spirit, cleanser of all sin and shame,
5b keep pure and clear our spirits' inward sight,
6a so that we may behold the Most High Father
6b whom only the eyes of a pure heart can see.
7a You inspired the prophets to proclaim beforehand the glorious praises of Christ;
7b You strengthened the apostles to carry Christ's victorious sign throughout the world.
8a When through His Word God created the fabric of the earth, the sky, and the oceans,
8b You, O Spirit, brooded over the waters, spreading upon them Your divine power.
9a You cause water to be fruitful, so that souls may have new life;
9b by Your inbreathing humans are made spiritual beings.
10a The world, divided by languages and customs, You have made one, O Lord;
10b You call idolaters back to the worship of God, O best of teachers.
11a Therefore, Holy Spirit, graciously hear us who pray to You;
11b without You all prayers are vain and unworthy of God's hearing.
12a You, O Spirit, have taught the saints in every age by embracing and indwelling them by Your divinity;
12b on this day You gave to Christ's apostles extraordinary gifts never before heard of in any age;
13 You have made this day to be glorious.[48]

For this sequence Notker uses a melody known in West Francia as *Cithara* ('Lute') but at St Gall as *Occidentana* ('Western').[49] In the West the Ascension sequence *Rex omnipotens* ('Almighty King') was set to it. Richard Crocker points out that this piece is largely a retelling of the Ascension story from Acts 1, whereas Notker makes only oblique references to the account in Acts 2 of the coming of the Holy Spirit.[50]

Notker, of course, is too much of a theologian to be content with a simple re-telling of the story. Rather than concentrating on the dramatic events in Acts 2, he prefers to celebrate the gracious work of the Spirit in the lives of ordinary Christians in every age.

In verse 3 the Spirit is the light of God's love, which casts out from human hearts the darkness of fear. There is a probable echo in verse 4 of St Ambrose's morning hymn *Splendor paternae gloriae* ('O splendour of God's glory bright'), which has the lines

The Stammerer of St Gall: Notker's Sequences

> The Spirit's sanctifying beam
> upon our earthly senses stream.[51]

Both writers use the words *infunde* ('pour') and *sensibus* ('senses'), as does the author of the hymn *Veni, creator spiritus* ('Come, O Creator Spirit, come'):

> Inflame our senses with light,
> pour love into our hearts.[52]

This hymn was almost certainly written during Notker's lifetime; its ascription to Rabanus Maurus is based on the shaky testimony of a tenth-century Fulda manuscript.[53] Notker may have known it: both poets describe the Spirit in terms of anointing, but they may have been independently influenced by the Confirmation part of the baptismal liturgy, where anointing is followed by the prayer for the Spirit's sevenfold gifts.

Verses 5 and 6 recall Matthew 5:8: 'Blessed are the pure in heart, for they shall see God', and verses 8 and 9 celebrate the Spirit's work in Creation (Genesis 1:2), and in bringing new life through the water of Baptism. Notker uses the same verb for 'make fruitful' (*fecundare*) as the prayer said at the blessing of baptismal water. At this point in the prayer the priest breathes three times over the water.[54] Notker may well have had this ceremony in mind as in verse 9 he links the life-giving water with the Spirit's inbreathing. There is also a probable echo here of the divine inbreathing of the breath of life in Genesis 2:7.

In verse 10 Notker sees the gift of tongues as part of the Spirit's work of bringing greater unity to humankind, thus reversing the confusion of languages in the Tower of Babel story (Genesis 11:7). The Spirit is the 'best of teachers', for he is the Paraclete promised by Jesus in John 14:26, who 'will teach you all things'. Notker returns to the theme of the Spirit as teacher in verse 12a; here his words recall the Pentecost Collect, where the light of the Spirit has 'taught the hearts of the faithful'. Perhaps something of Notker's own devotional experience can be sensed in this verse, when he describes the inspiration and guidance of the Spirit in terms of a loving embrace.

This sequence joins *Johannes Jesu* and *Laudes salvatori* in that very select group of Notker's works which found favour outside Germanic territory. It became the principal Pentecost sequence in most European churches and remained so throughout the Middle

Ages. In the fifteenth century the Benedictine nuns of Barking Abbey in Essex adorned it with a delightful ceremony: while it was being sung, the abbey servants scattered flowers of various sorts around the choir, symbolizing the diverse gifts of the Spirit in 1 Corinthians 12:4.[55]

As Trinity Sunday was unknown in the ninth century, Pentecost marks the end of the Proper of the Seasons. *Sancti spiritus assit* makes a fitting climax to Notker's celebration of God's saving acts in Christ, which began with the Nativity.

THE SAINTS

Notker provided sequences for nine feast-days in the Proper of the Saints, from John the Baptist on 24 June to All Saints on 1 November. There are also pieces for the Commons of Apostles, Martyrs, Confessors, and Holy Women.

Notker's flair for playing creatively with biblical images is shown in the sequence for St John the Baptist, *Sancti baptistae*. He asks the saint to pray that Christ may always visit His faithful people

> and be pleased to make His dwelling-place within them, and allow them to be clothed in the fleece of that Lamb whom your finger pointed out as the one who takes away the sins of the world, so that, in company with the angels, we may be worthy to follow Him, clothed in white, through the shining portal, John, friend of Christ![56]

In John 1:29 the Baptist points out Jesus as the Lamb of God who takes away the sins of the world. Notker links this with the white-robed multitude of the redeemed in Revelation 7:9 by implying that the white robe is the fleece of the Lamb. This striking image is making the theological point that Christ Himself is the Christian's robe of righteousness – as St Paul wrote in Romans 13:14 'Put on the Lord Jesus Christ'. In Revelation 7 those in white robes stand before the Lamb, whereas in the sequence they follow Him. There is probably a liturgical influence at work here, namely the Magnificat antiphon at Second Vespers of All Saints' Day: 'O how glorious is the kingdom in which all the saints rejoice with Christ! Clothed in white robes they follow the Lamb wherever He goes.'

The phrase 'John, friend of Christ' refers to the Baptist's description of himself as the 'friend of the bridegroom' in John 3:29.

The Stammerer of St Gall: Notker's Sequences

Sancti baptistae came to be sung in most European churches on 24 June. A measure of its popularity in England is that its last line 'Amice Christi, Johannes was used as a refrain in the fifteenth-century carol 'Pray for us the Prince of Peace', though the carol is actually addressed to that other dear friend of Christ, St John the Apostle.[57]

Notker conveys another theological message through a linking of images in *Laurenti David*, his sequence for St Laurence's Day, 10 August. Laurence, according to tradition, was martyred by being roasted on a grid-iron; he made light of his sufferings, saying to his torturer 'you have me well done on one side, turn me over and eat!'.[58] Notker links this gruesome scene of martyrdom with the meal shared by the Risen Christ with His disciples in Luke 24:41–3. In the Vulgate version Jesus eats a piece of roasted fish and a honeycomb, and shares what is left with the disciples. The two halves of the sequence's sixth verse point the contrast between the torturer and the saint:

> The wicked prefect of the city is grieved to be conquered by
> a roasted fish, the food eaten by Christ; having feasted on
> honeycomb, the guest at the Lord's table rejoices because he is
> to rise with Christ.[59]

By making this link Notker leads the mind away from the details of Laurence's death to that hope of Resurrection which sustained the martyr in his sufferings. The love of Christ, as the poet said earlier in this sequence, 'makes his soldiers spendthrifts with their blood'.

The love of Christ also enables women to mount the 'ladder to heaven' in *Scalam ad caelos*, the last sequence in the book, set for feasts of Holy Women.[60] The ladder-image comes from Jacob's dream in Genesis 28:12, but in the sequence the foot of the ladder is guarded by the dragon-serpent, representing the spirit of evil. The serpent plays the same rôle in the first sequence Notker wrote, *Laudes Deo concinat*; in both pieces the poet celebrates Christ's victory over sin and death by His Incarnation, Cross, and Resurrection.

Peter Dronke has sensitively explored the imagery in this sequence, and he notes Notker's boldness in celebrating the lives of women of all sorts: not only virgin martyrs but also wives, mothers, and former prostitutes. He also points out an overarching theme in Notker's work, the unity between earth and heaven

'With Angels and Archangels'

achieved by Christ: 'Notker's poetry is never a quest, he never prays *for* anything; prayer for him is objectless, it is nothing but a realisation, again and again, of the bonds between earth and heaven in which all his thought moved.'[61] Notker's interweaving of imagery from the Bible and the liturgy, his theological insight, his deep devotion, and his poetic imagination all combine to make his book of sequences a rare treasure. Dronke justly describes him as 'one of the greatest of medieval poets'.[62]

✠ 5 ✠

English Exuberance: The Winchester Troper

The Vikings, who had forced the priest from Jumièges to flee with his chant-book to St Gall, practically destroyed the Church in England. They had sacked Lindisfarne in 793, and York Minster, with its library and school where Alcuin had taught, was burned to the ground in 867.[1]

Alfred the Great (d. 899) resisted the Danes in his kingdom of Wessex and began a revival of the Church. This came to fruition in the time of King Edgar (d. 975), whose royal capital of Winchester had the monk Ethelwold as its bishop from 963. About the year 972 Edgar and Ethelwold summoned a council to order the life of the English Church; this produced the document *Regularis Concordia*. Among its liturgical directions are the instructions for performing the dramatized trope *Quem quaeritis* at the Easter Sepulchre (see Chapter 3).

This English monastic revival, promoted by a monk and an enlightened ruler, recalls the collaboration between Benedict of Aniane and Louis the Pious in arranging the Council of Aachen in 817 (see Chapter 3). Just as the Carolingian reform provided the impetus for writing the first tropes and sequences, so the Winchester revival also led to fresh creativity and delight in liturgical poetry.

Ethelwold wanted the worship of his church to conform as far as possible to the practice of Benedictine houses on the continent. While he was abbot of Abingdon, before he moved to Winchester, he invited monks from Corbie to come and provide examples of their practice, and further continental influences came to Winchester from Ghent and Fleury (St Benoît-sur-Loire), since monks from those houses were present at the council.[2]

'With Angels and Archangels'

As a result of these influences the repertoire of sequences and tropes at Winchester was broadly Anglo-French. Several pieces, however, are only found in the Winchester sources; these are probably home-made products, giving a flavour of the local style. The chants are contained in two manuscripts: Cambridge, Corpus Christi College 473 of the late tenth century, and Oxford, Bodleian Library, Bodley 775, from the early eleventh. They have been edited by Walter Frere,[3] and the sequences from the Oxford manuscript are in an appendix to the Surtees Society's edition of the York Missal.[4]

One of the pieces not found elsewhere is the Easter sequence *Pange turma*, which shows something of the unsophisticated exuberance of the Winchester style:

1   Ring out praises to Christ, all in this throng, with heart and mouth,
2a celebrating together
2b the wonderful Easter sacraments.
3a O what blessings!
3b O such wonders!
4   Lasting till the end of time,
5a they sparkle in highest heaven,
5b they shine with brilliance on earth.
6a For while so many things fill the holy Catholic Church with wonder,
6b the gracious joys of this present festival are still more excellent
7   in their especial splendour.
8a Therefore let bright voices sound together
8b and let them re-echo around the world.
9   Rejoice with sweetest singing
10a for Christ has condemned night and trodden down eternal death;
10b today He returns above with a splendid victory.
11a Mysteries ordained before the world began are fulfilled on this radiant day;
11b the sacred words of the prophets' predictions are unveiled in its glorious light.
12a Christ, the spotless Lamb of God, has defeated death and has arisen today in immeasurable glory.
12b Rejoice, O Catholic Church, our Mother; be glad and exult, as you spread out far and wide throughout the whole world:
13 let your songs combine together, sung with joyful eager hearts.

14 Christ on this bright day has conquered death, and in His mercy has restored you to your heavenly homeland.
15 Let all sing Alleluia.[5]

In contrast to Notker's theological meditations and his interweaving of strands from the Bible and the liturgy, this sequence is a simple expression of joy at the Resurrection. Its main focus is the Church's celebration of this mystery, particularly the part played in it by the singers themselves; Christ's victory over death is not mentioned until verse 10.

The title of the melody is *Pascha nostrum*, a reference to the Alleluia-verse for Easter Day 'Christ, our paschal lamb, has been sacrificed' (1 Corinthians 5:7). The usual Easter sequence sung to this tune was *Concinat orbis* ('Let the world sing together'). The melody was also known as *Cignea* ('Swan-like'), possibly because the unusually short verses 2 to 5 were reminiscent of a swan's slender neck.

References to singers and exhortations to sing, such as these in *Pange turma*, were common in Anglo-French sequences. There is, of course, biblical precedent for them in several of the psalms, for example, Psalm 98 (97): 'O sing to the Lord a new song'. Wolfram von den Steinen contrasts the French emphasis on the singers and the music they make with the German tradition, started by Notker, where the focus is much more on the subject-matter of the sequence. In Germany, he says, 'the sequence has something to say', whereas in France 'the sequence likes to sound well'. He goes on to say that England steers a middle course: French in having an 'a'-vowel at the end of each line, but German in giving a clear grammatical structure to the text.[6]

Pange turma certainly hangs together grammatically but its real essence could perhaps be described as 'mood music': an exuberant outpouring of Easter joy.

Some biblical imagery does make an appearance in *Laus harmoniae*, a sequence for St John the Evangelist:

> Let harmonious praise resound, alleluia!
> A wondrous child is here, born of a mother made fruitful by the Lord's grace; John the Evangelist proclaims His divinity.
> Like an eagle he fixes his eyes on the high mysteries of Godhead, his inward sight rising above everything in creation.
> As his clear mind contemplates these exalted things, his voice

openly declares 'In the beginning the Word was with the Father from all eternity'.[7]

Here the exhortation to sing is confined to the first line; the poet soon turns to the Incarnation and to the evangelist's work in unfolding its mystery. St John's feast-day is a mere two days after Christmas, so it makes liturgical sense for the poem to begin with the birth of Christ and then to echo the Johannine prologue, which is the Gospel for Christmas Day (John 1:1–14). In Notker's *Johannes Jesu* (see Chapter 4) St John gains his insight into Christ's divine nature through leaning on the Lord's breast; this Winchester poet uses the image of the clear-sighted and high-flying eagle to convey the saint's perception of heavenly mysteries. The eagle is the traditional symbol of St John; the other three evangelists also have their emblems, whose biblical source is the four living creatures in Revelation 4:7. This passage is itself derived from the four-headed creatures of the chariot-vision in Ezekiel 1:10. The assigning of emblems to Matthew, Mark, Luke, and John follows Ezekiel's order of man, lion, ox, and eagle. St John's symbol is certainly the most appropriate of the four, and this poet makes effective use of it.

There are several allusions to St John's Gospel and his Revelation in *Lyra pulchra*, one of the sequences for ordinary Sundays not found outside Winchester:

> Let lovely angel-harps make music to the King for ever, and let our voices sing to him 'alleluia'.
> He, the Lamb and the Bridegroom, unlocked the secret oracles of the prophets with the key of mercy; He came to this earth, proceeding from a Virgin,
> so that the lovely presence of His humanity might save those whom His divine majesty had created.
> O wonderful kindness! By this means joys have returned, sins have perished, and a captive world has been set free.
> Nature is amazed, because a Virgin has given birth;
> never has the world seen such a wonder.
> His humanity grew, taken from a Virgin Mother;
> His divinity is always with His Father.
> He who is eternally Alpha and Omega took on our fleshly limitations.[8]

Both 'Lamb' and 'Bridegroom' are descriptions applied to Jesus

English Exuberance: The Winchester Troper

by John the Baptist in John 1:29 and 3:29 respectively. The phrase 'proceeding from a Virgin' recalls the link made in two ancient hymns between the bridegroom-image and the virgin birth of Christ. St Ambrose in 'Come, thou Redeemer of the earth'(see Chapter 1) and the author of 'Creator of the stars of night' take the psalmist's likening of the rising sun to 'a bridegroom coming forth from his chamber' (Psalm 19 [18]:5) and apply the image to the birth of Jesus: 'Thou camest, Bridegroom of the bride ... proceeding from a virgin shrine'.[9]

Further biblical and liturgical allusions cluster around the poet's use of the word 'key'. The letter to the Philadelphian church in Revelation begins 'The words of the holy one, the true one, who has the key of David, who opens and no one shall shut, who shuts and no one opens' (Revelation 3:7). This echoes the prophecy to Eliakim in Isaiah 22:22 and is itself echoed in the fourth of the Great 'O' Antiphons, 'O Key of David', sung before and after the Magnificat at Vespers in the last week of Advent.[10] In the antiphon Christ, the Key of David, is asked to open the prison-house and set captives free; in the sequence the key opens up the hidden meaning of the prophecies which foretold his coming. It is the 'key of mercy' because Christ is the incarnation of God's merciful love, who brings joy, forgiveness, and liberty to captives.

The phrase 'Alpha and Omega' is another Johannine reference. The first and last letters of the Greek alphabet used as a divine title express the all-encompassing nature of God's being. 'I am Alpha and Omega' occurs three times in Revelation, at 1:8, 21:6, and 22:13.

The exuberance of the Winchester style does burst out in *Lyra pulchra* at 'O wonderful kindness!' but the poem also displays some careful theological thinking about the Incarnation, and is almost Notkerian in its use of biblical and liturgical echoes. This happy blend of thinking and feeling is perhaps an example of that 'speculative-affective synthesis' which Martin Thornton found to be an enduring element in English spirituality.[11] The confluence of doctrine and devotion is not, of course, exclusively English; it too is a Notkerian characteristic. At least one of Notker's works was known at Winchester; the troper contains his *Scalam ad caelos*, the sequence for feasts of Holy Women.[12]

Gloria resonante also draws on the Bible and the liturgy, and does so in a strikingly original way. After the first introductory verse the whole body of the sequence is a prayer addressed to Christ by His bride, the Church:

1. With resounding glory of cymbals let the sweet voice of the Church thus burst forth:
2a. 'To You, O Christ, be honour and endless praises, new and fresh as the spring-time;
2b. as David sang in his psalm, You shone before the rising of the morning star.
3a. Mighty Word of God, in mercy You took on human form;
3b. the altar of the Cross, that sacred altar, bore You up.
4a. From that pure stock, which cleansed the world, You brought me forth,
4b. Your Church, leaving the synagogue to go astray.
5a. Therefore I pray that, through the wounds of Your Cross and Your rose-red streams,
5b. You will fill the children I bear You with the grace which flows from heaven.
6a. Defend them with faith, that they may overcome evil,
6b. and may rejoice for ever in Your starry palace,
7. sharing the crown of Your Godhead.'[13]

The mention of resounding cymbals suggests that the voice of the Church is joining in the chorus of praise described in Psalm 150. In verse 2b there is an explicit reference to Psalm 110 (109):3, which in the Vulgate version reads 'From the womb before the morning star I begot you'.

The poet's meditation on the Crucifixion begins by seeing the Cross as an altar, a place of redemptive sacrifice. Verses 3b and 5a clearly echo the Easter Office Hymn *Ad cenam Agni*:

> Upon the altar of the Cross
> His Body hath redeemed our loss,
> And tasting of His roseate blood
> Our life is hid with Him in God.[14]

The English word 'stock', like the Latin original *stirps*, can mean both 'family lineage' and 'the lower part of a tree-trunk'. This double meaning allows the poet to make an imaginative link between Christ's streaming wounds as he hung on the tree of the Cross and the blood and water which flow in the act of giving birth. Thus in verse 4a the sufferings of Christ are the birth-pangs of the Church. She in turn would bring countless offspring to birth in the waters of Baptism, and so the streaming wounds also represent the abundant grace which she prays will flow from heaven into the hearts of her children.

Theology and poetic imagination come together in this sequence as they also do in *Lyra pulchra*. The similarities between the two suggest that they may have been written by the same person. Both begin with earthly voices blending with the music of angelic instruments – harps in *Lyra pulchra* and cymbals in *Gloria resonante*; both contain echoes of biblical and liturgical texts; there is a common delight in the use of compound words such as *homifera(m)* ('bringing humanity'), which occurs in both pieces, as does the idea that mercy (*clementia, clemens*) prompted God to send His Son into the world.

Sequences, of course, are meant to be sung. The following piece, *Laude Christum*, was sung on the feasts of Virgins:

1   Let us sing beautiful praises to Christ,
2a who adorns the virgins with an eternal crown.
2b Full of splendour is the hall of heaven's glory,
3   where the great light of Godhead humbly brings to all their joyful rewards.
4   There are holy peace and perfect love; the people shine like golden spring's fresh growth.
5   No night is there, but only the radiance of eternal day.
6   There life flourishes without death or disease; all are youthful, vigorous, and lovely.
7   Thousands of angels in sweet-sounding companies sing joyful praise, eagerly crying 'Holy, holy, holy' through all the ages of eternity.
8   There the streets are gleaming with bright and sparkling gold;
9   There the most stupendous walls rise upwards of precious costly jewels constructed.
10 There the virgin whose festival day we celebrate radiantly shines wreathed in glory. May we be led there, aided by her loving prayers.[15]

Several biblical passages lie behind this lyrical description of the glories of heaven. Verse 7 reflects Hebrews 12:22: 'You have come to Mount Zion and to the city of the living God, the heavenly Jerusalem, and to innumerable angels in festal gathering.' The angels' song of 'Holy, holy, holy' comes from Isaiah's vision of the temple in 6:3; it is echoed in Revelation 4:8 and again in the Sanctus-chant in the Eucharistic liturgy. Revelation 21:18–23 describes the holy city, whose jewelled walls and streets of shining gold are lit by the glory of God.

In verse 3 the poet adds a striking image of his own: that of God as the servant at the heavenly banquet, who fulfils the guests' needs and brings them gifts which make their joy complete. Perhaps there is a scriptural echo here too: in Luke 12:37 the master who finds his servants awake on his return makes them sit at table and comes and serves them.

This touch of poetic individuality and the wealth of biblical allusion in *Laude Christum* suggest that the author of the previous two sequences may have written this one too. He seems to be fond of vernal imagery: in verse 4 the saints in heaven flourish like the spring-time, and in verse 2a of *Gloria resonante* the praises offered to Christ are fresh and spring-like.

Although the words of *Laude Christum* are only found at Winchester, its melody, with minor variants, was sung in many parts of Europe. At Winchester it was called *Dulcedine paradisi* ('With the sweetness of Paradise') but elsewhere it was usually known as *Adducentur* from the Alleluia-verse for feasts of Virgins: 'The virgins that be her fellows shall be brought unto the king' (Psalm 45:14 [Vulgate 44:15]). In England and France it was sung to an Advent sequence, *Jubilemus omnes* (see Chapter 2), while the text set to it in Germany was Notker's *Stirpe Maria* for the feast of Mary's Nativity. Dom Anselm lists no fewer than 203 manuscripts containing the melody.[16]

The composer of sequences, fitting his texts to the long melodies following the Alleluia, had much more space to work in than the trope-writer, who had the added challenge of trying to dove-tail his words into those of a pre-existing text (see Chapter 2). Tropes often give the impression of being little more than verbal padding, but sometimes they enrich and illuminate their base-text. One such piece is *Caelica suspirans*. Like many tropes it is written in classical hexameters and it is skilfully blended with its base-text, which is the Introit for the Commemoration of St Paul on 30 June. The words of the Introit are in capitals:

> Sighing for the joys of heaven, Paul, Christ's vessel, wished to lay aside his fragile flesh, saying I KNOW WHOM I HAVE BELIEVED, AND I AM SURE, since for me to die is gain and to live is Christ, THAT HE IS ABLE TO GUARD WHAT HAS BEEN ENTRUSTED TO ME and to save my flocks from eternal death UNTIL THAT DAY.[17]

English Exuberance: The Winchester Troper

The Introit is from 2 Timothy 1:12 and the trope puts Paul's words into their context. By means of scriptural allusions the poet creates a thumbnail sketch of the apostle's life, faith, and work. The phrase 'Christ's vessel' recalls his conversion and apostolic call: in Acts 9:15 the Lord says to Ananias 'He is a chosen instrument (vessel) of mine to carry my name before the Gentiles'. The phrase occurs again in the Alleluia-verse of this Mass: 'Great is Paul, the chosen vessel, and truly worthy to be glorified'.

Paul's longing for heaven is expressed in the near-quotation of Philippians 1:21: 'For to me to live is Christ, and to die is gain'. Paul goes on to say 'My desire is to depart and be with Christ, for that is far better. But to remain in the flesh is more necessary on your account' (vv. 23–4). With this passage clearly in mind, the trope-writer holds together Paul's longing for heaven and his pastoral care for the flocks entrusted to him, the congregations which he founded and nurtured.

The poet's embroidering of this Introit-chant has produced a much more vivid picture of St Paul than the words of the Introit alone. His work should therefore have made it easier for his brethren to pursue the Benedictine ideal of letting their hearts and minds be in tune with their voices as they celebrated the apostle in their Eucharistic liturgy. As well as enriching the monks' communal worship, the trope's biblical allusions might also have provided food for their personal meditations.

The Pentecost trope *Lucida culmina* might also have been a stimulus for meditation. Its theme is the creative work of the Spirit, as it depicts in miniature the wonder and beauty of the sky, the earth, and the sea. It decorates the Introit *Spiritus Domini*, from Wisdom 1:7: 'The Spirit of the Lord has filled the world, and that which contains all things has knowledge of the voice' (translation from Vulgate). The trope elaborates the word *omnia* ('all things'), using the flowery and exuberant language that was characteristic of the Winchester style:

> The shining heights of the starry heavens and the foundations of the earth, keeping within their bounds the blue waters of the wave-wandering sea.[18]

The Saxon monastic culture of Winchester only flourished for a relatively short time. Not much more than a decade after the Oxford manuscript of the Troper was written came the fateful events of 1066, after which Norman customs were strictly imposed upon English monasteries and tropes to the Proper of the Mass virtually disappeared.[19]

Elsewhere in Europe the eleventh century was a time of gradual change in the style of sequence-writing, with rhythm and rhyme beginning to make their appearance. A well-known product of this transitional period is the Easter sequence *Victimae paschali* ('Christians, to the Paschal Victim'). It is traditionally ascribed to Wipo (d. 1050), chaplain to the imperial court at Aachen, and it contains such lines as 'Speak, Mary, declaring what thou sawest wayfaring', where the translation reflects the rhymes in the original text.[20]

By the end of the century sequences were being written that were rhythmical and rhymed throughout. They had a regular pattern of verses, each typically consisting of four lines of rhythmical trochaic tetrameter, but they still differed from hymns in that the melody changed after each pair of verses, as it did in the earlier form of the sequence. In the twelfth century the new style would achieve its full flowering, especially in France.

✠ 6 ✠

Paris Fashions: The Regular Sequence

Paris in the twelfth century was a place of intellectual ferment where new forms of Christian life and thought came together and sometimes reacted against each other. Students flocked to the Paris schools to hear teachers such as William of Champeaux (d. 1121) and Peter Abélard (d. 1142), who sharpened their pupils' minds by the question-and-answer method of teaching, and laid the foundations of scholastic theology. They emphasized the importance of reason in the search for theological truth.[1]

The older monastic tradition tended to distrust reason, and held that the way to know God was through worship, prayer, and contemplative love. The Cistercian William of St Thierry (d. c.1148), a great friend of St Bernard (d. 1153), wrote 'Love itself is our knowledge'. In an age of monastic and clerical laxity the Cistercians, led by St Bernard, were determined to return to the early simplicity of St Benedict's Rule. Their devotion to Christ was warm and emotional, but their life was austere.[2]

A third element was added to the religious life of Paris by the Victorines, who achieved a creative synthesis of reasoned doctrine and heartfelt devotion. The abbey of St Victor grew up around the hermitage outside Paris to which William of Champeaux had retired in 1108 after being out-argued in the schools by his former pupil Abélard. The community which he founded there followed the Rule of the Augustinian Canons Regular. This was a new form of monasticism associated with Pope Gregory VII's programme of reform for monks and clergy in the late eleventh century. The canons of St Victor lived a mixed life of contemplation and activity; the monastic elements of worship, prayer, and study were balanced by teaching and pastoral work in the suburbs that soon came to be built around their abbey at the foot of Mont Ste Geneviève on the left bank of the Seine.[3]

'With Angels and Archangels'

Schoolmen, Cistercians, and Victorines had their own distinctive attitudes to liturgical poetry. The Cistercians used office hymns, since these had been approved by St Benedict, but tropes and sequences had no place in their austere liturgy. Their aim was to use only those hymns which had been written by St Ambrose himself, and some monks went to Milan in search of genuinely Ambrosian texts. The results were inconclusive, and the hymnal they compiled was far from satisfactory.[4]

The scholars had no such reservations about liturgical poetry. Abélard composed a book of hymns and sequences at the request of his beloved former pupil Héloïse, who had become prioress of the 'Paraclete', Abélard's earlier place of retreat near Nogent-sur-Seine. The nuns there were using the new Cistercian hymnal, and Héloïse's sharp intellect was well aware of its flaws. She wrote to Abélard 'The syllables are often so uneven that the verses cannot easily be fitted to melodies, without which they are not hymns at all'.[5]

The hymns sent by Abélard in response to this letter show his inventiveness in their unusual verse forms and metres. The best-known is *O quanta qualia sunt illa sabbata* ('O what their joy and their glory must be'),[6] which he set for Saturday Vespers. In a Matins hymn, *Deus, qui tuos erudis*, he celebrates the 'fruitful table of Holy Scripture', abounding with various delightful dishes which provide a feast for the mind. Here he shares the traditional patristic view that biblical texts can be understood in three senses: the historical, the mystical, and the moral.

In *Lignum amaras* he applies Old Testament typology to the Cross, referring to Exodus 15:25, where Moses sweetens the bitter waters of Mara with the wood of a tree: 'Once bitter waters turned into sweetness when wood was placed there; so does the Cross make sweet for the saints the pains that they suffer.'[7] Unfortunately the manuscript breaks off in the course of the hymn for St Mary Magdalen's Day (22 July), and the part containing the sequences is lost. There may, however, be a survivor: the Annunciation sequence *Mittit ad Virginem* was ascribed to Abélard by the sixteenth-century scholar Clichtoveus. It begins 'Not just an ordinary angel is sent to the Virgin; humankind's Lover sends down an archangel in all his brave splendour' (Gabriel's name means 'God's Fortitude' according to Gregory the Great's 34th Homily on the Gospel, read at Michaelmas Matins).

Paris Fashions: The Regular Sequence

The dactylic rhythm is suggestive of Abélard's style, but the attribution is by no means certain. The piece seems to have been more popular in England and Germany than in France. It is absent from the thirteenth-century Parisian sources but is found at that time in several English manuscripts. At Hereford it was sung on the feast of the Annunciation (25 March), and in the Uses of Sarum and York it was among the sequences provided for Votive Masses of the Blessed Virgin Mary. York specified its use in such Masses during Advent, and with the same designation it makes a surprising appearance in the German Cistercian convent at Kaisheim-bei-Donauwörth. In most un-Cistercian fashion the nuns there had no fewer than fifty-nine sequences in their repertory at the beginning of the fourteenth century.[8]

In the twelfth century it was the Augustinians, including the Victorines, who were the first to embrace the new 'regular' style of sequence-writing. At the royal abbey of St Denis, to the north of Paris, the Benedictines were more conservative. They retained the older type of sequence, and the new 'regular' sort did not appear there until the later thirteenth century.[9]

The most widespread and influential of the early regular sequences, *Laudes crucis*, may have come from one of the schoolmen, if the uncertain attribution to Hugh of Orléans is correct. The new verse form embodies a new liveliness of thought and an ingenuity in the use of the Bible which reflects the intellectual vitality of twelfth-century Paris.

THE HOLY CROSS: LAUDES CRUCIS ATTOLLAMUS

1a Let us now the Cross be praising
and our voices be upraising;
in the Cross we all rejoice.

1b Let our singing heavenward glide;
that sweet wood on which Christ died
should be praised with sweetest voice.

1c May our lives and voices blend,
for, when strife and discord end,
then the sound is sweet and choice.

2a Servants of the Cross, sing praise!
Joyful life and endless days
are the gifts the Cross bestows.

'With Angels and Archangels'

2b Let us all our homage pay
to the saving Cross today,
tree whence our salvation flows.

3a O how blest and brightly gleaming
was this shrine of our redeeming,
reddened by the Lamb's dear blood!

3b He, the spotless Lamb, took hence
this world's sin and its offence,
and our ancient foe withstood.

4a This the ladder stretching high,
by which sinners, doomed to die,
to the King of Heaven are drawn.

4b Reaching to earth's furthest places,
on the Cross God's love embraces
all His creatures once forlorn.

5a Back in time this mystery reaches,
for the Cross, as wisdom teaches,
was foreshadowed in the Law:

5b wood made bitter water sweet;
streams gushed forth at Moses' feet,
summoned by the rod he bore.

6a Where a doorway bore this mark,
those within could face the dark
of that dread Egyptian night;

6b all their first-born sons were spared,
no angelic sword was bared
to unleash its deadly might.

7a In Sarepta gathering wood,
set to bake her son's last food,
this poor widow yet believed

7b that the oil and flour would last,
and, her faith still holding fast,
she salvation's hope received.

8a Once in ancient types concealed,
now to us have been revealed
all the blessings of the Cross;

8b Christ has won the heart of kings,
He alone salvation brings,
all His foes will suffer loss.

9a Through the Cross is victory given
to the faithful who have striven;
sicknesses away are driven,
and all evil things have fled.

9b Captives find their liberty,
new life comes to those set free;
to their former dignity
all things by the Cross are led.

10a Hail, O Cross, victorious tree,
from its sin the world you free!
Earth's green trees could never see
such a precious fruit or flower.

10b Medicine for all that ails us,
healing, when disease assails us;
when our human striving fails us,
save us by your mighty power.

11a Lord, whose blood did consecrate
that dear Cross we celebrate,
hear Your servants who adore You;
after this life, we implore You,
bring us to Your palace bright.

11b For our sakes You meekly bore
bitter pain and anguish sore;
at the last to that fair shore
take us, that for evermore
we may share Your joy and light.[10]

The sequence begins in time-honoured French fashion with an exhortation to sing, but the poet gives a distinctive touch to this conventional opening. The singers are urged to sing sweetly, to give fitting praise to the 'sweet wood' of the Cross. This is a reference to the Alleluia-verse *Dulce lignum*, sung before the sequence in Masses of the Holy Cross: 'Sweetest wood, and sweetest iron! Sweetest weight is hung on thee.'

It is itself a quotation from the Passiontide office hymn *Pange, lingua, gloriosi proelium certaminis* ('Sing, my tongue, the glorious battle'),[11] written by Venantius Fortunatus (d. 600) to celebrate the gift of a relic of the Cross to the abbey at Poitiers, where he was bishop.[12]

In verse 1c the writer suggests that truly harmonious praise needs the voice to be in tune not just with the mind and heart but also with the sweetness of a holy life. He uses the word *symphonia* ('sounding together'), which is interpreted by the philosopher and poet Alan of Lille (d. 1203) to mean 'the harmony of the concordant soul and mouth and deed'.[13]

After this introduction the focus of the poem moves from the singers to the Cross itself, the place of Christ's redemptive sacrifice. In verse 4 the poet considers its physical shape: the upright part reminds him of Jacob's ladder uniting earth with heaven (Genesis 28:12) and the promise of Jesus that, lifted up, he would draw all people to himself (John 12:32). The Cross's horizontal beam, upon which Christ's arms were outstretched, suggests the reaching out of God's love to embrace all creation.

There follows a veritable cascade of Old Testament types relating to the Cross, beginning in verse 5b with the incident used by Abélard in *Lignum amaras* where wood sweetens the bitter waters of Mara in Exodus 15:25. Then comes another miracle from Exodus (17:5–6) when Moses strikes the rock at Horeb with his rod and streams of water gush out onto the parched ground.

To modern eyes these types of the Cross appear strained and far-fetched; it seems that any wooden object in the Old Testament will serve the purpose. For the literate medieval Christian, however, regular sequences could have a double function. Their short rhythmical verses made them easily memorable, and so, as well as enriching communal worship, they could also be used as resources for individual meditative prayer. The connections they make between various biblical texts could open up fruitful lines of thought and lead to fresh insights. The link between the Cross and the rod that drew forth life-giving streams might lead the mind to the scene depicted in John 19:34, where blood and water flow from the pierced side of Christ. Tradition associates this scene with the life-giving sacraments of Baptism and the Eucharist; it could also recall Jesus' words to the Samaritan woman in John 4:14, that he can give living water which wells up to eternal life. Given a little rumination, the most unpromising of typological links can sometimes yield spiritual nourishment; if the mind is given time to follow these paths of biblical association, fresh insights can be gained into the mystery of the Cross.

A slow, meditative use of devotional texts was recommended by St Anselm to Queen Matilda of England when he sent her a book of meditations in 1104. In his covering letter he wrote: 'They are not to be read straight through or quickly, but a little at a time with serious concentrated thought. The reader is not intended to read the whole of any of them, but only as much as seems enough to awaken the desire to pray, for that is their purpose.'[14] Anselm is describing the Benedictine practice of *lectio divina*, spiritual reading, which can be applied to the Bible or to any devotional text, including sequences, as a way leading into prayer.

In verse 6 the poet goes further back into the Exodus story to the night of the Passover. The Israelites were instructed in Exodus 12:7 to mark the doorposts and lintel of their houses with the blood of the lamb they had slaughtered, so that the angel of death would pass over them and spare their first-born sons. The poet assumes that these marks would be in the form of a cross. A literal translation of verse 6a is 'There is no safety in a house unless a person fortifies the doorway with a cross' (*Nulla salus est in domo nisi cruce munit homo superliminaria*). Medieval Christians believed that the sign of the cross was a powerful defence against the forces of evil, and this verse strongly suggests that it was a common practice to protect the doorways of houses with this sign. Each Easter the singing of the *Exultet* reminded worshippers that 'This is the Paschal Feast wherein the true lamb is slain, by whose blood the doorposts of the faithful are consecrated', and an Easter house-blessing in the Roman Ritual contains an explicit reference to that Passover incident.[15]

There is no mention in the house-blessing of a cross being marked on the fabric of the building, but this would seem a natural thing to do when blessing a house, given the large number of crosses involved in the consecration of a church. Twelve were marked on the inside walls, a further twelve on the outside, and all were anointed by the bishop with the oil of chrism. In some places the four corners of the church and the doorposts were also anointed.[16] The singing of *Laudes crucis* accompanied the anointing in northern France.[17]

Incised crosses can often still be seen on church doorways. While most are probably pious graffiti, some may be original marks of consecration. This seems especially likely where they are set in special stones, as at Malpas in Cheshire, where a red sandstone church has a doorway cross cut in a block of white sandstone.

Evidence for domestic doorway crosses has largely disappeared or been obscured by rebuilding, but the realm of folklore may contain a couple of hints of their existence. Church doorway crosses often have holes incised at the ends of the arms and in the middle, probably to represent the Five Wounds of Christ in his head, both hands, feet, and side. Such a cross would be easy to cut into a wooden house doorway and might explain the enigmatic verse in the folksong 'Green Grow the Rushes O': 'Five for the symbols at your door'. Some traditional farmhouses had a saltire cross cut into a post beside the inglenook fireplace in order to ward off evil. Two examples of these 'witch-posts' can be seen in the Ryedale Folk Museum at Hutton-le-Hole in North Yorkshire.

So far the typology in the poem has suggested that the Cross sweetens suffering, produces streams of life-giving water, and enables Christ's people to share in his Paschal victory over death. For his final Old Testament type the poet turns in verse 7 from the Law to the Prophets. The connection between the Cross and the widow's firewood in 1 Kings 17:9–16 is another tenuous one, but the emphasis is on the woman's faith in God's promise through Elijah that the supply of flour and oil would not fail. It is, of course, through faith that Christians come to know the redeeming love of God revealed on the Cross.

In verse 8a the poet sums up his use of typology in terms which echo St Augustine's well-known epigram describing the relationship between the two Testaments: 'The New is in the Old concealed; the Old is in the New revealed'.[18]

At verse 9 the structure of the verses changes from six lines to eight lines. The increased number of rhymes conveys the feeling that the poem is building up to a climax as the poet recounts more of the blessings brought by the Cross. The emotion intensifies further in verse 10, where the Cross is addressed directly. There is another clear echo here of Fortunatus's hymn:

> Faithful Cross! Above all other, one and only noble tree!
> None in foliage, none in blossom, none in fruit thy peer may be.

The climax finally comes in the ten-lined verse 11, where the Lord Himself is addressed in a heart-felt prayer that, through His saving death on the Cross, His people may come to share in the glories of heaven.

In the thirteenth century St Thomas Aquinas used the melody of *Laudes crucis* when he composed his sequence for the new feast of Corpus Christi, *Lauda, Sion, Salvatorem* ('Laud, O Sion, thy salvation').[19] In using this melody he may well have been seeking to emphasize the theological link between the Cross and the Eucharist, the sacrament in which Christians 'proclaim the Lord's death until he comes' (1 Corinthians 11:26). The above translation of *Laudes crucis* can be sung to the tune of *Lauda Sion* provided that the melody of verse 1 is sung three times and St Thomas's verse 9 is omitted.

Margot Fassler has pointed out that individual sections of this melody were sometimes detached and re-arranged in new patterns, like pieces of a mosaic, for use in other sequences. A particularly ingenious example of this practice is the sequence *Gaude, Roma* ('Rome, rejoice') in honour of St Peter. Here the melody from verse 11 lines 3 and 8 of *Laudes crucis* is inverted in allusion to the tradition that St Peter was crucified upside down. Thus G B D D E C D D becomes D B G G F G A G and is fitted to the words *Ergo Petro crux paratur* ('So a cross is made for Peter').[20]

The guide for anchoresses known as *Ancrene Wisse* provides evidence that *Laudes crucis* was used in personal devotion as well as in liturgical worship. An anchoress lived an enclosed life of prayer in a cell usually attached to a church – a good example survives at Chester-le-Street to the north of Durham. She would have a window looking into the church so that she could share in its worship, and a 'window on the world' where she could give counsel to those who sought it. *Ancrene Wisse* was written in the thirteenth century, probably by one of the Dominican friars of Chester. Among the devotions it prescribes are five Greetings of the Cross, to be said by the anchoress in the morning and at midday as she knelt before her crucifix. Three of these are antiphons from the Divine Office, another is the first verse of an earlier Holy Cross sequence, *Salve, crux sancta* ('Hail, holy Cross, noble tree') and the last is verse 10 of *Laudes crucis*. The anchoress was to beat her breast at the words 'When our human striving fails us'.[21]

In liturgical use *Laudes crucis* lasted until the end of the Middle Ages as the main sequence for both feasts of the Holy Cross, the Finding on 3 May and the Exaltation on 14 September, with *Salve, crux sancta* as an alternative.[22]

THE RESURRECTION: ZYMA VETUS EXPURGETUR

1 Purge away the former leaven,
and the Risen Lord of Heaven
newly greet with praise sincere.
All our hopes now come to flower

'With Angels and Archangels'

    on this day, whose wondrous power
    was foretold by Law and Seer.
2 Egypt in its might was shaken
    and God's people safely taken,
    freed from all their bondage sore.
    Iron furnace had confined them,
    bitter slavery did bind them,
    labouring with mud and straw.
3 Now breaks forth the voice of gladness,
    praise of God drives out all sadness;
    this, the day the Lord has made,
    brings us triumph and salvation,
    ending grief and desolation,
    freeing us from death's dark shade.
4 Good things, once to sight forbidden,
    shadowed in the Law lay hidden,
    till with Christ fulfilment came.
    Open now stands Eden's Garden,
    Christ's own blood has brought us pardon,
    blunted is the sword of flame.
5 'Child of laughter', in whose stead
    once a ram its life-blood shed,
    signifies the joy we gain.
    Joseph rises from the pit,
    Christ ascends in heaven to sit,
    after death and bitter pain.
6 Aaron's serpent-rod, consuming
    Pharaoh's serpents grim and looming,
    safe from all their evil might;
    brazen serpent, wholeness bringing
    to the sick, whose wounds were stinging
    from the fiery serpents' bite.
7 Christ his hook has deftly wielded,
    with pierced jaw the snake has yielded;
    in the cockatrice's lair
    his young hand the weaned child places,
    and the world's old foe outfaces,
    who then flees in his despair.
8 Those who mocked the balding seer,
    when to Bethel he came near,
    feel Elisha's anger sore.
    David, seen as gripped by madness;
    scapegoat, bearing sin and sadness;
    flying bird, ensnared no more.

Paris Fashions: The Regular Sequence

9 With a jaw-bone wreaking slaughter,
Samson loved a Gazan daughter;
him the Gazans sought to kill.
But the city's gates he shattered,
and he bore them, torn and tattered,
to the heights of Hebron's hill.

10 Thus did Judah's mighty Lion
break apart death's gates of iron,
and the third day rose again.
As the Father's voice resounded,
Christ took up to life unbounded
countless souls with Him to reign.

11 Just as Jonah once remained
three days in the whale contained,
then, alive, his freedom gained,
so did Christ rise from the tomb.
See the bride's bouquet in flower,
spreading wide its fragrant dower;
synagogue now fades in power,
but the Church is in full bloom.

12 Death and life have fiercely striven,
to Life's Prince is victory given,
Christ the captives' bonds has riven,
many share His glorious reign.
Joy returns with this new morning,
night's tears vanish at its dawning;
life slays death, its power scorning,
gladness now has come again.

13 Christ the victor, Christ the way
leading to eternal day;
by Your dying Death You slay;
grant that at Your feast we may
joyfully behold Your face.
Bread of life and fruitful vine,
living water, pure and fine,
feed us, cleanse us, Lord Divine,
and from all Death may design
guard and save us by Your grace.[23]

Zyma vetus was written by the best-known composer of regular sequences, Adam of St Victor (d. 1146). He began his career in the Cathedral of Notre Dame; in 1098 he appears in its records as a subdeacon and he subsequently rose through the ranks to become Precentor, the canon in charge of all the sung parts of the liturgy. It seems that he grew dissatisfied with the life of a secular cathedral canon and wished for the more regulated life of an Augustinian, and so around the year 1133 he joined the Abbey of St Victor. Here he came under the influence of Hugh of St Victor (d. 1141), a distinguished theologian who held together the importance of both reasoned doctrine and contemplative prayer. Hugh placed equal emphasis on each of the three traditional 'senses' of scripture: the literal, the mystical, and the moral. He also saw the whole of Creation as 'a book written by the finger of God', its beauty pointing beyond itself to the eternal beauty of its Creator.[24]

Adam's Easter sequence is a profoundly scriptural meditation on the Paschal mystery of the Resurrection, and is biblically based from its very first line. St Paul's exhortation in 1 Corinthians 5:7 to celebrate the Christian Passover with the unleavened bread of sincerity and truth forms part of the Alleluia-verse *Pascha nostrum*, sung before the sequence on Easter Day. In making this thematic link Adam is following the example of the author of *Laudes crucis*, where the 'sweet wood' of the Cross echoes the Alleluia *Dulce lignum*.

Adam then announces the main subject of his poem, the tracing of the various ways in which the Resurrection was foreshadowed in the Old Testament. The first and most obvious prefiguration is the story of the Exodus, recounted each year at the Easter Vigil. Just as the Israelites were wonderfully enabled to escape from slavery and death in Egypt, so Christ delivers His people from the slavery of sin and the fear of death by His Passion and Resurrection. The forced labour of making bricks is described in Exodus 5:6–7, and Egypt is called 'the iron furnace' in Deuteronomy 4:20, 1 Kings 8:51, and Jeremiah 11:4.

There is another reference to the day's liturgy in verse 3: the Easter Gradual chant, sung before the Alleluia and Sequence, is Psalm 118 (117):24, 'This is the day which the Lord has made; let us rejoice and be glad in it'.

In verse 4 Adam returns to his consideration of how Christ fulfilled the promises and prefigurations of the Old Testament. He has a scriptural warrant for his method in Hebrews 10:1: 'the Law has but a shadow of the good things to come instead of the true form of these realities'. The words 'shadow' and 'form' indicate the influence of Plato (d. 347 BC), who taught that the things of this world are mere shadows or copies of their true essence or 'form', which is eternal. Book 7 of the *Republic* contains the well-known comparison of human life to people living in a cave, unable to see the real objects outside except for their shadows as they are cast on the cave's wall. For the author of Hebrews the shadows of the Old Testament find their solid reality in Christ, just as the earthly temple is a copy of the true sanctuary of heaven (9:24). Platonism continued to influence Christian writers throughout the patristic and medieval periods, and is especially evident in the work of the Victorines. A Platonic lens helped them to picture the relationship not just between the two Testaments but also between the things of earth and the things of heaven.

In the second half of verse 4 Adam begins a series of brief allusions to Old Testament types, the flickering shadows which herald the coming of Christ. He starts, appropriately enough, with the Book of Genesis and the Garden of Eden. The redemptive work of Christ has opened Paradise to all; the flaming cherubic sword of Genesis 3:24 no longer has power to bar the entrance. In highlighting the sword of flame Adam demonstrates his poet's instinct for choosing a striking visual image which makes a vivid impression on the mind.

Adam then moves further into the Book of Genesis, to the stories of the Patriarchs. Isaac's name means 'laughter' (Genesis 21:5–6) and is applied here to the joy of the Easter celebration. Isaac is also saved from death when a ram is killed in his stead (Genesis 22:13), and Joseph is raised from the waterless pit as Christ was raised from the grave (Genesis 37:24, 28).

In verse 6 Adam comes to the Books of Exodus and Numbers, and again shows his poetic individuality in using the image of the serpent. Normally this is a symbol of evil, but here God's power transforms it into something that overcomes evil and brings healing: Aaron's serpent devours those of Pharaoh in Exodus 7:12, and the bronze serpent of Numbers 21:9 heals the victims of snakebite who look upon it. Being raised up on a pole this serpent is a type of the Cross, an instrument of painful death transformed for Christians into the means of healing and salvation.

Adam turns in verse 7 from the Law, the Books of Moses, to the rest of the Old Testament, the Prophets and Writings. In this verse the serpent has resumed its normal hostile character in the shape of the sea-monster Leviathan. Only Christ can meet the challenge given to Job of piercing its jaw with a hook (Job 41:1). The cockatrice or basilisk in Isaiah 11:8 is another snake-like symbol of evil, rendered unable to hurt or destroy by the royal child of David's line who brings in God's kingdom.

The anger of Elisha, mocked for his baldness in 2 Kings 2:23–4, seems an unlikely type for Adam to choose. It may refer to the mockery Christ endured during his Passion, but perhaps a more likely antitype is the Cleansing of the Temple. 'Bethel' means 'House of God', and Jesus was provoked to righteous anger by the sight of the traders in the Temple turning his Father's house into a market-place. After this incident his disciples remembered that it was written, 'Zeal for thy house will consume me' (John 2:17; Psalm 69:9 [68:10]). 'Zeal' (*zelus*) was the word Adam used for Elisha's anger.

Verse 8 continues with another obscure type, the apparent madness of David in 1 Samuel 21:14. The friends of Jesus said 'He is beside himself' in Mark 3:21, but Adam may be pursuing his theme of people who escape from death like Isaac and Joseph in verse 5. David feigned madness in order to escape death at the hands of Achish, king of Gath.

The scapegoat of Leviticus 16:21–2 presents a much clearer parallel to the redemptive work of Christ. The goat carries away the sins of the people, and in John 1:29 the Baptist hails Jesus as the Lamb of God who takes away the sin of the world. The verse ends with another of Adam's vivid poetic images. The bird of Psalm 124 (123):7, having escaped death in the fowler's snare, takes flight into freedom and new life – a delightful picture which expresses the liberation and joy brought to Christ's people by His Resurrection.

In verses 9 and 10 Adam begins to apply his types to Christ more explicitly. The mighty Samson escapes death in Gaza by shattering the city's gates, and Christ bursts open the gates of death (Judges 15:15; 16:1–3). Another biblical text underlies this image of the Resurrection: in Psalm 107 (106):16 the Lord 'shatters the doors of bronze, and cuts in two the bars of iron' as He leads prisoners out of darkness and gloom. Christ is called the 'Lion of Judah' in Revelation 5:5; the phrase is derived from the Blessing of Jacob in Genesis 49:9: 'Judah is a lion's whelp; ... he couched as a lion; ... who dares rouse him up?' For Adam it is the Father's voice that wakes His Son from the sleep of death. Perhaps the poet knew the legend in the Bestiary that lion-cubs were born dead and after three days were wakened to life when their father came and breathed on them.[25] Adam probably also knew the Easter hymn *Chorus novae Jerusalem* by Fulbert of Chartres (d. 1028). Here too Christ is the Lion of Judah, but it is His own voice rather than the Father's that rouses the dead of former ages.[26]

From verse 11 Adam follows the pattern of *Laudes crucis* by increasing the number of lines to the verse as his poem builds to its climax. Jesus applies the 'sign of Jonah' to Himself in Matthew 12:40, and the Resurrection has caused His Bride the Church to bloom and flourish like the cluster of henna-blossom in Song of Solomon 1:14 (Vulgate 1:13).

The conflict between Death and Life in verse 12 echoes a line in the eleventh-century Easter sequence *Victimae paschali*: 'Death and life have contended in that combat stupendous.'[27] The joy of the new dawn of Easter is expressed in language that recalls Psalm 30:5 (29:6): 'Weeping may tarry for the night, but joy comes with the morning.'

Adam again follows the structure of *Laudes crucis* in making his final verse a direct prayer to Christ. Here he uses imagery from St John's Gospel, including some of the 'I am' sayings: Way (14:6), Bread of Life (6:35), True Vine (15:1), and Living Water (4:10, 14).

There are at least thirty scriptural references in *Zyma vetus*, a fact which makes it a rich resource for meditation. It seems to lend itself to the well-known meditative scheme 'Picture, Ponder, Pray': Adam provides a wide choice of biblical images such as the bird released from the snare, which can be pictured in the mind, applied to the Resurrection, and turned into prayer.

In terms of its liturgical performance this sequence was widely sung in France and England, being set in some Sarum manuscripts for Easter Monday and at York for Easter Friday.[28]

THE HOLY SPIRIT: LUX IOCUNDA, LUX INSIGNIS

1. Light of joy and glory bright,
from the throne in heaven's height
sent as fire to Christ's dear friends,
hearts and tongues with love igniting,
so our tongue, at His inviting,
sweetly with our heart's love blends.

2. Christ's own promise to His bride
He fulfilled when Eastertide
ended on the fiftieth day.

'With Angels and Archangels'

    He, the Rock of our salvation,
    pours forth honey's sweet libation,
    oil that soothes all grief away.

3 Sinai's commandments came
    not in tongues of living flame
    but on tablets cut in stone.
    In the upper room enflamed,
    varied tongues one faith proclaimed,
    hearts were filled with love alone.

4 O how happy was that day,
    decked in festival array,
    when the Church was brought to birth,
    when three thousand souls believed
    and were in her arms received,
    living first-fruits from the earth!

5 In the Law first-fruits were bread;
    now, made one by Christ the Head,
    Jews and Greeks one faith can own.
    He the two has firmly blended
    and their separation ended,
    Christ the precious Cornerstone.

6 Both are vessels new and willing,
    ready for the Spirit's filling;
    as Elisha did renew
    oil to soothe a widow's care,
    so, if we our hearts prepare,
    God will fill us with His dew.

7 This new wine, this heavenly dew
    shrinks from lives that are untrue
    and from peaceful ways depart;
    for the Holy Paraclete
    cannot find a dwelling meet
    in a dark divided heart.

8 Kind Consoler, come and teach
    our poor spirits, fill our speech,
    warm our hearts, for where You reach
    nothing harmful finds a place.
    Happiness, and pleasant things,
    health that from contentment springs,
    all the sweetness plenty brings,
    come from Your abundant grace.

9 Light that streams from every quarter,
    seasoning each son and daughter,
    You anoint baptismal water

> with regenerating might.
> Praise to You for Your salvation,
> making us a new creation;
> we, by grace a holy nation
> once were children of the night.
>
> 10 Gift and Giver, grace abounds
> through Your gifts, our heart resounds
> with Your love that knows no bounds;
> let our tongues their skilful sounds
> in your praises now employ.
> Author of all good, bestow
> Your forgiveness here below.
> In Your new life may we grow,
> and, renewed in Christ, may know
> all the fullness of Your joy.[29]

This sequence may also have been written by Adam; it is certainly Victorine in its blending of theology and devotion. It begins with the light and fire of the first Christian Pentecost (Acts 2:3). The poet reminds the singers that they too can be like the apostles if they allow the Spirit to unite their hearts and tongues in expressing God's love.

In verse 2 the outpouring of the Spirit, promised by Christ in Acts 1:4–5, is seen as fulfilling one of the verses in the Song of Moses. Here God's loving care for His people is described in a series of vivid images, among which are the lines 'he made him suck honey out of the rock, and oil out of the flinty rock' (Deuteronomy 32:13).

The Jewish Pentecost on the fiftieth day after Passover celebrated the giving of the Law on Sinai (Exodus 24:12). The poet contrasts the hard stone tablets given to Moses with the living flames of the Spirit bringing the new law of love. The three thousand new believers of Acts 2:41 are seen as living first-fruits, as opposed to the Old Testament's first-fruits of bread as in 2 Kings 4:42.

Verse 5 celebrates the work of the Spirit in uniting Jews and Gentiles into one new people of God. The poet draws on the theology of Ephesians 2:14–22, where Christ has broken down the wall that separated the two races and has become the cornerstone binding together the new temple in which Christians are the living stones.

The new vessels in verse 6 recall the words of Jesus in Mark 2:22 that new wine needs to be contained in new wine-skins. In the story of Elisha and the widow in 2 Kings 4:1–7 the oil continued to flow as long as there were empty vessels ready to contain it. Oil and dew are found together in Psalm 133 (132), where the oil on Aaron's head and the dew of Hermon express the joy of brothers dwelling in unity. Dew also occurs as an image of the Holy Spirit in the Pentecost post-communion prayer: 'Pour out your Holy Spirit upon us, Lord, and cleanse our hearts; make them fruitful by the inward sprinkling of his dew'.[30]

In verse 7 the poet applies his message to himself and his community, stressing the need for a sincere intention to live together in peace. He then follows the Victorine custom of increasing the size of his closing verses, but instead of waiting until the last verse to turn his poem into a prayer he addresses the Holy Spirit directly from verse 8 onwards.

Verse 9 refers to the regenerative power of the Spirit in Baptism; the images of light, seasoning, and anointing have both scriptural and liturgical associations. The Spirit enables Christians to be 'salt of the earth' and 'light of the world' in accordance with the words of Jesus in Matthew 5:13–14. In the liturgy of Baptism salt is placed in the candidate's mouth and oil is poured into the font when baptismal water is blessed on Holy Saturday. Light also shines on this water when wax from the Paschal Candle is dripped into it, or the candle itself is lowered into the font while the priest prays for the descent of the Holy Spirit to make the water a fruitful source of new birth.[31]

Lux iocunda may not be as tightly packed with biblical types as *Zyma vetus* but it still contains plenty of images which could be pondered and turned into prayer. In twelfth-century Paris it was sung at Notre Dame and Ste Geneviève as well as at St Victor; in England it appears in some Sarum manuscripts and in fourteenth-century missals from Worcester, Norwich, and Lincoln. At York it was divided into two, with the first seven verses being sung on the Thursday after Pentecost and the rest of the sequence on the following day.[32]

The following verses give a flavour of another Victorine sequence in honour of the Holy Spirit, *Qui procedis ab utroque*:

> You proceed, O Comforter,
> from the Father and the Son:
> give us tongues to speak your praise,
> set our minds and hearts ablaze

with your flame, O Holy One.
All things live and move in you,
loving warmth of sanctity:
bond of love that joins in one
God the Father and the Son,
equal in divinity.
Shining light of love divine,
bring our darkened hearts release:
chase the shadows which we dread,
guide our steps, that we may tread
paths of justice and of peace.
Fears and worries melt away
in the warmth of your blest fire:
may the joyful love you bring
lead to our true flourishing
and fulfil our hearts' desire.[33]

There is a notable absence of biblical allusions in this piece, and its style is more warm and emotional than *Lux iocunda*. Margot Fassler thinks it dates from the generation after Adam: its Trinitarian theology, especially the idea that the love between Christians should reflect the love between the divine Persons, is reminiscent of the treatise on the Trinity written by Richard of St Victor (d. 1173).[34]

This poet sees the Holy Spirit as the light and fire of God's love, binding together the Persons of the Trinity and uniting Christians with God and with one another. The use of light as an image of God is certainly scriptural, especially in the Johannine writings, for example, 'God is light, and in him is no darkness at all' (1 John 1:5). It is also a prominent idea in the work of the neo-Platonist theologian known as Dionysius (Denis) the Pseudo-Areopagite (*c*. 500). His writings had been influential in Paris since the ninth century, when John Scotus Eriugena translated them from Greek into Latin and Abbot Hilduin of St Denis wrote his *Life of St Denis*. Hilduin's Denis was a composite figure because the abbot had confused the identities of three men called Dionysius/Denis: the Areopagite converted by Paul in Acts 17:34, the bishop of Paris martyred with his companions in the third century, and the early sixth-century theologian.

Suger, the twelfth-century abbot of St Denis, was a great enthusiast for Dionysian ideas, especially his emphasis on light as a divine image, and his Greek view of the Trinity. This was the concept known as *perichoresis* ('processing around'), whereby

'With Angels and Archangels'

the Persons of the Trinity remain distinct but interpenetrate one another in an eternal dance. Suger rebuilt his church to embody these ideas; when it was consecrated in 1144 light flooded into it through the great Gothic windows around the apse, and the movement of the processions to and from the side-chapels reflected the mystery of the Trinity. The abbot also insisted that the harmonious relations between the divine Persons should be mirrored in the peace and love that ought to prevail among the brethren, so that their earthly worship might be at one with the praises of the angels and saints.[35]

The author of *Qui procedis* with his focus on light, Trinitarian theology, and unity, portrayed in words the themes which Suger embodied in the fabric and ceremonial of his church. It is surprising then that this sequence is not in any of the surviving manuscripts from St Denis, but only in those from St Victor and Notre Dame. It was however still being sung in Paris in the sixteenth century, since it is commented on by Clichtoveus in his *Elucidarium* of 1517.[36]

EVANGELISTS

Two sequences in the Victorine style in honour of the evangelists show a more typical use of biblical typology and symbolism. They are *Plausu chorus laetabundo* ('Come sing, ye choirs exultant'), translated by Jackson Mason in *English Hymnal* 179, and *Iocundare, plebs fidelis* ('Rejoice, faithful people'). Both pieces display ingenuity in finding biblical foursomes and applying them to the four evangelists. The river that flowed out of Eden and divided into four streams (Genesis 2:10) is compared to the Gospels, which bring grace and new life from Christ their source. The four carrying-poles for the Ark of the Covenant (Exodus 37:3–4) enabled that special focus of God's presence to be amongst His people, just as the Gospels bear witness to the incarnate presence of God in Christ.

The most elaborate symbolism in these pieces comes from the four living creatures in Ezekiel 1:10 and Revelation 4:7. The author of the Winchester sequence *Laus harmoniae* (see Chapter 5) had applied the image of the eagle to St John, whose mind soared heavenward to penetrate the mysteries of the eternal Word. These Victorine poems use the eagle in a similar way and then go on to the other three creatures. St Matthew is the man, since his Gospel begins with the genealogy tracing the human descent of Jesus from David and Abraham; St Mark is the lion, bearing witness to the Resurrection, when the Father's voice roused from death the young Lion of Judah; St Luke is the ox, an animal of sacrifice signifying the sacrificial death of Jesus on the Cross. Ezekiel's vision yields a further piece of symbolism in that the wheels of the creatures' chariot represent the literal sense of Scripture and the wings the mystical or contemplative sense.

The closing verses of *Iocundare* on the theme of the rivers of Paradise illustrate the Victorines' delight in Creation and their conviction that the realms of Nature and Grace belong together. The life-giving river reveals God's goodness in providing the means for His creatures to grow and flourish, and it is also a symbol of the grace which flows from Christ through the writings of the evangelists. There is also another Victorine synthesis here, the blending of theology and affective devotion:

> Four streams through Eden's garden flow,
> causing living things to grow;
> trees and plants their blossoms show,
> joyful in life's fertile force.
> These streams flow from Christ, the spring;
> down from heaven His grace they bring,
> to His people offering
> health and sweetness from life's source.
> Those who to these waters throng
> find their thirst grows still more strong;
> tasting love, for love they long,
> and for its fulfilment sigh.
> May we to their teaching cleave,
> and sin's tainted waters leave,
> and be drawn, as we believe,
> closer to our home on high.[37]

Iocundare was sung at St Victor and at Notre Dame on feasts of evangelists, and was added to a late thirteenth-century Sarum manuscript[38] as an alternative to *Laus devota mente*. At York it was set for the feast of St Luke and *Plausu chorus* was assigned to the other evangelists.[39]

Iocundare illustrates the Victorines' rootedness in Scripture and their positive view of the natural world, seeing it as a mirror of God's goodness. *Qui procedis* hints at the influence of Dionysian ideas: Hugh had written a commentary on the Pseudo-Areopagite's *Celestial Hierarchies* and Richard drew heavily upon this in his writings on contemplation. Richard taught that in the higher stages of contemplative prayer the intellect and the imagination are left behind and the soul can experience 'ecstasy', a state of being 'outside oneself'. In this state light is infused directly into the soul from above in a ray of divine revelation.[40]

The two Benedictine nuns who are the subjects of the next chapter experienced a form of ecstasy which included visions. In their lives and work they interwove the strands of Bible, poetry, and liturgical worship in their own distinctive ways.

✣ 7 ✣

Poetry and Ecstasy in the Rhineland: Hildegard of Bingen (d. 1179) and Elisabeth of Schönau (d. 1165)

HILDEGARD OF BINGEN

On All Saints' Day 1106 an eight-year-old girl was enclosed in a cell attached to the monastery of Disibodenberg, which stands on a hill overlooking the valley of the River Nahe some twenty miles south-west of Bingen in the Rhineland. The girl was Hildegard, the daughter of Hildebert and Mechtild of Bermersheim; she was their tenth child and so her parents resolved to dedicate her to God as a tithe-offering. She was enclosed with her mentor, the saintly anchoress Jutta of Sponheim; a cousin of Jutta's lived there too and did the domestic work.

Jutta's sanctity attracted a number of young women to come asking to live under her guidance. In 1112 a convent was built for them and the sixteen-year-old Hildegard became a Benedictine nun. The site of the convent had Celtic roots, as did Notker's abbey of St Gall: Disibod and Gallus were both seventh-century Irish monks whose cells became places of attractive holiness.

After Jutta's death in 1136 the sisters elected Hildegard as their abbess. In 1141 she had a vision in which she was told 'Say and write what you see and hear', and so she began to write her best-known work, *Scivias* ('Know the ways'). This is a remarkable blending of the Bible with an integrated theology of Creation and Redemption which is reminiscent of the Victorines. A miniature illustrating one of the manuscripts of this work depicts Hildegard receiving a direct infusion of heavenly light, very much in the manner of Richard of St Victor's description of contemplative prayer.[1]

'With Angels and Archangels'

She had been aware of a light within herself since early childhood. She wrote 'In the same way that the sun, the moon, and the stars are reflected in water, in that way do I see Scripture, discourses, virtues, and human actions reflected in that Light ... I write whatever I see or hear in the Light'. These perceptions did not involve her bodily senses but came to her while she was fully conscious and wide awake.[2]

Hildegard's writings were read at the Synod of Trier in the winter of 1147–8, where they gained the influential approval of both Pope Eugenius III and St Bernard. Her wisdom and prophetic insight attracted all sorts of people to seek her advice and her prayers, including the Emperor Frederick Barbarossa and King Henry II and Queen Eleanor of England.

Her delight in God's handiwork in the natural world led to her becoming expert in the healing properties of herbs and in the best ways to cultivate them. Her skills as a healer were offered not just to her fellow nuns but also to the poor of the surrounding area.

Prompted by a vision, Hildegard moved her nuns sometime around 1150 to what was then a desolate hill, the Rupertsberg, at Bingen where the Nahe flows into the Rhine. The community continued to grow and flourish at its new location, and in 1165 she founded a daughter-house in an abandoned Augustinian abbey at Eibingen on the other side of the Rhine above Rüdesheim.

Hildegard the prophetic visionary, abbess, and healer was also a gifted poet and musician with a highly individual style. She collected her liturgical poetry and music into a work called *Symphonia armoniae celestium revelationum* ('Music of the harmony of heavenly revelations'). The title suggests that she heard the words and music of her compositions with her inward ear during her ecstasies – 'I write whatever I see or hear in the Light', as she told her biographer, Guibert of Gembloux. The word *symphonia* ('sounding together') is a reminder of the Benedictine ideal of consonance between the voices of the singers and their hearts and minds, so that the praises of the nuns might be in tune with the heavenly worship of the angels and saints.

The liturgical poetry in *Symphonia* consists of antiphons and responsories for use in the Divine Office, and sequences to be sung at Mass. Hildegard ignored the rhythm and rhyme of the newly fashionable 'regular' sequence and preferred something closer to the 'classical' style that Notker used. In both words and music,

Hildegard of Bingen (d. 1179) and Elisabeth of Schönau (d. 1165)

however, she followed her own distinctive path, abandoning Notker's one-note-per-syllable rule and often setting several notes to a single syllable of text. In Notker's sequences the two halves of each verse match each other in number of syllables because they were sung to the same melody; there is no such match in Hildegard's sequences because she does not repeat her melodies in the second half of the verse but embellishes and develops them. Peter Dronke has published the text and music of her sequence for St Maximinus of Trier, *Columba aspexit*, where these features of her style can be seen, or they can be heard in the recordings of her music which are fortunately now available.[3]

This is her sequence in honour of the Holy Spirit, *O ignis spiritus*:

1a O fire of the Spirit, the Paraclete, life of all living creatures; in Your holiness You shape and form all things and bring them to life.

1b In Your holiness You give Your healing unction to those whose fragile lives have been broken; in Your holiness you tend their infected wounds.

2a O gentle breath of sanctity, O fire of love; O taste of sweetness in the heart, and inner fragrance of goodness.

2b O spring of clearest water on which we gaze, and see that God is gathering together those who are far off, and is seeking the lost.

3a O breastplate of life, hope which binds together all the body's limbs and girdles them with goodness, save those whom You have blessed.

3b Watch over those whom the enemy has imprisoned, and release them from their bonds, since Your divine power longs for their salvation.

4a O strong, safe pathway, stretching everywhere on earth and reaching every height and depth, You hold together all things, and bind them into one.

4b Through You the clouds glide, the breezes fly, stones become damp, springs gush forth into flowing streams of water, and the earth distils its moisture in green growth.

5a You also guide unfailingly all those whom Your inbreathed wisdom has instructed and made glad.

5b Praise be to You, for Yours is the voice which sounds in our praising, and You are the joy of our lives. As You give us Your shining gifts, Your strength is our hope and our glory.[4]

'With Angels and Archangels'

Hildegard's compositions are the fruits of the revelations she experienced, and so it is not surprising that this piece, like most of her poems, breathes an air of ecstatic wonder. She conveys the sense of wonder very effectively by her repeated use of the vocative ('O fire of the Spirit', 'O gentle breath of sanctity') as she contemplates the many aspects of the Spirit's life-giving work.

The poem begins with two biblical images and the echo of a phrase in the Creed. The Spirit is the Pentecostal fire experienced by the apostles in Acts 2, and Hildegard makes it clear in verse 2a that this fire is the fire of love. The Spirit is also the Paraclete promised by Jesus in John 14:16 and 26. No single English word can do justice to the connotations of 'Paraclete'; its sense includes Comforter, Consoler, Encourager, Strengthener, Advocate. The Creed describes the Spirit as 'the Lord, the Giver of Life', and this is the dominant theme of the sequence.

The holiness of God's Spirit is emphasized three times in verse 1, perhaps a reference to the seraphic hymn 'Holy, holy, holy' in Isaiah 6:3 which is repeated in the Sanctus-chant of the Mass. Hildegard was herself experienced in tending the sick and wounded, and it is clear from this verse that she saw this as an aspect of God's healing and life-giving work. Like the Victorines she regarded God's activity in Creation and Redemption, in Nature and Grace, as parts of an indivisible whole. The Paraclete gives inward strength and comfort to human spirits, and also outward healing to bodies through natural remedies; both are the work of the same life-giving Spirit.

All the five bodily senses are involved in Hildegard's celebration of the Spirit's activity: the fire and water in verse 2 are visual images, the breath of sanctity can be felt like a gentle breeze, its sweetness tasted and its fragrance smelled. The sense of hearing comes in verse 5: as the sound of her words and music filled the convent church, the Spirit was audibly inbreathing those praises of God.

Several of these images have biblical associations. The word *spiritus* means 'breath', and in Genesis 2:7 God breathes into man's nostrils the breath of life. In Isaiah 44:3 the outpouring of God's Spirit is likened to streams of water falling on dry ground, and in John 7:38–9 Jesus promises the living water of the Spirit to all who believe in Him.

Hildegard of Bingen (d. 1179) and Elisabeth of Schönau (d. 1165)

The breastplate in verse 3, safely enclosing and protecting the wearer, recalls the spiritual armour described in Ephesians 6:13–17. Verse 4a echoes two passages from the Book of Wisdom which are used in the liturgy. Wisdom 1:7 is the Introit-chant for Pentecost: 'The Spirit of the Lord has filled the world, and that which holds all things together knows what is said.' Wisdom 8:1 forms part of the first Great 'O' Magnificat antiphon in Advent, *O Sapientia*: the Spirit of Wisdom 'runs from one end of the earth to the other, mightily and sweetly ordering all things.'

The concept of greenness in verse 4b was an important one for Hildegard. A literal translation of her Latin would be 'the earth sweats greenness' (*terra viriditatem sudat*). For her, greenness expressed the life-giving power of the Spirit both in Creation and, as can be seen in the next sequence, in Redemption. As she wrote in one of her prose works, 'The living Spirit goes forth, is embodied in green fertility, and produces fruit that is Life'.[5]

O viridissima virga

1. O greenest branch, hail! You appeared in the oracles of holy men, blown by the Spirit's breath.
2. When the time came, you blossomed among your boughs. Hail, hail to you, because the warmth of the sun upon you drew forth a fragrant balm.
3. For a beautiful flower bloomed within you, which gave its scent to all fragrant herbs that had been dry,
4. and they all appeared in full greenness.
5. The heavens sent their dew upon the grass, and the whole earth was made glad because her womb brought forth wheat, and in her the birds of heaven had their nests.
6. Then food was made for humankind, and great joy for all who shared the feast. Therefore, O sweet Virgin, in you no joy is wanting.
7. Eve despised all these things,
8. but now praise be to the Most High.[6]

This Marian sequence shows the close co-inherence of Creation and Redemption in Hildegard's thought. She begins with the messianic prophecy in Isaiah 11:1–2 that the Spirit of the Lord shall rest upon the branch which will spring up from the root of Jesse. She applies the image of the branch to Mary, whose openness to the Spirit's life-giving grace means that the branch is 'most green'. The

'With Angels and Archangels'

breath of the Spirit has also blown upon the prophets, inspiring them to prefigure the Incarnation.

In verses 2–5 Hildegard develops the image of the branch; it grows and produces the precious flower which is Christ, whose fragrance spreads over the dry earth and makes it green. The earth's flourishing comes about because the heavens have sent their dew upon it – another image which points to the Incarnation. Several biblical texts are echoed in these verses:

> The wilderness and the dry land shall be glad, the desert shall rejoice and blossom (Isaiah 35:1);
> May he be like rain that falls on the mown grass, like showers that water the earth! (Psalm 72 [71]:6);
> Shower (Vulgate *Rorate*, 'Send dew'), O heavens, from above, and let the skies rain down righteousness; let the earth open, that salvation may sprout forth (Isaiah 45:8).

In the second half of verse 5 the imagery takes an unexpected turn, like the sudden transformations which happen in dreams – the poems are, of course, the result of Hildegard's visions. The branch has grown into a tree in which birds can make their nests, but now it produces wheat. This will become the food which is Jesus, the Bread of Life, who gives strength and joy to the human heart.

Here too the imagery seems to develop under the influence of scriptural texts:

> I would feed you with the finest of the wheat (Psalm 81:16 [80:17]);
> Thou dost cause the grass to grow for the cattle, and plants for man to cultivate, that he may bring forth food from the earth ... and bread to strengthen man's heart. The trees of the Lord are watered abundantly ... in them the birds build their nests (Psalm 104 [103]:14, 15, 17);
> On this mountain the Lord of hosts will make for all peoples a feast ... This is the Lord; we have waited for him; let us be glad and rejoice in his salvation (Isaiah 25:6, 9).

In this piece Hildegard draws her imagery from the Psalms and from Isaiah. Her theology has much in common with the Victorines but she uses the Bible in a markedly different way. A typical Victorine sequence, such as Adam's Easter poem *Zyma vetus*, is a carefully constructed mosaic of Old Testament types, each of which relates in its own way to the poem's theme. Hildegard works in a more fluid medium, like a potter with clay; she moulds and

Hildegard of Bingen (d. 1179) and Elisabeth of Schönau (d. 1165)

shapes her biblical material, incorporates it into her imaginative world, and transforms it as her vision develops.

Her sequence in honour of St Rupert, patron of her Rupertsberg convent, draws much of its imagery from the description of the heavenly Jerusalem in Revelation 21:

O Ierusalem

1a O Jerusalem, city of gold, decked in royal purple.
1b O construction of highest goodness, you are light which never grows dark.
1c For you are clothed with the dawn and arrayed in the sun's warm brightness.
2a O blessed childhood, shining in the dawn, and O praiseworthy youth, aflame in the sun.
2b For in these early years, O noble Rupert, you shone like a jewel. Therefore you could not be hidden away among foolish men, just as a mountain is not concealed by a valley.
3a Your windows, Jerusalem, are beautifully decorated with topaz and sapphire.
3b As you shine brightly among them, O Rupert, you stand out from those whose way of life is lukewarm, like a mountain crowned with roses, lilies, and purple flowers showing itself openly to a valley.
4a O tender flower of the field, and O sweet greenness of fruit, and O burden without weight, which does not bend down the heart to sin.
4b O noble vessel, which is not defiled or consumed by dancing in the cave of the old serpent, and which is not weakened by wounds inflicted by the ancient destroyer.
5   The Holy Spirit makes music in you, for you are joined to the choirs of angels, and you are clothed in the Son of God, having no stain in you.
6   What a lovely vessel you are, O Rupert! In your boyhood and youth you longed for God in holy fear, and in the embrace of love, and in the sweetest fragrance of good works.
7   O Jerusalem, your foundations were laid with brightly gleaming stones; these are the publicans and sinners, who were lost sheep. But they were found by the Son of God and they ran towards you and were placed within you.
8   Then your walls flash with living stones, who by their eager good will and devotion have flown up to heaven like clouds.
9   And so your towers, O Jerusalem, shine brightly with

> the redness and whiteness of the saints and with all the splendours of God, which are for ever yours, O Jerusalem.
> 10 Therefore, O inhabitants of Jerusalem crowned with splendour, and you, O Rupert, who are their fellow-citizen, help us who serve and labour here in exile.[7]

Hildegard makes an interesting theological link in verse 1a between the heavenly Jerusalem and the Cross. The phrase 'decked in royal purple' (*ornata regis purpura*) is a quotation from verse 4 of Venantius Fortunatus's Passiontide hymn *Vexilla regis* ('The royal banners'):[8]

> O Tree of beauty, Tree of light,
> O Tree with royal purple dight.

In applying this image to the holy city Hildegard is reminding her sisters that the saints are in heaven because of the redemption achieved by Christ. The city's eternal brightness comes from the light of God's glory, and its lamp is the Lamb who was slain (Revelation 5:12; 21:23).

In the following verses the dawn's radiance grows into full sunlight, as Rupert grew from childhood into youth. His holy life made him shine out like a jewel, or like a flower-studded mountain rising above a valley. The theme of flowers leads Hildegard to some words of the bride in the Song of Solomon: 'I am a flower of the field' (2:1; RSV translates this as 'rose of Sharon'). The bride goes on to compare her beloved to an apple tree whose fruit was sweet to her taste (2:3). In verse 4a the poet is perhaps contrasting the sweet green fruit which is Rupert with the forbidden fruit of Genesis 3:3 that bowed Adam and Eve down under the burden of sin.

Rupert's avoidance of sin is described in verse 4b in terms that echo St Paul's warnings in 1 Corinthians 10:7–10 about avoiding the sins into which the Israelites fell in the time of Moses:

> Do not be idolaters as some of them were; as it is written, 'The people sat down to eat and drink and rose up to dance' ... We must not ... grumble, as some of them did and were destroyed by the Destroyer.

The cave may be an allusion to the basilisk's den in Isaiah 11:8.

In verse 5 Rupert sings with the Spirit among the angel-choirs because he is clothed in Christ's robe of righteousness; he has, in St Paul's words, 'Put on the Lord Jesus Christ' (Romans 13:14).

Hildegard of Bingen (d. 1179) and Elisabeth of Schönau (d. 1165)

He is therefore without stain, like the bride in Song of Solomon 4:7, and deserves his place in the holy city, which is also seen as a bride in Revelation 21:9–10.

In verse 7 Hildegard gives her own distinctive twist to the biblical imagery. The foundation-stones of the new Jerusalem are not the twelve apostles as in Revelation 21:14, but the publicans and sinners, the lost sheep of Luke 15:3–7, who were found by Christ and brought to their heavenly home.

The phrase 'living stones' (*vivis lapidibus*) in verse 8 also occurs in the first verse of the office hymn for a church's Dedication Festival, *Urbs beata Jerusalem* ('Blessed City, heavenly Salem').[9] Both hymn and sequence draw this image from 1 Peter 2:5: 'Like living stones be yourselves built into a spiritual house'.

It is not clear what Hildegard means in verse 9 by 'the redness and whiteness of the saints'. Perhaps red signifies the martyrs and white the virgin saints, or perhaps red refers to the blood of the Lamb, in which the multitude in Revelation 7:14 have washed their robes and made them white.

A dominant theme in this sequence is Rupert's place within the structure of the holy city, which is the Bride of Christ, the Church. There is an interplay between the individual and the corporate, between Rupert's own holy life and his status as part of the Church, the mystical Bride. For this reason Hildegard can apply to a male saint her bridal references from the Song of Solomon: 'flower of the field' (2:1) and 'there is no stain in you' (4:7).

Bridal imagery expressing the corporate aspect of sainthood is clearly seen in the opening verses of the sequence for St Ursula, whose cult was centred on Cologne, some seventy miles down the Rhine from Bingen:

O Ecclesia

O Church, your eyes are like sapphires
and your ears like the mount of Bethel;
your nose is a hill of myrrh and incense
and your mouth like the sound of many waters.
Truly faithful to her vision,
Ursula loved the Son of God;
she left behind the love of this world,
and she gazed into the sun.
She called to that most beautiful young man, saying:
'With great desire I have longed to come to you,

'With Angels and Archangels'

and to sit beside you at the heavenly marriage-feast;
rushing towards you along a strange and unknown path,
like a cloud rushing across a sky of clearest sapphire-blue.'[10]

In the sequence for St Rupert the Church is pictured as the New Jerusalem; here she is explicitly seen as the Bride of Christ. Hildegard begins both pieces by addressing the Church before she turns her attention to the individual saint. This emphasis on the corporate aspect of sainthood is a reminder that a holy life cannot be achieved in isolation from the Church, and also that Ursula's deep love of Christ is an example for all Christians to follow. The vivid imagery from the Song of Solomon expresses Christ's delight in his bride the Church – a delight that embraces not just Ursula but potentially extends to include all the baptized.

The eyes of the bride in the Song of Songs are not compared specifically to sapphires, but they are presumably blue since they are likened to 'pools of Heshbon' (7:4).

The 'mount of Bethel' or 'Bether' comes from 2:17 (RSV translates as 'rugged'), and the 'hill of myrrh and incense' is at 4:6. 'Many waters cannot quench love' says the bridegroom at 8:7, but the phrase 'sound of many waters' occurs in Revelation 1:15.

In verse 3 of the sequence Hildegard's imagination transforms the sapphire of the bride's eyes into the blue of the sky, where the wind-blown cloud is carried swiftly along its high, unknown path. So, too, the saint follows her own strange and unknown path, which will lead her to her beloved Lord.

Hildegard's creative rule-breaking was not confined to the textual and musical form of her sequences, but extended also to the way in which her nuns celebrated their liturgical festivals. They would let their hair flow down beneath veils of white silk; on their heads would be garlands of wrought gold or crowns bearing the sign of the Cross and the emblem of the Lamb of God; gold rings would be on their fingers as they sang in choir. The poet and abbess was thus expressing in outward and visible form the biblical imagery she used in her sequences, as her sisters celebrated their status as brides of Christ in the Eucharistic foretaste of the marriage-supper of the Lamb.[11]

In summarizing her poetic achievement, Peter Dronke wrote: 'Hildegard's images are traditional; what is new is the alchemy for which she uses them, and which produces a poetic effect profounder than any explication can hope to suggest.'[12]

Hildegard of Bingen (d. 1179) and Elisabeth of Schönau (d. 1165)

Monastic ruins survive on the Disibodenberg but nothing above ground remains of her convent at Bingen. Most of it was destroyed during an attack by Swedish forces in 1632, and the rest was blown up by the builders of the railway in 1857. Some of the stonework, however, was incorporated into a vaulted cellar on part of the site, and this still exists beneath the modern building at Am Rupertsberg 16. It forms a highly atmospheric chapel, which is cared for by the Rupertsberger Hildegardgesellschaft and is open on Sunday afternoons in summer. Here a Mass is celebrated on her feast-day, 17 September, and at this time too her relics are carried in procession at the daughter-house she founded at Eibingen, which is still a flourishing convent. Among the woods and vineyards of the Rochusberg, just east of Bingen, is the Hildegardforum, where there is a herb-garden such as Hildegard would have tended, similar to the one Walafrid Strabo delighted in at Mittelzell on Reichenau.[13]

ELISABETH OF SCHÖNAU

Hildegard and Elisabeth were alike in several ways: both were Benedictine nuns who often suffered from poor health, and both were visionaries who gave prophetic messages to leading churchmen. Elisabeth, however, had her own distinctive way of combining the strands of Bible, poetry, and worship.

Hildegard's visions came to her while she was fully awake but Elisabeth received hers during states of unconsciousness which she described as 'falling into ecstasy'. When she regained consciousness she would find herself saying sentences from the Bible or the liturgy which related to the vision she had seen. Liturgical words and actions were often the triggers which brought on an ecstatic vision. Although not a composer of poems as Hildegard was, Elisabeth showed her poetic imagination in her vivid descriptions of the visions themselves.

Hildegard's convent at Bingen lay close to the busy trade-route of the Rhine Valley. Schönau is only about a dozen miles to the north, but its situation is much more remote and secluded, near the village of Strüth in the valley of the Mühlbach. In 1114 a Benedictine priory was founded here as a daughter-house of Schaffhausen in Swabia; in the mid–1120s it became an independent abbey which was a double house of both monks and nuns, with the convent buildings being separated from the monastery by some thirty yards.[14]

Elisabeth's parents entrusted her to the care of the Schönau nuns when she was twelve years old in 1141; she was probably clothed as a Sister at the age of eighteen, and she had her first visions in 1152 when she was twenty-three. She described what she saw in her states of ecstasy to her brother Ekbert, also a Schönau Benedictine, who recorded her words in three 'Books of Visions'. There is evidence that he had studied at St Victor, where there was great interest in ecstasy as part of contemplative prayer (see Chapter 6). In one of her visions Elisabeth saw the soul of one of his friends, whom she called 'that famous master Adam' – this was perhaps the great liturgical poet who died in 1146.[15]

Elisabeth's humility made her reluctant to give any sort of publicity to her visions, but Hildegard and Abbot Hildelin both persuaded her to make them known, so that others might benefit from them. In 1156, following a visit to Hildegard, she began to dictate a further set of visions to Ekbert; this resulted in the 'Book of the Ways of God', a title which shows the influence of Hildegard's *Scivias* ('Know the Ways').

Despite her frail physical health she was elected Superior of the convent. This was an office held for life; she was in charge of the nuns but under the authority of the Abbot. Her duties included the entertainment of visitors, and this could sometimes interfere with the contemplative side of her life. On one occasion she said 'My prayers were hindered that day by the presence of guests'.[16]

When she had been Superior for about eight years, Elisabeth's health finally broke down, and she died at three in the afternoon of Friday, 18 June 1165. Ekbert noted that this was an appropriate day and time for one who had such a deep devotion to the Lord's Passion. In contrast to Hildegard's long life of eighty-one years, death came to Elisabeth when she was only thirty-six.

Elisabeth's account of her visions soon turns to the things of heaven, but it begins with a ghostly encounter in the convent chapel. Pentecost 1152 was a spiritual low-point for Elisabeth. She was feeling ill, depressed, and unable to pray. She did not feel well enough to attend Mass and tried instead to read her Psalter, but before completing the first psalm she threw the book across the room in despair and even considered ending her own life. The depression lasted for several days until the evening of 29

Hildegard of Bingen (d. 1179) and Elisabeth of Schönau (d. 1165)

May, the feast of St Maximin of Trier. On that evening she was at Compline with her Sisters in the convent chapel when she saw a small ghostly figure, the size of a child, but wearing a monk's habit. She immediately became gravely ill, and the Sisters took her to the chapter-house where she lay trembling on the floor. The Gospel-book was fetched and they began reading St Luke's Passion narrative. Elisabeth could still see the ghost, and when they reached the verse 'And Satan entered into Judas', the figure started smiling and dancing for joy, but at the end of the Passion Gospel it disappeared.

Elisabeth interpreted this experience as an apparition of the Devil, and it was at this time of spiritual and emotional crisis that her liturgically based visions began. She saw the Holy Spirit in the form of a dove, and the Virgin Mary during her Saturday Mass. The illness and anguish persisted, however, and Elisabeth gave this account of what happened next:

> The Sisters and Reverend Brothers came together and saw how my soul was troubled. They decided that communal prayers should be made for seven consecutive days, and that they should do penance for me before the Lord, and that on each of the days a special Mass should be celebrated for me in my distress. Among the seven Masses was one of the Holy Spirit, which was due to be sung on the Thursday. I looked forward to it with great longing, hoping that I should receive some consolation on that day. The longed-for day came, and while the Brothers were celebrating Mass I was lying down and praying with the Sisters. And my heart opened up, and I saw an immense light in Heaven, and a dove of great beauty (like the one I had seen earlier proceeding from the light) came down to me. With outstretched wings it circled my head three times, and then flew back up to Heaven.
>
> After this on the Friday, while the Mass of the Cross was being said and I was lying down, a glorious sign of the Cross in Heaven was shown to me, as if on the left side of the Divine Majesty.
>
> On the Saturday, when the Mass of the glorious Virgin was being celebrated, I saw her again in heavenly brightness, worshipping in the presence of the great Majesty. As the Sacred Ministers in the sanctuary were devoutly singing her praises in the sequence 'Hail, bright Star of Ocean' (*Ave praeclara*) and they reached the verse 'Pray, O Virgin, that we may be made worthy of that Bread from Heaven', she fell on her face and

> completely prostrated herself in prayer, and she remained like that until the beginning of the Gospel. From that day to this, on almost every Saturday and whenever her Mass is celebrated on other days, I regularly see the same vision.'[17]

This passage illustrates the very firm link between Elisabeth's visions and the liturgy. On each of the three days described here it was the celebration of the Mass which provided the springboard for her flights of contemplation. Even her initial ghostly experience took place during the liturgical Office of Compline, and her contemplative prayer was to remain closely related to the liturgy for the rest of her life. This is perhaps her most distinctive feature when she is compared to other visionaries, although Julian of Norwich's visions of the Passion were stimulated by a piece of domestic liturgy, when a priest approached her sick-bed and held up his crucifix as he began the Order of the Visitation of the Sick.[18]

Her account of the Lady Mass demonstrates Elisabeth's firm belief that earthly liturgy really does take place 'with angels and archangels and with all the company of heaven'; the realms of earth and heaven interpenetrate one another. Elisabeth's vision assures her that the Virgin in heaven actually does pray when the singers of the sequence ask her to. This incident clearly made a deep impression on the Schönau Sisters, as the thirteenth-century Cistercian Caesarius of Heisterbach mentions it in his *Dialogus miraculorum* ('Dialogue of Miracles') of *c.* 1223. He says that in his day the convent was still observing Elisabeth's directive that a *venia* should be sought (that is, a genuflexion made) at the verse *Audi nos* in that sequence. This verse, which runs 'Hear us, for your Son honours you and denies you nothing', occurs about half-way through the last section of the sequence – the part during which Elisabeth saw the Virgin at prayer. *Ave praeclara* was perhaps the best-loved Marian sequence in medieval Germany. Two vernacular versions of it survive as witnesses to its popularity.[19]

Her vision on the feast of SS Peter and Paul in 1152 established an abiding pattern in Elisabeth's prayer life, in which biblical verses and liturgical texts both played a part:

> At First Vespers on the feast of the blessed apostles Peter and Paul I fell into ecstasy, and I saw those glorious princes standing in the splendour of that great light with the emblems of victorious martyrdom. With faces turned towards me they came down into the air above our earth, and in front of them

> came the blessed Virgin Mother of our Lord Jesus. Peter stood still and made the sign of the cross over me, and I greeted him, saying 'You are the shepherd of the sheep, the prince of the apostles ...' Looking at Paul also I seized upon these words of his: 'I have fought a good fight, I have finished the course ...' When they had returned into the realm of light, I recovered from my ecstasy. From then on, by the grace of the Lord, each saint whose festival we celebrated appeared to me on his feast-day in heavenly light.[20]

Her words to Paul come from 2 Timothy 4:7, and her greeting of Peter would have been sung during the Night Office as part of the responsory following the fifth lesson at Matins. The complete verse is 'You are the shepherd of the sheep, the prince of the apostles; God has given you all the kingdoms of the world, and therefore you have been entrusted with the keys of the kingdom of Heaven'. During First Vespers of Michaelmas she has a vision of three archangels, and when she recovers from her ecstasy she finds herself saying the verse from Revelation 8:3: 'An angel stood beside the altar of the temple having a golden censer in his hand', which is the first psalm antiphon at Matins on this feast.

Her visions during Holy Week and Eastertide 1153 contain vivid imaginings of the Passion, Resurrection, and Ascension. After her ecstasy on this feast she comes to herself with words from St Luke's Ascension-narrative (24:50) and the Magnificat antiphon 'O King of glory, Lord of hosts, who today has ascended in triumph above all the heavens, do not abandon us as orphans but send to us the promise of the Father, the Spirit of truth'.[21]

In the first of her Pentecost visions that year her imagination is again caught up into the events commemorated in the liturgy:

> After this, on the day of Pentecost before Mass began, I was in ecstasy, and I saw again the disciples in the house I mentioned earlier, and the mother of the Saviour was with them. And it happened that, while they were sitting down, something like a flame of fire came down upon each of them with great force. And immediately they all got up together and went out full of cheerfulness and confidence to preach the word of God among the people. When I had seen this, I came to myself again and quickly took up these words: 'The Holy Spirit, proceeding from the throne, invisibly entered the hearts of the apostles ...'
>
> When the Introit of the Mass began, I came into ecstasy again and I saw a vividly bright ray of light from heaven which

> reached down to the altar. And down the middle of it came the beautiful dove which I often see, carrying in its beak something red, like a flame of fire. This looked rather larger than it did when I had seen it before. First, the dove hovered with outstretched wings over the priest's head, and then it seemed to give him a drop of what it carried in its beak. It did the same to the other ministers in the sanctuary, those who were vested for their readings, and then settled on the altar. When I came out of my ecstasy, I asked the Superior to warn the Sisters to pray devoutly, hoping for something which did in fact happen afterwards. For when we went up for Communion at the end of Mass, I slipped through the hands of the Sisters who were supporting me and fell heavily into ecstasy. And as each one received Communion, I saw the dove fly towards her and give her some of what it carried in its beak.[22]

As she recovers from the first ecstasy, she again quotes spontaneously from the day's Office-liturgy: this time it is the responsory following the third lesson at Matins. The three visions which she had on this day are bound into a theological unity by means of the image of Pentecostal fire. First she sees it descending on the apostles, then the dove brings it to the sacred ministers at the altar, and finally each of the Sisters partakes of it as she receives Communion. Elisabeth's imagination ingeniously combines two symbols of the Holy Spirit: the fire and the dove. The Spirit is seen not just as a bond between the priests and nuns of Schönau, but also as a link stretching across the ages, which unites the whole of that liturgical community with the disciples in the Upper Room.

These Pentecost visions allowed Elisabeth to experience the reality of the Holy Spirit's presence in the worshipping life of the Church. Her ability to portray Christian doctrines in vivid images also included the Trinity and the Communion of Saints. As well as her regular Saturday vision of Mary she had a Sunday vision of the Trinity. This had its roots in an incident on the afternoon of 22 July 1152. On that day Elisabeth was not well enough to go to Vespers, and so she and the Superior read the psalms privately in the chapter-house, after which, noticing that it was raining outside, she had a vivid mental picture of a rainbow. At that moment the Sisters came out of chapel and into the cloister, and then they all stopped and stood looking up into the sky. The Superior wondered what they could be looking at, and Elisabeth said 'I think they can see a rainbow.' The two went out to join them and, of course, a

Hildegard of Bingen (d. 1179) and Elisabeth of Schönau (d. 1165)

rainbow it was. Elisabeth's subconscious clearly started to work on the rainbow image and to make connections with Revelation 4. On the following Sunday she had the first of her visions of the Trinity: she saw the whole company of the saints in light, and in the midst of them an ineffably glorious Majesty on a throne surrounded by a rainbow. On the right of the throne sat the Son of Man, and on the left was a cross of light. Though there was no explicit image of the Holy Spirit, the fact that there were three central figures taught her that this was a vision of the Trinity. She says, 'In a way I cannot explain I knew that one Divinity is truly in three Persons, and the three Persons are one divine Substance.' Perhaps her words here echo the Sunday Preface of the Trinity: 'one God, one Lord, not one only Person, but three Persons in one Substance'.[23]

When particular saints appear to her on their festivals, they usually do so within the context of her Sunday vision of the Trinity. In Elisabeth's scheme of visually realized doctrine the saints do not get in the way of her relationship with God, but are seen in their proper places. Thus the words which conclude her vision on the feast of the Beheading of John the Baptist begin with the Trinity, and then move outward to the saint of the day by way of Mary and the angels:

> To You be praise, glory, and thanksgiving, O holy, blessed, and glorious Trinity! Pray for us, Blessed Virgin Mary, that we may be made worthy of the promises of Christ. May all the holy angels of God pray for us in the sight of the Lord. Among those born of woman none has arisen greater than John the Baptist.[24]

This recurring Sunday vision roots Elisabeth's meditations on the Communion of Saints in the doctrine of the Trinity, and gives to her visionary world a pattern of repetition combined with variation. Perhaps this mirrors a similar pattern in the liturgy, where the frequently repeated elements of the Ordinary combine with the variable ones of the Proper.

During her contemplative ecstasies Elisabeth's imagination, fed by the Bible and the liturgy, allowed her to see beyond the sacramental symbols in her convent chapel and glimpse something of what those symbols represented. On Maundy Thursday 1153 she had this experience of what is a very early instance of the custom of elevating the chalice:

'With Angels and Archangels'

> During Mass I saw, as I usually do, everything that was done around the altar, and, while the priest was saying the Canon and was lifting up the chalice in the sight of God, above the chalice I saw the Lord Jesus as if hanging on the cross, and blood seemed to flow down into the chalice from His side and feet.[25]

In her Candlemas vision that year Elisabeth sees the earthly worship at Schönau as partaking in a heavenly liturgy involving Mary, Simeon, and a company of virgin saints:

> At Mass on the Purification of St Mary I began to feel very weak before the Gospel, and as soon as it had been read I passed into ecstasy and saw Our Lady coming down a beam of light. She came and stood at the right hand side of the priest, and beside her was a venerable old man with a long white beard. When the Sisters offered their candles into the hands of the priest, she returned towards heaven, and then a great company of noble virgins came to meet her with shining candles. They waited for a while outside the beam of light, and then joyfully followed her back to heaven.[26]

The last two extracts show that Elisabeth's visions often had a double focus: she remained aware of all that was happening in the sanctuary, but also saw the citizens of heaven interacting with the earthly liturgy. Mary and Simeon stand specifically at the right hand side of the priest; Mary returns to heaven precisely when the Sisters come to present their candles at the Offertory.

Most Christians need to expend some meditative effort if they are to perceive those connections between earth and heaven which came spontaneously to Elisabeth in her visions. Anne L. Clark points out that monastic liturgical life was understood to mirror the continuous celestial liturgy, and she rightly emphasizes the continuity between Elisabeth's contemplative experiences and ordinary Christian prayer:

> As the liturgy itself offers a structure of connection to the otherworld, Elisabeth's experience offered a consolidation – a making solid of – that connection ... Elisabeth understood her own life of prayer to be the context of her visionary experience ... It was a heightening of rather than a divergence from the usual experience of prayer.[27]

Elisabeth's writings became widespread remarkably soon after her death. By 1181 the English Cistercian Roger, of Forde Abbey in Dorset, had obtained a copy of the first Book of Visions, and

Hildegard of Bingen (d. 1179) and Elisabeth of Schönau (d. 1165)

this was rapidly disseminated in England and France. Her fame, however, did not last long; she was to share with Hildegard a period of obscurity which lasted until the nineteenth century. In 1883 Ferdinand Roth, who published her 'Visions and Letters', set off from St Goarshausen in the Rhine Valley and walked over the hills to Schönau. When he got there he found no trace of any local devotion to Elisabeth, but the parish priest at that time had enclosed what was reputed to be her skull in a glass reliquary in the church. The priest told Roth that, when he first came to the parish in the 1860s, Elisabeth was virtually unknown in the place, and he had found the skull used as an ornament on his predecessor's desk.[28]

Schönau is still a secluded rural hamlet, and Elisabeth's skull remains in its reliquary above the altar of the Baroque church which stands on the site of her convent.

It might be useful to note which particular elements of the liturgy stimulated the visionary heightenings of Elisabeth's prayer-life, on the assumption that what helped her to pray might help others too. The poetry and music of the *Ave praeclara* sequence played an important part in her Saturday vision, and the events in the Gospel came vividly into her mind during the ceremonial drama of Candlemas and Holy Week. As well as the highlights of the liturgical year there is a pattern of dramatic climaxes within the structure of each Mass, consisting of Gospel, Consecration, and Communion. It often happened that Elisabeth went into her contemplative ecstasies at precisely these points in the service.

The next chapter explores some of the ways in which biblical images and ceremonial drama combined to give a vivid experience of the Gospel message to medieval Christians, enabling them to be drawn further into the mystery of God's love revealed in Christ.

It seems fitting to end this chapter with a sequence in honour of Elisabeth, which Joseph Kehrein published from a source in the *Acta Sanctorum*:

Salve felix Elisabeth

1 Hail, Elisabeth most blessed,
virgin fragrant as the rose!
Through your life, renowned and saintly,
God His mighty wonders shows.

'With Angels and Archangels'

2. Rapt in holy contemplation
of God's high mysterious ways,
in His boundless love rejoicing,
on the Trinity you gaze.

3. Hail, most highly favoured daughter
of the blessed Mother-Maid!
You were often in her presence
as in ecstasy you prayed.

4. On their own appointed feast days
saints appeared in heavenly light.
God in graciousness revealed them
to your mystic inner sight.

5. Hail, bright spring of holy learning!
Fountain whence sweet waters flow,
sprinkling honeyed drops of wisdom,
teaching us our God to know.

6. Fairest tree in Schönau's woodlands,
clothed in springtime's verdant green;
leafy boughs surround you, countless
as the visions you have seen.

7. As you turned your eyes to heaven,
its fair portals were unsealed;
saints came through its gates to meet you,
and its mysteries revealed.

8. Mirror of the Father's goodness,
shining with His image true,
dear delight of saints and angels;
great the love they bore to you.

9. When the Sacrament was carried
in the sacred pyx enclosed,
you beheld Christ's precious Body;
His Real Presence was disclosed.

10. Now, most kindly saint, exalted
into heaven (as we believe),
through your loving intercession
let us all God's grace receive.

11. Think of us, and all who love you
in this humble house of prayer;
may we know your gracious guidance
and in your protection share.[29]

✠ 8 ✠

Poetry in Motion:
Ceremony, Symbol, and Allegory

CEREMONY AND SYMBOL

Most lay people in the Middle Ages could not understand the words used in church services because they did not know Latin. By about the year 800 Late Latin had mutated in the western Frankish empire into the Romance languages, and Latin was completely foreign to the more recently converted Germanic peoples of the eastern part of the empire.[1] The Carolingian reformers, however, were careful to promote preaching and teaching in the vernacular; intercessions were also in the mother-tongue in many places, including England, where they were known as 'The Bidding of the Bedes'.[2]

Despite the language barrier Christians could still participate in worship and learn more about the Faith through visual imagery and symbolic actions. The interior walls of the church would be a blaze of colour, with paintings illustrating various parts of the biblical narrative of salvation from the Garden of Eden to the Last Judgement, which was often depicted above the chancel arch. Within this arch and on top of the Rood Screen was a portrayal of the central mystery of the Faith: the figure of Christ crucified, the Son of God pouring out His life in loving redemptive sacrifice for the salvation of humankind. Whenever the Eucharist was celebrated at one of the altars in the church, the living memorial was made of that great act of redemption.

The risen and glorified Christ had promised His disciples that He would be with them always (Matthew 28:20). A powerful symbol of his presence was the reserved Sacrament, which in England was usually enclosed in a hanging pyx suspended above the High

Altar. If the worshipper's eyes were directed eastwards, they would be led from Christ on the Cross to Christ enthroned in glory, yet still dwelling sacramentally with his people. Following the fashion of Cluny, the pyx often took the form of a dove, symbolizing the presence and power of the Holy Spirit in the Church.

Since most lay people only received Communion at Easter, blessed bread was given to everyone at the end of Mass on other Sundays. The infrequency of lay Communions meant that from the early thirteenth century the dramatic climax of the Mass was the Elevation, when the priest lifted up the newly consecrated Host and showed it to the people. Squints were cut through walls and holes were bored through screens to enable as many people as possible to see this action, and to greet and adore the sacramental presence of Christ. 'Jesu, Lord, welcome thou be, in form of bread as I thee see' was a greeting commonly used in England; it was part of a fourteenth-century elevation prayer recommended by John Myrc in his *Instructions for Parish Priests*.[3]

By going to church on the great festivals the Christian could experience the Gospel story as its events unfolded over the course of the Church's Year. Candlemas, the last feast of the Christmas season, was especially rich in visual imagery and symbolic actions. Its official name was 'The Purification of St Mary the Virgin'; it takes place on the fortieth day after Christmas, 2 February, and commemorates the events recounted in Luke 2:22–32 when the child Jesus was presented by His parents in the temple at Jerusalem. The blessing of candles on this day derives from verse 32 of the Gospel: the old man Simeon takes the child in his arms and calls him 'a light for revelation to the Gentiles, and for glory to thy people Israel'. Simeon's song, the *Nunc Dimittis*, was sung while the blessed candles were distributed to the people, and then everyone walked with them in procession, their faces illuminated by that symbol of Christ, who brings the light of God's love to the world.[4]

Those who knew Latin could enjoy the poetic language of the prayers which were used to bless the candles. These contained several references to biblical texts on the theme of light, providing a broad scriptural context for the Gospel of the day: 'The people who walked in darkness have seen a great light' (Isaiah 9:2); 'Light rises in the darkness for the upright' (Psalm 112 [111]:4); '[God] called you out of darkness into his marvellous light' (1 Peter 2:9).[5]

Ceremony, Symbol, and Allegory

The candles were blessed with a petition that wherever they were lit or placed, whether on land or on water, the forces of evil might be banished and health of body and soul might be given. There was therefore a strong incentive for the worshipper to take the candle home, but custom required that it should be presented to the priest at the Offertory. The resulting tension is expressed in a story recounted in the thirteenth-century *Golden Legend*, which bears some similarities to Elisabeth of Schönau's Candlemas vision (see Chapter 7):

> One Candlemas Day a certain noblewoman was unable to attend Mass because her chaplain was absent. As she was praying in her chapel, she had a vision in which she was present at a heavenly liturgy celebrated by Christ himself. Mary and a crowd of virgins were there with lighted candles, and at the Offertory they all genuflected and presented their candles to the priest. Everyone in the sanctuary waited for the woman to come and offer her candle, but she refused, despite repeated requests to do so by angelic messengers. Eventually an angel was despatched with orders to take the candle from her by force, and a fierce struggle ensued, which ended when the candle broke in two. The angel went away with the top half, leaving the bottom half in the woman's hand. There the vision ended and the lady was back in her chapel; but the half-candle was still in her hand! She regarded it as a gift from Our Lady, graciously given despite her behaviour at the heavenly Mass, and kept it safely, finding later that it worked many miracles of healing.[6]

This story is depicted in the chapel at Eton College, and forms part of a series of Miracles of the Virgin in the Lady Chapel frescoes at Winchester Cathedral.[7]

In the early fifteenth century the Candlemas liturgy in St Margaret's, King's Lynn sent Margery Kempe into an ecstatic vision of the Presentation of Christ:

> When the said creature beheld the people with their candles in church, her mind was ravished into beholding Our Lady offering her Blissful Son to the priest Simeon in the Temple... Then was she so comforted by the contemplation in her soul... that she might full evil bear up her own candle to the priest, as other folk did at the time of offering, but went wavering on each side like a drunken woman.[8]

Margery (c. 1373–1438) was unusually devout, being a weekly communicant, and unusually emotional, often becoming a nuisance because of her loud weeping in church, but she does illustrate the impact which the liturgy could have upon a layperson's devotional life. Eamon Duffy quotes both Margery's vision and the *Golden Legend* story in *The Stripping of the Altars*, and he goes on to say,

> The Candlemas ceremonies were designed to summon up the scenes they commemorated, and the quest for the visionary vividness which made Margery unsteady on her feet lay behind the tendency in late medieval England to elaborate and make more explicit the representational and dramatic dimension of the liturgy.[9]

Not long after Candlemas comes the penitential season of Lent, another period of forty days, excluding Sundays, in preparation for Easter. Its biblical background is the forty-day fast made by Jesus in the wilderness (Matthew 4:2), which echoes the fasts of Moses (Exodus 34:28) and Elijah (1 Kings 19:8). Ash Wednesday, the first day of Lent, was characterized by the biblical symbol of ashes being placed on the heads of everyone in church. The prayer blessing the ashes referred to the example of the people of Nineveh, who put on sackcloth and ashes as a sign of their repentance (Jonah 3:5–6). The ceremony was also a reminder of mortality: when the priest imposed the ash on each person, he echoed God's words to Adam in Genesis 3:19, 'Remember you are dust and to dust you shall return', although in England the word 'dust' (*pulvis*) was replaced by 'ash' (*cinis*).[10]

The absence of meat from the Lenten diet was accompanied by a visual fast in church: the splendour of the sanctuary was hidden from view by a white veil which hung across the whole width of the chancel, and veils also covered the crosses and statues. The purpose of this was to heighten the dramatic effect of the joyful unveiling at Easter, when the bells rang out and all the church's colourful symbolism was revealed in celebration of the Resurrection.

During Lent the veil was raised on Sundays and feasts but kept down on weekdays except at the Gospel. The fourteenth-century books from Exeter Cathedral and St Mary's Abbey, York provide for it to be raised also at the Elevation, emphasizing the importance of Christ's words in the Gospel and his presence in the Sacrament. At the abbey in York a black cloth was placed in the middle of the reredos veil behind the high altar, so that the elevated Host could be seen clearly.[11]

Ceremony, Symbol, and Allegory

Ceremonial drama abounded in the last week of Lent, Holy Week, which leads up to the great festival of Easter, the climax of the Church's Year. On the week's first day, Palm Sunday, the whole congregation was involved in celebrating the events recounted in Matthew 21:1–9, where Jesus enacted Zechariah's prophecy (9:9) that Sion's king would come to her in humility, mounted on an ass. He was met by crowds of people, who laid green branches down before Him and shouted 'Hosanna to the Son of David'.

The ceremonies in church began with the blessing of flowers and branches. As at Candlemas and on Ash Wednesday the prayers of blessing contained allusion to the Old Testament, in this case to Genesis 8:11. Just as the green olive leaf which the dove brought to Noah heralded an emerging new world of peace, so Christ's approaching death would lead to the new life of the Resurrection.[12]

When the branches had been distributed, two processions were formed: one representing Jesus and His disciples, and one consisting of the congregation with their branches to represent the crowd. The two processions left the church separately and met outside. In the smaller procession the church's relics were carried on a platform called a *feretrum*, from which was suspended a pyx containing the reserved Sacrament. The carrying of the Sacrament on this day was an English custom introduced in the eleventh century by Lanfranc, the first Norman Archbishop of Canterbury. It was virtually unknown in France except at Bec, where Lanfranc had been abbot. He was involved in a controversy with Berengar of Tours over Eucharistic doctrine in which he strenuously defended the reality of Christ's presence in the Sacrament. This may have influenced his desire to have Christ sacramentally represented in the Palm Sunday procession.[13]

When the two processions met, the deacon read the Palm Gospel (Matthew 21:1–9) and then in the Sarum (Salisbury) Use three clerks turned to the people and sang *En rex venit mansuetus*:

> Now your King comes meekly to you,
> daughter of Jerusalem;
> seated on a beast of burden
> humbly, as the seers foretold,
> who His coming had predicted
> in their oracles of old.
> This is He who comes from Edom,

> from Bozrah with garments dyed;
> in these robes of kingly beauty
> His royal progress now he makes,
> not with war-horse nor with chariot,
> but the way of love He takes.
> This is He, a lamb unblemished,
> who to slaughter was consigned;
> through His death new life is given,
> death and hell by Him were killed.
> Thus the ancient prophets' writings
> now by Him have been fulfilled.[14]

These verses, written in rhythmical trochaic tetrameter, allude to several Old Testament texts which draw out more of the significance of Christ's entry into Jerusalem. The poet begins with the prophecy quoted in the Gospel, Zechariah 9:9, where Sion's king comes to her in humility. The second verse refers to Isaiah 63:1, which was seen as a prediction of Christ's Passion: 'Who is this that comes from Edom, in crimsoned garments from Bozrah, he that is glorious in his apparel, marching in the greatness of his strength? 'It is I, announcing vindication, mighty to save.' The poet points out the paradox that, though Christ's demeanour is anything but war-like, he will achieve a mighty victory over death itself. Verse 3 contains allusions to the unblemished Passover lamb of Exodus 12:5, and to the Suffering Servant of Isaiah 53:7, who is led like a lamb to the slaughter. There is also an echo of the first psalm-antiphon at Lauds on Holy Saturday: 'O death, I will be your death; hell, I shall be your destruction.'

The procession then moved to the place of its second station, where boy choristers sang a much older hymn than *En rex venit*, Theodulf's *Gloria laus et honor* ('All glory, laud and honour'),[15] its elegiac couplets evoking the classicism of the Carolingian Renaissance. At Orléans, where Theodulf had been bishop, it was sung from the city gate, and this also happened at Canterbury in Lanfranc's time. At Salisbury Cathedral there must have been an especially ethereal quality to the sound of this hymn, as the choristers were hidden from view in a high gallery inside the west wall, and they sang through quatrefoil openings in the facade. The row of statues in front of these openings would have given the impression that the saints were adding their own hosannas to those of the people below.[16]

Ceremony, Symbol, and Allegory

When the procession had re-entered the church, it made a final station in front of the unveiled crucifix on the Rood Screen. Here the choir sang the antiphon *Ave rex noster*: 'Hail our king, son of David, redeemer of the world ... whom the Father sent as a saving victim.'[17] This marked a change of mood from the joyful hosannas of the procession to the more sombre tone of the Mass that then followed, in which the Gospel was the St Matthew Passion.

On the Wednesday of Holy Week the Lenten Veil was involved in a final moment of drama before being put away for another year. The Gospel of the day was the St Luke Passion, and when it came to the verse (23:45) 'and the curtain of the temple was torn in two' the veil was suddenly removed. In the fifteenth century the nuns of Barking were able to effect a realistic 'tearing in two': their veil consisted of two curtains which met in the middle and were drawn apart at this point; William of Malmesbury in the twelfth century hinted at a similar arrangement.[18] Among the Gilbertines (England's only native Religious Order) and in the Sarum Use the veil was caused to fall down at this verse.[19] In houses of Benedictine monks the veil seems to have remained in place during this Gospel; at St Mary's, York about the year 1400 it was drawn aside at the *Agnus Dei* and then, as ordered by Lanfranc in the eleventh century, removed after Compline.[20]

During Mass in cathedrals on Maundy Thursday the bishop consecrated the holy oils to be used that year in his diocese in the sacraments of Baptism, Confirmation, and the Anointing of the Sick. Before the oils were blessed the choir sang a hymn dating from Carolingian times, *O Redemptor, sume carmen*. Three boys sang the refrain 'O Redeemer, accept the song we sing to you' between verses sung by the choir. One of these mentions the olive branch brought by the dove to Noah in Genesis 8:11; the dove is identified with the Holy Spirit, and the ark with the Church:

> Come to us, O Holy Spirit,
> who across the flood did search,
> and once brought a branch of olive
> to the ark of Holy Church.
> Bless, eternal King of Heaven,
> this fruit of the olive tree;
> let it be a living sign, which
> from all harm may set us free.[21]

The Kiss of Peace was not given at Mass today, because on this night Judas betrayed Jesus with a kiss (Matthew 26:48–9).

The word 'Maundy' is a corruption of the Latin *mandatum* ('commandment'), and derives from Jesus' words in John 13:34: 'A new commandment I give to you, that you love one another even as I have loved you.' This verse was sung during the Washing of Feet, a ceremony commemorating the washing of the disciples' feet by Jesus in John 13:1–15. At York Minster the archbishop washed the feet of the poor before those of the clergy.[22]

In the Roman Rite parts of another Carolingian hymn were sung during this ceremony, *Congregavit nos*, written by Paulinus of Aquileia (d. 802) for a synod at Friuli in 796:

> The love of Christ has gathered us in one:
> let us rejoice and all be glad in him;
> let us revere and love the living God
> and love each other truly from our hearts.
> Where charity and love are, there is God.[23]

The fifteenth-century *Ordinale* of the Gilbertines added further biblical symbolism to the Maundy ceremony: the feet of the poor were washed, kissed, and touched with the hair, recalling the loving ministrations to Jesus of the woman in the Pharisee's house in Luke 7:38.

Maundy Thursday was also the day when the church's altars were stripped of their hangings and washed. Here too the Gilbertines had detailed instructions incorporating biblical symbolism. The altars and crucifixes were first beaten with hyssop twigs to commemorate the scourging of Jesus in John 19:1. Then wine was poured into the five consecration crosses in the altars and into the places of the five wounds in the crucifixes: the crown of thorns, the nails in each hand, the nail through the feet, and the wound in the side made by the soldier's spear (John 19:34). Finally the altars and crucifixes were washed with water, the wine and water representing the blood and water which flowed from the spear-wound.[24]

The minds of those who took part in these ceremonies would have been led from the events of the Last Supper to those of the Passion, in preparation for the more extended contemplation of that saving mystery which the following day's liturgy would provide.

The Gospel on Good Friday was the St John Passion. The verse 'They parted my garments among them' (19:24) was given a dramatic illustration by the removal of two linen cloths from the altar by two servers, one to each side.[25] The Solemn Prayers followed the Gospel, and then the cross was brought in and unveiled in three stages. While the clergy venerated it, the Reproaches were sung, and during the veneration by the people the choir sang Fortunatus's hymn *Pange lingua* ('Sing, my tongue, the glorious battle').[26] As a sign of penitence and devotion the people approached the cross barefoot and on their knees; for this reason the ceremony was popularly known in England as 'Creeping to the Cross'.

No Mass was celebrated on Good Friday but the priest received Communion with the second of the three Hosts consecrated on Maundy Thursday, the first having been consumed on that day. To enact the burial of Christ the third Host was placed with the cross in the Easter Sepulchre. In some places this was a temporary wooden structure and in others a permanent recess in the north wall of the chancel. Lamps were lit around it and a watch was kept. Margery Kempe records the powerful effect which these ceremonies had on her, making the events of the Passion vividly present in her mind:

> On a Good Friday, as the said creature beheld priests kneeling on their knees and other worshipful men with torches burning in their hands before the Sepulchre, devoutly representing the lamentable death and doleful burying of Our Lord Jesus Christ after the good custom of Holy Church, the memory of Our Lady's Sorrows, which she suffered when she beheld His Precious Body hanging on the Cross, and then buried before her sight, suddenly occupied the heart of this creature drawing her mind wholly into the Passion of Our Lord Christ Jesus ... wounding her with pity and compassion, so that she sobbed, moaned, and cried.[27]

Throughout the later Middle Ages and well into the twentieth century the Easter Vigil was celebrated on the morning of Holy Saturday. The compiler of the *Ordinale* of St Mary's Abbey, York was aware of the anomaly of celebrating in the day time a liturgy which contained several references to night and darkness. He explained that the Vigil was originally held at night but was brought forward because of human frailty and the previous day's fast; those wishing to receive Communion today would have been fasting from the previous midnight. It was not until the 1950s that the Vigil was restored to its ancient and appropriate time during the hours of darkness.[28]

The rite began with the blessing of the New Fire, although in some places this happened on Maundy Thursday and the fire was kept burning until the Vigil. Ritual fires had been part of the culture of the pagan peoples of northern Europe; the Church used fire in its Easter ceremonies to symbolize the light of Christ rising from the darkness of death. Sometimes the fire was kindled by refracting the sun's rays through a crystal, but on cloudy days a spark was struck from a flint. The leaping of the spark from the stone onto the tinder was a sign of the Risen Christ springing to new life from the rocky tomb.

The spark struck from the rock was used as an image of the Resurrection by Prudentius (d. c. 405) in his hymn *Inventor rutili* ('Gracious Lord, Creator of shining light'). This was sung as the flame from the New Fire was carried into church to light the Easter Candle.[29] The flame was transferred by means of a candle on the top of a pole called a 'spear' (*hasta*). At Winchester St Ethelwold's *Regularis Concordia* (c. 970) records that the top of the spear took the form of a serpent with the candle in its mouth.[30] In some places there was a triple candle, in case a single flame should be blown out by the wind. The Gilbertines were even more cautious, having five candles on their spear with a sixth enclosed in a lantern.[31]

The spear and the serpent are symbols which refer to the Passion: the soldier's spear that pierced the side of Christ in John 19:34, and the serpent lifted up on a pole in Numbers 21:9. This was seen as foreshadowing the Cross because those who looked upon it found healing and new life. The Gilbertines called the stand for their Paschal Candle a 'tree' (*arbor*); the Tree of Life was an epithet often applied to the Cross. There was further Passion symbolism in the widespread practice of inserting five grains of incense into the Paschal Candle, or into its stand if the candle was too high to reach. The grains were inserted in the form of a cross, and represented the Five Wounds. This cluster of Passion symbols at the Easter Vigil conveys a theological message: the Cross and the Resurrection belong together as parts of the one Paschal mystery of Redemption.

In many large churches the proportions of the Easter Candle were enormous. In Durham Cathedral the stand itself reached as high as the triforium and occupied almost the whole width of the choir. Upon it was placed a piece of wood as high as a man, and on top of that was the Paschal Candle. It was so high that it had to be lit by means of a device lowered from the roof. In some places, including York, such a device took the form of a dove, which descended with a candle in its beak – a reminder of the fire of the Holy Spirit. The St Mary's *Ordinale* describes the lighting of the Candle by an abbey servant, who climbed up the church wall with some of the New Fire in a lantern. All the lights in the church were lit from the Paschal 'because the fire of the Holy Spirit proceeds from Christ, and all the children of the Church are illuminated by Christ'.[32]

The Candle was lit during the Easter Proclamation, the *Exultet*; the deacon singing it paused at the phrase *rutilans ignis* ('shining fire') to allow the lighting to take place. Easter is the Christian Passover, and so the *Exultet* is rich in biblical allusions to chapters 12 to 15 of Exodus, which tell the story of the Passover and the escape from Egypt. The lighted Candle is a vivid symbol of the pillar of fire in Exodus 13:21; this was a sign of the Lord's presence with His people as He set them free from death and slavery and led them through the Red Sea towards the Promised Land. Since New Testament times Christians have seen these events as foreshadowing the Cross and Resurrection, by which Christ leads His people away from the bondage of sin and death, and towards the promised glory of heaven.

The readings which followed the *Exultet* expressed in various ways the Easter theme of new life with God. The readings varied in number but always included the Creation story in Genesis 1 and the crossing of the Red Sea in Exodus 14:24–15:1.

New life was also celebrated in the next part of the service, the liturgy of Baptism. The Blessing of the Font contained a comprehensive summary of the part played by water in the biblical story of salvation. It included the moving of God's Spirit over the primeval waters (Genesis 1:2), the flood's washing away of evil from the world (Genesis 7), and the four rivers of Paradise, which brought fruitfulness to the earth (Genesis 2:10). To illustrate these the priest scattered water from the font towards the four points of the compass. The prayer also referred to the bitter waters of Mara, made sweet by wood (Exodus 15:23–5), the water from the rock struck by Moses' rod (Exodus 17:6), and the flowing streams of grace which bring joy to the city of God (Psalm 46:4 [45:5]). The references from the New Testament were to the water made wine at Cana (John 2:1–11), the Baptism of Jesus in the Jordan (Mark 1:9), his walking on the Sea of Galilee (Mark 6:48), and the water mingled with blood which flowed from his side (John 19:34).[33]

The climax of the Font Blessing came when the priest prayed for the descent of the Holy Spirit:

> Let the power of the Holy Spirit come down upon the fullness of this font ...

He sang this petition three times, each time at a higher pitch, while lowering the Easter Candle more deeply into the water with each repetition. By its third immersion it was resting on the bottom of the font; the priest held it there as he breathed three times across the surface of the water, straight ahead, and then diagonally left and right. Before removing the Candle he sang:

> ... and let the whole substance of this water be made fruitful for rebirth.[34]

In the Sarum Use the Paschal Candle was not carried to the font because of its size and the height of its stand, which at Salisbury reached to about thirty-six feet. As a rather tame substitute some wax was dripped into the font from another candle, which had been lit at the New Fire.[35]

Several Franco-Roman sacramentaries from the ninth century refer to 'candles' in the plural being placed in the font. Amalarius of Metz, writing about the year 830, describes how all the baptismal candidates lowered their own candles into the water, creating a scene which recalled the descending flames of the first Christian Pentecost.[36]

At this climax of the Font Blessing three biblical symbols of the Holy Spirit were brought together: the Water of Life (John 7:38–9), the Breath of God, renewing the face of the earth and bequeathed by Jesus to the apostles (Psalm 104 [103]:30; John 20:22), and the sending down of Pentecostal fire (Acts 2:3).

Oil of Unction and Oil of Chrism were then poured into the font, but at York this only happened if there were candidates to be baptized.[37]

The final part of the Vigil was the first Mass of Easter, and during the Gloria all the bells rang out to celebrate the Resurrection. In York relations were sometimes strained between the monks of St

Mary's Abbey and the canons of the Minster; mindful of this, the monks tactfully refrained from ringing their bells unless those of the Minster had already sounded.[38]

During Matins at St Mary's on Easter morning the Abbot, Prior, and Sub-Prior, vested in either white or red copes with matching stoles and maniples, brought the Blessed Sacrament from the Easter Sepulchre; all the church's torches were lit, all the bells were rung, and the organ sounded. The Sacrament was carried in procession round the choir during the singing of the *Te Deum*.[39]

Easter Matins at Barking Abbey included two dramatic enactments. The first represented the 'Harrowing of Hell', the Risen Christ's liberation of the souls of the dead. When Dame Katharine of Sutton was Abbess (1358–76), she decided that it should take place at this time in order to 'root out spiritual torpor'. The nuns with some clergy, holding palms and unlit candles, were shut inside St Mary Magdalen's Chapel. The officiant and two deacons approached the chapel, accompanied by the cross, a banner, and a thurible. Taking the cross the officiant knocked three times on the door with it, each time singing at a gradually higher pitch: 'Lift up your heads, O gates! and be lifted up, O ancient doors! that the King of glory may come in. (Psalm 24 [23]:7)'

Then the doors were flung open and those inside were dragged out. After this the dramatized trope *Quem quaeritis* was performed at the Easter Sepulchre (see Chapter 3). The Blessed Sacrament in a crystal was then taken from the Sepulchre, shown to the people, and carried in procession to the altar of the Holy Trinity.[40]

A longer procession took place after Terce and before the principal Mass. At St Mary's, York it went round the outside of the church if the weather was fine, accompanied by the singing of Fortunatus's hymn *Salve, festa dies* ('Hail thee, Festival Day').[41] The *Ordinale* says that this Easter procession is the origin of the procession before Mass on all the other Sundays of the year, 'so that, like the apostles, we may see the Lord in Galilee'.[42] Each Sunday has something of the flavour of Easter about it, since it is the first day of the week, the day on which Christ was raised to new life. The mention of Galilee is a reference to the angel's words to the women in Matthew 28:7, 'He is going before you to Galilee; there you will see Him'. The place where the procession ended was known as the Galilee, and the name still survives in some places, such as the cathedrals at Durham and Lincoln.

'With Angels and Archangels'

During the regular Sunday procession the people and the church's altars were sprinkled with holy water. Outside Eastertide this ceremony had a penitential character; it was accompanied by the *Asperges* chant, taken from Psalm 51:7 (50:9): 'Thou shalt purge me, O Lord, with hyssop, and I shall be clean; thou shalt wash me, and I shall be whiter than snow.' In Eastertide the symbolic associations of water changed from the idea of cleansing to that of abundant life. The accompanying chant in the Easter season was *Vidi aquam*: 'I beheld water which proceeded from the right side of the temple, and all they to whom that water came were made whole, and they say, 'alleluia, alleluia'.' The text has its main scriptural source in Ezekiel's temple vision in chapter 47, where the water flowing from the temple becomes a river, which brings life and flourishing wherever it reaches. In Johannine theology the true temple is Christ Himself; Jesus 'spoke of the temple of His body' (John 2:21), and water flowed from His side on the Cross (19:34). In Revelation there is no temple in the holy city, for at its heart is the throne of God and of the Lamb, from which flows the river of the water of life (21:22; 22:1).[43]

The Sunday procession also included the singing of the Litany of the Saints, in which Christians in heaven were asked for the support of their prayers. This reminded earthly worshippers that they were joined in one communion with the whole company of heaven, within the fellowship of the mystical Body of Christ.

Much longer litany-processions took place on the Rogation Days, the three days leading up to the feast of the Ascension on the Thursday of the fifth week after Easter. These processions had been instituted about the year 470 by St Mamertus, Archbishop of Vienne in the Rhône Valley. They were acts of petitionary prayer for the protection of the land from the earthquakes and volcanic eruptions which had been troubling the area. In Carolingian times they were used as opportunities for instruction in the Faith (see Chapter 3 II); in medieval England they were seen as banishing the forces of evil and asking a blessing on the growing crops. They also ensured that parishioners knew where their parish boundaries were; the procession would stop at a boundary marker, a stone or prominent tree, and a Gospel would be read, often the one appointed for Ascension Day (Mark 16:14–20). The place-name Gospel Oak is a surviving reminder of this custom.

The processions from cathedrals ended at some other church in the city or its suburbs, where Mass was celebrated. In York this element of neighbourliness was sometimes compromised: on Rogation Monday the Minster usually visited St Mary's Abbey and *vice versa*, but the *Ordinale* instructs the abbey Sacrist to make sure the processions can pass each other in the wider part of Bootham without having to wait too long. It once happened that the two sets of alms-boys had a fight, during which each side broke or stole their opponents' holy water sprinklers. Since then the Minster did not always wish to come to St Mary's, in which case the monks went instead to St Matthew's Hospital in the Horsefair. The destination on Tuesday was St Leonard's Hospital, and on Wednesday the procession went through the fields beside the River Ouse as far as Clifton.[44]

Several banners were carried at the head of the procession in front of the cross. In the Sarum Use and at Exeter in Bishop Grandisson's time (*c.* 1337) the leading banner depicted a dragon and the second a lion. The carrying of images of these two beasts while walking in procession might suggest an allusion to Psalm 91 (90):13: 'Thou shalt tread underfoot the lion and the dragon.' On Rogation Wednesday, however, the dragon was relegated to a position behind all the other banners, with the lion then being at the procession's head. This would indicate that only the dragon was a symbol of evil, whereas the lion was an image of the Risen Christ, the victorious Lion of Judah (Revelation 5:5) who overcame the dragon, as in St Fulbert of Chartres' hymn *Chorus novae*, 'Ye choirs of New Jerusalem':

> How Judah's Lion burst his chains,
> And crushed the serpent's head.[45]

The early-fifteenth-century *Ordinale* of the Gilbertines says that the first two Rogation Days represent the times of nature and the written law; the third day, when the dragon is at the back, symbolizes the time of grace. At St Mary's, York the dragon's retreat was more gradual: he was at the front on Monday, in the middle on Tuesday, and at the back on Wednesday. He was clearly a satanic figure, being described as 'laughing and proud'; he was conquered 'by the grace of Christ and by prayers'.[46]

At Pentecost the Office of Terce had a special importance because it took place at the third hour of the day, the time when the Holy Spirit descended upon the apostles (Acts 2:15). The Gilbertines were instructed to light lamps around the altar and to sing the Office 'with great devotional fervour of heart and voice'.[47] The Order's founder, St Gilbert of Sempringham (d. 1189), was influenced by the austere liturgical style of the Cistercians. Among the Benedictines, however, the medieval flair for ceremonial drama was much more in evidence. At St Mary's, York the altar was censed by seven monks in white copes – the Abbot, Prior, and five senior brethren – during the Office Hymn *Veni, Creator* ('Come, O Creator Spirit, come').[48] The *Ordinale* says:

> It is certainly permissible for a white dove, either a live one or a representation (*sive viva, sive ymaginaria*), to descend with clouds at the beginning of the hymn *Veni, Creator* to represent the coming of the Holy Spirit, and for seven candles to be lit as a sign of his seven gifts, with the Blessed Virgin and the apostles looking up to heaven.[49]

Presumably an abbey servant would have been somewhere up aloft waiting for the hymn to begin, when he would either release the live dove or lower the representation. This seems to have been a large piece of stage scenery incorporating the dove, clouds, seven candles, and the figures of the Virgin and the apostles.

A similar device was used by the Benedictine nuns of Barking Abbey. Its early fifteenth-century *Ordinale* says that during the *Veni, Creator* 'the dove descends in the midst of the choir with seven candles'. The seven gifts of the Spirit derive from the Vulgate version of Isaiah 11:2, where they are given as 'wisdom, understanding, counsel, fortitude, knowledge, piety, and the fear of the Lord'.

The variety of the Spirit's gifts, as indicated by St Paul in 1 Corinthians 12:4–11, was beautifully illustrated at Barking when the servants scattered flowers of various sorts around the choir during the singing of Notker's Pentecost sequence *Sancti Spiritus assit* (see Chapter 4).[50]

With each passing year the Church's rites and ceremonies gave the worshipper a chance to experience afresh the saving events of the Gospel. Those with little knowledge of Latin could still be drawn into these events through symbolism and ceremonial; Margery Kempe's experiences at Candlemas and on Good Friday show how powerfully impressive the liturgy could be. Christ's Cross and Resurrection, the redemptive mystery at the heart of the Gospel, is shown forth in every celebration of the Mass. The medieval worshipper was able to enter more deeply into this mystery at any time of the year by using the form of meditation known as liturgical allegory.

ALLEGORY

Allegory was inherited by the first Christians from Judaism as a means of understanding Scripture. A scriptural text was thought to contain more than just its literal sense; it could also point to deeper truths. An example in the New Testament is the way St Paul uses the two sons of Abraham to illustrate the contrast between the freedom enjoyed by Christians and the law-bound religion of Judaism. Isaac was the son of the free woman Sarah (Genesis 21:2), and her slave Hagar gave birth to Ishmael (Genesis 16:15). 'Now this is an allegory', says St Paul in Galatians 4:24, and he goes on to explain that Hagar 'corresponds to the present Jerusalem, for she is in slavery with her children. But the Jerusalem above is free, and she is our mother' (4:25–6). St Paul accurately calls this an allegory, because a symbol has just one point of connection between itself and the thing symbolized, but an allegory has more than one such link.

By the late fourth century the ceremonial of the Eucharist was being given an allegorical interpretation, for example, in Antioch by Theodore of Mopsuestia. He told his baptismal candidates that when the bread and wine were being carried towards the altar they were to think of Christ being led towards his Passion. The placing of these gifts on the altar represented the laying of his body in the tomb, and the cloths spread upon the altar signified his grave-clothes. The moment of Resurrection came at the Epiclesis, the prayer for the descent of the Holy Spirit upon the bread and wine.[51]

In seventh-century Gaul the writer known as Pseudo-Germanus gave an allegorical exposition of the Gallican Mass.[52] After the adoption of the Roman Rite in the Carolingian Empire the Western Church had one of its most prolific and influential allegorists in Amalarius of Metz, who was writing around the year 830. Despite the vehement opposition of Agobard and Florus (see Chapter 3. IV) Amalarius's imaginative approach to the liturgy offered to those who did not understand the words of the Mass a chance to meditate upon aspects of the life of Christ.

'With Angels and Archangels'

One of Amalarius's outline-meditations begins with the choir singing the Introit and Kyrie, which is compared to the chorus of prophets foretelling the coming of Christ. The Epistle represents the preaching of John the Baptist, the Alleluia the apostles' joyful response to their call, and the Gospel the teaching of Christ, which would then be expounded in a vernacular sermon. When the people surged forward to present their gifts at the Offertory, the worshipper could think of the crowds on Palm Sunday, and then of Christ's prayer in Gethsemane as the priest began the low-voiced recitation of the Canon. The celebrant's bowing of his head at the prayer *Supplices te* was the cue for a meditation on Christ's death, with the centurion's cry being represented by the audible beginning to the prayer *Nobis quoque*. The uniting of the sacramental Body and Blood at the Commixture symbolized the Resurrection, a fitting climax to the meditation.[53]

Amalarius's fertile imagination produced numerous alternative allegorical schemes, allowing the individual worshipper a wide choice of subjects for meditation. The subdeacons, for example, were a particularly visible feature of the liturgy in those days, since they stood behind the altar facing the priest and congregation. During the Canon they stood with heads bowed, and then they raised their heads at the *Libera nos* ('Deliver us') just before the Commixture. Amalarius says they could symbolize either the apostles, who were sad until delivered from evil at the Resurrection, or the secret disciples like Joseph of Arimathaea, or again the women who persevered in the presence (*facies*, 'face') of Christ in his Passion.

The number of these alternative suggestions for meditation is evidence not just of Amalarius's ingenuity but also of his insight into devotional psychology. He was aware that every congregation would contain people of varying temperaments: a meditative pathway which suited one person would not be found helpful by another. By providing a range of options he was clearly trying to make his work pastorally useful, so that as many people as possible might be enabled to enter more deeply into the Divine Mysteries.

Many writers throughout the Middle Ages followed Amalarius in applying allegorical interpretations to the liturgy. In the early twelfth century Honorius Augustodunensis compared the priest at the altar to a *tragicus*, an actor in a tragedy – that is, a serious drama as opposed to a comedy. He wrote: 'By his actions in the theatre of the Church our actor portrays Christ's battle to Christian people, and impresses upon them the victory of his redemption.' Honorius suggested that, when the priest turned to the congregation after the Offertory and said *Orate, fratres* ('Pray, brethren') the people might think of Christ's request to his disciples to pray while he underwent his agony in the Garden of Gethsemane (Mark 14:38). The silently recited Secret prayer could suggest the silence of the Suffering Servant as he is led like a lamb to the slaughter (Isaiah 53:7). The priest's extended hands as he prayed at the altar would recall Christ's arms outstretched on the Cross, and the chant of the Preface corresponded to his cry of dereliction (Mark 15:34).[54]

Allegorical interpretations were also given to the eucharistic vestments; the vesting prayers in use today derive from this tradition, some of them being enriched with biblical associations. The amice, which at first is put over the head before being lowered to fit around the neck, is likened to the 'helmet of salvation', part of the 'whole armour of God' in Ephesians 6:17. The alb recalls the multitude of the redeemed in Revelation 7:14, who have 'washed their robes and made them white in the blood of the Lamb'. The maniple on the left arm evokes the reapers of Psalm 126 (125):6, joyfully carrying their sheaves (*portantes manipulos*) after sowing in tears. The placing of the chasuble on the shoulders is a reminder of Jesus' words in Matthew 11:30, 'My yoke is easy and my burden is light'. Rupert of Deutz, a contemporary of Honorius, is thought to have been the first writer to give Christological meanings to the vestments. For Rupert the amice on the head was a sign of the Incarnation, in which Christ hid his divinity and clothed himself in our humanity.[55]

Shortly before his election as Pope in 1198 Innocent III wrote a treatise on the Eucharist called *De Sacro Altaris Mysterio* ('On the Sacred Mystery of the Altar'), in which he continued the tradition of relating ceremonial actions to the events of Christ's Passion. An example of this is his treatment of the hiding of the paten between the Offertory and the *Libera nos* ('Deliver us') prayer after the Our Father. In a said Mass the priest would hide the paten under the corporal on the altar, and in a solemn celebration the subdeacon would hold it concealed in the folds of the humeral veil hanging from his shoulders. Innocent took this as representing the behaviour of the disciples when Jesus was arrested in Gethsemane (Mark

'With Angels and Archangels'

14:50): they fled in fear and hid themselves, leaving Christ alone in his Passion.[56]

Innocent was a major influence on Durandus of Mende (d. 1296), whose allegorical work was very widely read in the later Middle Ages. By the year 1500 there had been forty-three printings of his *Rationale Divinorum Officiorum* ('Account of Divine Services').

In fifteenth-century England a priest known only as B. Langforde continued this devotional tradition in his book *Meditations in the Time of Mass*. It contains a meditative scheme on the Incarnation and two on the Passion. One of these bids the worshipper at the Offertory to 'Have meditation how our Lord, the Saviour of all mankind, most willingly offered Himself to His eternal Father, to be the sacrifice and oblation for man's redemption; and offer yourself to Him in return.' After the Elevation: 'Call to remembrance and imprint inwardly on your heart by holy meditation the whole process of the Passion from the Maundy (last supper) unto the point of Christ's death.' At the Our Father, a prayer containing seven petitions:

> Remember the seven words of great mystery which our Lord did speak hanging quick upon the cross in His great agony, distress, and pain of death; and specially follow the example of that holy word in the which He prayed for His enemies (Luke 23:34) ... See now that you likewise forgive all enmities.[57]

Christ's Passion was an especially important element in the devotional lives of late medieval Christians. Some villages never recovered from the effects of the Black Death in the mid-fourteenth century, and many people were all too familiar with poverty, pain, and bereavement. It was a source of strength and comfort to them to know that God's Son had Himself undergone great suffering in order to win for them the joys of eternity.

As the Middle Ages went on, the allegorical meanings given to the vestments became increasingly centred on the Passion. The alb was often decorated with four rectangular panels of embroidery called apparels: a pair above the hem, one at the front and one at the back, with another pair on the sleeves. A fifth apparel was attached to the amice, and in an Augsburg missal of 1555 these were seen as representing the Five Wounds. The girdle and maniple pointed to Christ's bonds at His scourging, and the chasuble recalled the purple robe.[58]

Ceremony, Symbol, and Allegory

The next chapter looks at some of the poems which were among the fruits of this Passion-centred devotional tradition.

✠ 9 ✠

The Poetry of the Passion

Among the pastures of Cheshire near Macclesfield stands Gawsworth Hall, a half-timbered Tudor manor-house which was the home of the Fitton family. In 1497 Randle Fitton became Rector of the neighbouring church of St James, and several family members have had the dates of their death written into the calendar of a missal of Sarum Use now in the Bodleian Library, Oxford.[1] The Gawsworth Missal and an Augustinian Collectar from Dublin[2] are the only two manuscripts which contain *Plangat Syon*, a sequence remarkable for its distinctive and rather cryptic use of biblical typology:

Plangat Syon

1a Mourn, O Sion, your Salvation,
mourn with bitter lamentation,
for your Spouse, who all creation
shepherds, by His flock is slain.

1b Mourn, for God's own Son divine,
in whose human life did shine
truth and graciousness benign,
now must suffer grievous pain.

2a Virgin, mourn the Son you bore,
stripped, and cut with lashes sore,
thorn-crowned head pierced red and raw;
now the Mother's grief flows free.

2b Mourn His body stained with blood,
nailed alive to that hard wood,
hands and feet fixed to the Rood,
hanging on the gallows-tree.

3a Christ endured that pain and shaming,
'Eloï, Eloï' proclaiming,
'lama sabtani' exclaiming;
death's approach would not delay.

The Poetry of the Passion

3b Virgin, mourn the myrrh and gall
    when His thirst held Him in thrall;
    'It is finished' hear Him call,
    as His life-blood ebbs away.

4a Mary to John's care commending,
    His last breath to God ascending,
    thus His life achieved its ending
    and redeemed the human race.

4b Sun and moon their light did hide;
    when a soldier pierced His side
    blood and water in a tide
    poured from Him in streams of grace.

5a Rocks are rent, the earth is shaken,
    bodies of the dead awaken
    and appear, their graves forsaken,
    at the Lord's expiring cry.

5b Mary, Queen of Heaven most fair,
    helping sinners by your prayer,
    mourn your Son, whose loving care
    led Him for our sins to die.

6a Mother of the Crucified,
    standing with Him as He died,
    that which Simeon prophesied
    pierced your spirit in that hour.

6b Virgin Mother of Messiah,
    virtue's bloom with grace afire,
    as foretold by Jeremiah,
    Rose that mourns the Lily-flower.

7a Moses had your grief foretold
    in the Pentateuch of old;
    Lamentation's letters hold
    portents of your anguish sore.

7b Bowed no more with grief tremendous,
    crowned in heaven, be pleased to send us
    prayerful help, and so commend us
    to the blessed Son you bore.

8a Christ, exalted now on high,
    humbled then in dust to lie,
    for our sins condemned to die,
    bearing evil's crushing might.

8b Christ, who followed suffering's way,
    grant that on the judgement day
    with Your blessed saints we may
    share eternal joy and light.

'With Angels and Archangels'

> 8c In Your mercy, Lord, behold us,
> may Your Mother's prayers uphold us
> and Your gracious love enfold us
> in Your heavenly palace bright.[3]

In the Gawsworth Missal *Plangat Syon* is appointed for use in the Mass of the Five Wounds. This cultus, like that of the Holy Name, belongs to the tradition of warm, affective devotion to Christ in His Sacred Humanity which spread through western Christendom during and after the twelfth century, due in large part to the influence of St Bernard and the Cistercians. Its emotional tone is illustrated by the 'Rosy Sequence', *Jesu, dulcis memoria* ('Jesu! – the very thought is sweet!'),[4] set for the feast of the Holy Name. After the thirteenth century, under Franciscan influence, this devotional tradition became especially focused on aspects of the Passion.

There is a private devotion to the Five Wounds in a late twelfth-century Benedictine psalter from Chester, but the liturgical observance is thought to have begun in the monastery of Fritzlar in Thuringia. In Germany it became a liturgical feast, but in fifteenth-century England it remained as a Votive Mass, usually said on a Friday as an alternative to the Mass of the Holy Cross. It would probably have been celebrated at the altar in the loft on top of the Rood Screen, at the foot of the great Cross.[5]

There is no especial emphasis on the wounds themselves in *Plangat Syon* but the actions which caused them are mentioned: the crowning with thorns in verse 2a, the nailing of hands and feet in 2b, and the piercing of the side in 4b. The poem has a wider focus, treating the whole Passion as seen through the eyes of Mary as she stood by the Cross (John 19. 25).

The first and last verses contain strong echoes of St Thomas Aquinas's Corpus Christi sequence, *Lauda Sion*:

> Laud, O Sion, thy salvation,
> Laud with hymns of exultation
> Christ, thy King and Shepherd true.[6]

In both poems 'Sion' represents the Church: the holy city, new Sion, appears in Revelation 21:2 as a Bride adorned for her Spouse. St Thomas bids the Church to praise Christ, her King and Shepherd, for the gift of himself in the Blessed Sacrament; the later poet bids the Church to mourn for him like his grieving mother, since the Shepherd has been killed by his own flock.

The Poetry of the Passion

Verse 6a recalls Simeon's prophecy to Mary when she presented the child Jesus in the Temple: 'A sword will pierce through your own soul also' (Luke 2:35). In the following two verses the poet develops the image of 'Sion' in a new way: as Mary focuses the eyes of the Church, new Sion, on the Passion, her grief is prefigured in the Old Testament by the mournful daughter of Sion in Lamentations and by Rachel's lament for her children. Rachel is a prominent figure in chapters 29–35 of Genesis but her mourning is not mentioned anywhere in the Pentateuch, the 'Books of Moses'. It does appear, however, at Jeremiah 31:15, the text quoted by St Matthew (2:18) in relation to the slaughter of the Innocents:

> A voice was heard in Ramah, wailing and loud lamentation, Rachel weeping for her children; she refused to be consoled, because they were no more.

'Lamentation's letters' are spelt out in the original text of verse 7a:

> *Virgo mater Christi Jesu,*
> *scribitur in threnisque vau,*
> *joth, hee, heth, lamet, tahu,*
> *Moysi pentatyco.*

A literal translation would be:

> Virgin Mother of Christ Jesus, it [*i.e.* Mary's grief] is written in the Pentateuch of Moses and in Lamentations: Vau, Iod, He, Heth, Lamed, Thau.

Lamentations is a series of alphabetical poems, each verse being preceded by a letter of the Hebrew alphabet. The names of the letters were chanted when Lamentations was used in the Holy Week Office of Tenebrae, thus making them familiar to many. The mournful daughter of Sion features in numerous verses and it is not clear which ones were in the mind of *Plangat Syon*'s author, but an application of the letters in his poem to the corresponding verses in Lamentations 1 yields the following result:

VAU (v. 6):	From the daughter of Sion has departed all her majesty.
IOD (v. 10):	The enemy has stretched out his hands over all her precious things.
HE (v. 5):	Her children have gone away, captives before the foe.
HETH (v. 8):	All who honoured her despise her ... yea, she herself groans, and turns her face away.

'With Angels and Archangels'

LAMED (v. 12): 'Is it nothing to you, all you who pass by? Look and see if there is any sorrow like my sorrow.'

THAU (v. 22): 'For my groans are many and my heart is faint.'

Woven into this Old Testament typology of Mary at the Cross is a striking piece of floral imagery in the last line of verse 6b: *Languet rosa lilio* ('Rose that mourns the Lily-flower'). The scriptural basis for seeing Mary as a rose is Ecclesiasticus (Sirach) 24:14 (Vulgate 24:18). Here the personified female figure of Wisdom, widely regarded as a prefiguration of Mary, describes herself as a 'rose in Jericho'. The passage would have been familiar because in the Sarum Use it formed part of the first reading at Mass on the feast of Mary's Assumption. For the twelfth-century poet Alan of Lille Mary is a 'blossoming rose which knows no thorn', and the rose-epithet is applied to her in several English lyrics from the thirteenth to the fifteenth centuries.[7]

The comparison of Christ to a lily is much more unusual. A well-known meditation on the Passion by John of Fécamp (d. 1078), *Candet nudatum pectus*, begins by focusing on the whiteness of the crucified Jesus; early in the fourteenth century it was turned into an English lyric, 'Whyt was hys nakede brest'. The renowned Yorkshire hermit Richard Rolle (d. 1349) quoted a version of this lyric, in which the Five Wounds are mentioned, in a spiritual letter known as *Ego dormio*:

> Naked es his whit breste, and rede es his blody side;
> Wan was his fayre hew, his wowndes depe and wyde.
> In five stedes of his flesch the blode gan down glyde.[8]

There is an association between Christ and lilies through the figure of the bridegroom in the Song of Solomon, who was often seen as a type of Christ, the Bridegroom of the Church. When the daughters of Jerusalem ask the bride where her beloved has gone, as they too wish to find him, the bride replies,

> My beloved has gone down to his garden, to the beds of spices, to pasture his flock in the gardens, and to gather lilies. I am my beloved's and my beloved is mine; he pastures his flock among the lilies.[9]

This passage is applied to Christ in the Ambrosian Office Hymn for feasts of virgins, *Jesu, corona virginum* ('Jesu, the virgins' crown'). Its second verse begins

The Poetry of the Passion

> Amongst the lilies thou dost feed,
> with virgin choirs accompanied.[10]

When the author of *Plangat Syon* refers to Christ as a lily, he is evoking the whiteness of his naked breast and perhaps also suggesting that Christ is the bridegroom offering love among the lilies of the garden. There was a strand in medieval English devotion to the Passion which made this same paradoxical connection between the Cross and the garden of love in the Song of Solomon. The fourteenth-century lyric *Quia amore langueo* ('For I languish with love') takes its refrain from Song of Solomon 2:5: 'Refresh me with apples, for I am sick [or 'I languish'] with love.' In this poem Christ's outstretched arms on the Cross are ready to embrace his beloved, the Christian soul, whom he invites into his garden: 'Mine arms ben spread to clip her me to ... Fair love, let us go play: apples ben ripe in my gardayne.'[11]

In *Plangat Syon*, since its main theme is the grieving Mother at the Cross, it is she who languishes with love for her Son.

Something similar to the poet's image of the Rose languishing for the Lily is depicted in a remarkable fifteenth-century wall-painting in All Saints' Church, Godshill on the Isle of Wight, which is known as 'the Church of the Lily Cross'. On the east wall of the south chapel is a mural showing Christ crucified on a three-branched lily. His open arms could be seen as being ready to embrace all who come to him, and they also seem to be stretching upwards as if to gather the lilies like the bridegroom in the garden. The wall beside the cross is patterned with stylized red roses, emblems of the grieving Mother.

Maestae parentis Christi ('Of the sorrowful Mother of Christ') is another sequence which uses Old Testament typology in its treatment of Mary at the Cross. It first appears in England in the edition of the Sarum Missal printed in Rouen in 1497, where it is set for the Mass of the Compassion or Lamentation of Blessed Mary. It is unusual in that parts of it are in classical sequence form while others have rhythm and rhyme like a regular sequence. Its style is florid and rhetorical, and only some of its thirty-eight verses are translated here.

The poet was clearly aware that anger is often a component of grief. In this extract Mary sees the unjust sufferings of her Son and vents her anger at the angel Gabriel:

> 'Why should You suffer like this, my sweetest Son?
> You have never done any wrong;
> why should You die nailed to a cross, as if You were a criminal?
> How can I go on living, when my Son endures such pain?
> Is this the grace which you brought to me, Gabriel,
> when you said "Hail Mary, full of grace"?
> I have the very opposite of what you promised me:
> instead of grace, I have pain and punishment.
> You called me the most blessed of all women;
> now, my grief and affliction are plain for all to see'.[12]

In the next extract the body of Jesus has been taken down from the Cross and is being held by Mary – a scene which Richard Pfaff likens to a fifteenth-century Pietà:[13]

> Such a tearful sight! The Mother sits, only half-alive, and holds in her bosom the lifeless body.
> She goes all over His wounds, the blood-stained places of the nails and scourges; she sees His temples surrounded by the wreath of thorns, and in His side the open doors of His heart. Such a weight of grief and groaning!
> With her gentle hands the Mother strokes her Son's limbs, once beautiful and now bruised.
> She embraces and kisses His face, which has become pale through suffering and cruel blows.
> Wringing her hands she cried aloud; she moistened the body with her weeping, her tears falling in drops like the dew.[14]

From this vivid portrayal of Mary as she cradled the body of her Son the poet turns to the mothers in the Old Testament whose tears prefigured the grief of Mary at the Cross:

> Whoever searches the scriptures will see women lamenting most bitterly. Taunted by her rival, Samuel's mother Hannah weeps as she prays and is thought to be drunk.
> Rachel's wailing voice resounded in Rama; she was grieving for her children and refused to be consoled.
> Naomi was sad and mournful when death snatched away her husband and her sons; Anna, mother of Tobias, cried when her son was sent to Rages by his father to retrieve his money.
> Hannah the mother of Samuel and Anna the mother of Tobias, Naomi, and Rachel (if we believe Jeremiah) all wept many tears.
> But no lament could be likened to the bitter tears of the Virgin Mary, Mother of Christ crucified, the true Messiah.[15]

The Poetry of the Passion

Plangat Syon features two mournful figures from the Old Testament, the daughter of Sion in Lamentations and Rachel in Jeremiah 31:15. *Maestae parentis* also has Rachel together with Hannah (1 Samuel 1), Naomi (Ruth 1), and Anna (Tobit 5:17). Both poets use the same phrase for 'bitterest lamentation(s)', *planctu(s) amarissimo(s)*, which may indicate a borrowing or may simply be coincidence.

The sorrows of Mary were the subject of devotional poetry as early as the twelfth century. The sequence *Planctus ante nescia* ('Lamentation was unknown to me before') is a Victorine product from Paris, the work of the abbey's Sub-prior, Godfrey of Breteuil (d. 1196):

> O my Son, my only sweetness, and my special joy,
> look upon Your mother's tears, and bring me some comfort.
> Your wounds torment my eyes, my mind, and my heart.
> What mother, what woman has ever known such joy as I knew, and such misery?
> In Your pain, the colour drains from Your face;
> it rushes and floods down in a tide of blood.
> Oh, the gentleness of Your heart, suffering such pain!
> Oh, the goodness of Your grace, dying so meekly!
> How true the words of faithful Simeon:
> now I feel within me that sword of grief which he promised;
> my sobbing, my sighs, and my tears
> are the outward signs of my inner wound.
> O Sion's children, run into His arms, as He hangs upon the cross;
> Those arms are there outstretched, ready to embrace all who love Him.[16]

This selection of verses from the sequence ends with the image of Christ's arms on the Cross being outstretched to embrace all who come to him, as in the English lyric *Quia amore langueo* quoted above. There is a similar idea in the Parisian sequence *Laudes crucis* (see Chapter 6), which would have been well-known to Godfrey. Here the horizontal beam of the Cross expresses God's love reaching to the ends of the earth, while the vertical beam is compared to a ladder by which sinners are drawn up to heaven. This recalls Jesus' saying in John 12:32 that, lifted up, He would draw all people to Himself:

> A ladder stretches up on high,
> by which sinners, doomed to die,
> to the King of Heaven are drawn.
> Reaching to earth's furthest places,
> on the Cross God's love embraces
> all His creatures once forlorn.

Godfrey's sequence appears in a missal printed in Paris in 1520 and intended for the Franciscan Order,[17] but there is no evidence that it was ever used liturgically, even at St Victor.

There is some bold imagery from the Song of Solomon in a sequence found in a fifteenth-century Darmstadt manuscript, *Ecce arbor salutaris* ('Behold the saving Tree'), in which the Cross is seen as a bridal bed:

> On this bed, with outstretched arms,
> pledging all love's perfect charms
> to His dearly cherished bride,
> here the Bridegroom gives His all:
> love poured out beyond recall,
> love, that heals her death-wounds wide.
> See, O bride, your fair Belovèd,
> all with rosy blushes covered;
> feast your eyes on His bright face.
> Let your heart's desire delight you,
> and love's eager bonds unite you;
> yield yourself to His embrace.[18]

The last two verses of Song of Solomon 1 suggest that the couple's bridal chamber is a woodland clearing overhung by trees. The bride says, 'Behold, you are beautiful, my beloved, and lovely! Our bed is flowery.' The bridegroom replies, 'The beams of our house are cedar, its rafters are cypress (1:15–16, Vulgate).' Later, the bride says, 'My beloved is all radiant and ruddy (5:10).' In the sequence the wooded setting of the bridal bed becomes the wood of the Cross, and the Bridegroom's ruddiness is not the sign of a healthy complexion but the redness of the blood He shed for love of the Bride.

A better-known scriptural type of the Cross appears in the previous verse: 'Here the bronze serpent is lifted up, whose precious blood has taken away our wounds. Stricken himself by the serpent and sharing in our sorrows, he offered himself to be looked upon.'[19] In Numbers 21:9 those who had received deadly bites from serpents were saved and healed by looking at the bronze serpent which Moses had raised up on a pole. Jesus applied this image to himself in John 3:14: 'As Moses lifted up the serpent in the wilderness, so must the Son of Man be lifted up, that whoever believes in him may have eternal life.'

By evoking these biblical texts the poet is conveying the message that all who gaze in faith upon the costly love of God revealed on the Cross are given healing for their inner wounds and a share in Christ's victory over death.

The usual sequence at the Mass of the Five Wounds was *Cenam cum discipulis* ('A supper with the disciples'). It is found in manuscripts from St Gall and Einsiedeln, and became widespread in England and northern Europe. Its earliest appearance in England is probably in a Sarum missal thought to have been written for the Benedictine monks of Durham in the first half of the fifteenth century.[20]

The poem tells the story of the Passion from the Last Supper to the piercing of Jesus' side after His death. This is mostly done by a narrative in the third person, but in some verses the poet addresses Jesus directly:

> How, my Jesus, could You bear
> such suffering to sustain,
> racked with thirst upon the cross,
> yet silent to remain?
> Could it be, beneath the weight
> of such oppressing pain,
> You thirsted still more deeply
> our salvation to obtain?
> Uttering Your life's last words
> while on the cross suspended,
> into God the Father's hands
> Your spirit You commended;
> with a mighty shout You died,
> Your final breath expended;
> thus for all was life regained,
> Your saving work was ended.
> I shun humility, and You
> the way of pride forsake;
> I transgress, my punishment
> upon Yourself You take.
> I eat the fruit and gall is given
> to You, Your thirst to slake;

'With Angels and Archangels'

> I seek a life of quiet ease,
> You suffer for my sake.[21]

The poet is meditating on three of the 'Seven Words' of Jesus on the Cross: 'I thirst' (John 19:28); 'Father, into thy hands I commend my spirit' (Luke 23:46) and 'It is finished' (John 19:30).'

In the last two verses of the sequence the poet reflects on the spear-wound from which came water and blood (John 19:34). This scene recalls the life-giving stream flowing from the temple in Ezekiel 47, and the living water promised by Jesus to the Samaritan woman in John 4:14:

> His body hung upon the cross,
> His lifeless arms stretched wide,
> no longer feeling pain; but when
> a soldier pierced His side,
> the spear transfixed His Mother's heart;
> in agony she cried,
> and saw the blood and water flow
> forth from the Crucified.
> Let all those who search for love,
> healing, and salvation,
> hasten to this stream and drink
> from its rich libation.
> Precious blood, which from our ills
> brings us liberation;
> living water, clear and sweet,
> fount of new creation.

Among the hymns which Peter Abélard wrote for Héloïse and her nuns (see Chapter 6) is this Good Friday hymn, *Solus ad victimam*:

> Walking alone, Lord, You go to Your sacrifice,
> victim of death, and our death's mighty conqueror.
> What can we say to You, knowing our poverty,
> You, who have freed us from sin and from slavery?
> Ours are the sins, Lord, and we are the guilty ones,
> You, in your innocence, take on our punishment;
> grant that our spirits may share in Your suffering,
> may our compassion respond to Your pardoning.
> Three sacred days are the time of our sorrowing,
> as we endure now the night of our heaviness,
> until the morning restores to us joyfulness;
> Christ, newly risen, brings gladness for tearfulness.
> Grant us, O Lord, to take part in Your suffering,
> that we may share in Your heavenly victory;

> through these sad days living humbly and patiently,
> may we at Eastertide see You smile graciously.[22]

Here Abélard, the sharp debater of the Paris schools, addresses a simple and humble prayer to Christ, whom he pictures on the way to the Cross. Rather than concentrating on the details of the Passion he takes a wider theological view, reflecting with penitence and gratitude on the benefits of Redemption: Christ's victory over sin and death.

Abélard also refers to the liturgical context of his hymn: it would be sung in Héloïse's convent at the mid-point of the *Triduum Sacrum*, the Sacred Three Days leading up to Easter. He adds a biblical allusion, comparing this time of penitential sadness to the night of sorrow in Psalm 30:5 (29:6): 'Weeping may tarry for the night, but joy comes with the morning.' This biblical echo provides a link between Passion and Resurrection; Abélard's theological insight perceived these as being two aspects of the same mystery of Redemption. Perhaps he also had in mind a text from the Good Friday liturgy which holds together the Cross and the Resurrection. During the Veneration of the Cross Psalm 67 (66) was sung with the antiphon *Crucem tuam* repeated after each verse: 'We venerate Your Cross, O Lord, and praise and glorify Your holy Resurrection, for because of the Cross joy has come to the whole world.'[23]

The Passion and Resurrection are also held together in the sequence *Surgit Christus* ('Christ arises'). This is found in a sumptuous St Gall manuscript known as Codex Brander.[24] It is a compendious collection of tropes and sequences compiled about the year 1507 by a priest called Joachim Cuontz in preparation for the beatification of Notker in 1513. *Surgit Christus* develops and re-uses part of Wipo's Easter sequence *Victimae paschali* ('Christians, to the Paschal Victim'). Wipo's poem contains a short dialogue between the choir and a voice or voices representing Mary Magdalen:

> Speak Mary, declaring what thou sawest wayfaring:
> 'The tomb of Christ, who is living, the glory of Jesu's Resurrection:
> Bright angels attesting, the shroud and napkin resting.
> Yea, Christ my hope is arisen: to Galilee he goes before you.'[25]

Surgit Christus extends this dialogue to include Mary Magdalen's experiences at the Crucifixion. A rubric in the manuscript indicates that the part of Mary is to be sung by three choirboys with good voices (*bene vociferati*):

1. Christ arises now in triumph; through a glorious victory
   the lamb has become a lion.
   By His death He has conquered death; He has unlocked its gates
   with the glory of His dying.
2. This is the lamb who hung upon the Cross
   and redeemed all the sheep of His flock.
   Since no one suffered such pain as He did,
   Mary Magdalen was consumed by burning grief.
3. *Choir* Tell us, Mary, what did you see as you gazed upon the Cross of Christ?
   Mary I saw Jesus stripped and lifted up on the Cross by the hands of sinners.
4. *Choir* Tell us, Mary, what did you see as you gazed upon the Cross of Christ?
   Mary His head crowned with thorns, His face stained with spittle and full of bruises.
5. *Choir* Tell us, Mary, what did you see as you gazed upon the Cross of Christ?
   Mary His hands pierced by the nails, His side wounded by the spear,
   the outpouring of the living fountain.
   I saw that He commended Himself to His Father,
   And that He inclined His head and sent forth His spirit.
6. *Choir* Tell us, Mary, what did you do after you lost Jesus?
   Mary I kept His weeping Mother company and brought her home. Then I lay down on the ground and wept for both of them.
7. *Choir* Tell us, Mary, what did you do after you lost Jesus?
   Mary When I had prepared the ointments, I went to the tomb but I did not find Him whom I loved; my grief was twice as great.
8. *Choir* O Mary, do not weep; now Christ is truly risen.
   Mary Indeed with many proofs I saw the signs of His rising.
9. *Choir* Tell us, Mary, what did you see on the way?
   Mary The tomb of Christ, who is living ...

The sequence concludes with the text and music of *Victimae paschali*, verses 4–9.[26]

The poet's re-working of Wipo's sequence not only holds together the Cross and the Resurrection but also gives a fresh perspective to meditation on the Passion by looking at it through the eyes of Mary Magdalen. The first line of verse 8 (*O Maria, noli flere*, 'Mary, weep not, weep no longer') is a quotation from the opening of a hymn by Philip the Chancellor (d. 1236) on the subject of Mary's encounter with Jesus by the tomb in John 20:11–18.[27]

The Poetry of the Passion

Mary's reply in verse 8 contains the phrase 'with many proofs' (*multis argumentis*), which comes from Acts 1:3.

In their own ways Abélard and the author of *Surgit Christus* both wrote about the Passion while also keeping the Resurrection in view. In the medieval observance of Holy Week the Easter Sepulchre had a similar dual focus: the Host and Crucifix were 'buried' there as the final act of the Good Friday liturgy, and the celebration of the Resurrection began there as they were triumphantly carried out on Easter morning (see Chapter 8). As Eamon Duffy put it, 'Expressing to the full as it did the late medieval sense of the pathos of the Passion, the sepulchre and its ceremonies were also the principal vehicle for the Easter proclamation of Resurrection.'[28]

Christ's Cross shows what it cost him to live a human life in union with God; his Resurrection opens the way for human beings to enter the realm of eternity. Through faith and Baptism Christians are united with Christ in his mystical body, the Church, and are brought into communion and fellowship with all the citizens of heaven. The Church's worship of God on earth was seen as a participation in the eternal adoration offered by the angels and saints.

The next chapter explores some of the ways in which poetic images in the Bible and the liturgy helped medieval Christians to realize the heavenly context of their earthly worship.

✠ 10 ✠

'With Angels and Archangels': Sharing the Worship of Heaven

The story goes that the Saxon King Edgar (d. 975) had gone hunting one Sunday morning, and had asked St Dunstan (d. 988), the Archbishop of Canterbury, to delay saying Mass until he returned. The saint was waiting vested at the altar when he had a vision of heavenly worship with angels singing to the Trinity this *Kyrie*-trope, beginning *Rex splendens*:

> O Lord, shining King of heaven's citadel,
> save Your people in Your loving kindness.
> The choirs of Cherubim unceasingly proclaim Your glory;
> the noble Seraphim respond with hymns of praise.
> The nine angelic orders worship You in their beauty;
> the Church throughout the world unites to sing to You;
> the sun, moon, and stars, the earth and sea all serve You,
> O Christ the King, enthroned on high.[1]

When the king finally arrived, Dunstan told him that he had already heard Mass and would not celebrate another that day. He forbade the king to hunt any more on a Sunday, and he taught the chant he had heard sung in heaven to his clerks.

The legend is recounted in the Plainsong and Medieval Music Society's edition of *Missa Rex splendens*;[2] it has no historical basis – the trope's origin is probably French – but both the story and the text of the trope illustrate the close relationship in the medieval mind between earthly and heavenly worship.[3]

The author of *Rex splendens* saw not just the Church but the whole creation as joining in the eternal chorus of praise. There is precedent in the Old Testament for the idea that all creation praises God, especially in the Song of the Three Children (the *Benedicite*) and in Psalm 98 (97):8, where rivers clap their hands and hills rejoice before the Lord.

Sharing the Worship of Heaven

When human voices sang praise to God, those of a speculative turn of mind saw a cosmological connection between earth and heaven as well as a theological one. The musical theorist Regino of Prüm (d. 915), working with a pre-Copernican concept of the universe, saw musical harmony as an image of cosmic harmony. He related the music of the spheres to the eight notes of the diatonic scale sung or played by human musicians. In ascending order from the earth, the spheres (each with its own governing planet or luminary) comprise: Moon, Mercury, Venus, Sun, Mars, Jupiter, and Saturn. Each of these was thought to 'sing' a note of the scale from A to G, and the Heavenly Sphere completed the octave with a top A.[4]

It was also believed that each sphere was presided over by one of the angelic orders: Angels, Archangels, Principalities, Powers, Virtues, Dominations, Thrones, and Cherubim, with the Seraphim higher still in a ninth sphere.

Jean Leclercq pointed out that many of the musical theorists were monks, who saw their scholarship as part of their monastic vocation:

> We can discern in the general intent of their study ... their awareness of the majesty of God. Their purpose is to help their brethren by means of ordered, unanimous song to join in the praise which the universe and the angels render to God, to sing in anticipation on earth the song they will continue in Heaven.[5]

The angelic music was normally, of course, inaudible to human ears, except at the Incarnation, when it was heard by the shepherds in Luke 2:8–20. This event was celebrated in a Christmas sequence which was popular in England and France, *Caeleste organum*:

> The harmonies of heaven resound today on earth;
> the angel-choirs on high sing of the Virgin Birth.
> Shepherds, keeping careful vigil, hear the angel voices
> singing songs of splendour, full of glory and of peace.
> The things of earth are now made one with things above:
> joy is ours, for God's own Word is joined to human flesh.
> Bright stars announce His birth,
> and starlight leads the shepherds into Bethlehem.
> These men, who live by leading flocks of sheep,
> find heaven's King among the animals.
> He whose sovereign power extends through all that's made
> lies here confined within a narrow manger.[6]

'With Angels and Archangels'

In his *Meditations* Eckbert of Schönau, Elisabeth's brother, related the songs of the angelic orders to David's ten-stringed lute in Psalm 33:3 (32:2); the tenth 'string', restored by Christ to sweet tunefulness, represented the praises offered by the Church on earth.[7]

Evelyn Birge Vitz has pointed out an example in the Grail literature of a heavenly vision associated with the liturgy. The French romance *La queste del Saint Graal*[8] has a scene where Lancelot enters a chamber flooded with light and full of angels with censers, candles, and crosses. A priest was celebrating Mass there before the Holy Vessel. At the Elevation three men were above his outstretched arms, two of whom placed the youngest into his hands.[9]

Liturgical visions were not, of course, confined to legend and literature but were sometimes experienced by real people with visionary gifts, such as Elisabeth of Schönau and Margery Kempe (see Chapters 7 and 8). Most worshippers, however, needed to be reminded of their communion with the citizens of heaven by the words of Scripture, by the poetry, music, and symbolism of the liturgy, and by the visual arts in their various forms: sculpture, paintings, and vestments.

Each year a church would keep its Dedication Festival, the anniversary of its consecration. The liturgy of this day contained a biblical text which was fundamental to the nature and purpose of the church building. The Introit of the Mass was taken from Genesis 28:17, Jacob's exclamation after his dream of the ladder linking heaven and earth: 'How awesome is this place! This is none other than the house of God, and this is the gate of heaven.' John 1:51 speaks of the angels ascending and descending upon the Son of Man; here Jesus is the new Jacob's Ladder, the true link between earth and heaven. Both these texts were probable influences on Notker's Dedication Festival sequence *Psallat ecclesia* (see Chapter 4).

Medieval churches were rich in reminders that those who entered them were stepping into 'the house of God and the gate of heaven'. In the porch there would be a holy water stoup where people could dip their fingers and sign themselves with the cross. This could remind them of their baptism, the sacrament of their new birth as children of God, members of Christ's mystical body, and inheritors of the kingdom of heaven. If the church's architecture was Romanesque – a style which spread rapidly in England after the Norman Conquest – the round-headed arch of the doorway would probably be carved with a zig-zag pattern known as chevron moulding. This was not merely ornamental but symbolized the rays of eternal heavenly light. There may also be carved foliage, representing fresh growth in the new life of Paradise. It seems much more plausible to interpret human faces entwined with foliage as images of heaven rather than as survivals of paganism. As Rita Wood explains,

> In the early part of the twelfth century, chevrons and geometric patterns were everywhere on doorways and chancel arches: they described the church as the place of light, the place where God is. As time goes on, the amount of foliage carved increases: this also describes Heaven, but now as the restored Paradise, the proper home of mankind... The 'green man' exhales the new spiritual life, leafy like the breath made visible in frosty air.[10]

There would also be more obvious reminders of the company of heaven: perhaps angels in the roof, and saints depicted in statues, in windows, on walls, and on the Rood Screen.

For the literate, the words of the Mass contained several references to the heavenly worship which formed the unseen background to the celebration of the earthly liturgy. The *Gloria* was known as the 'Angelic Hymn' because the shepherds in Luke 2:13 heard angels singing its opening words: 'Glory to God in the highest, and on earth peace to people of good will'. The *Sanctus* ('Holy, holy, holy') takes up the song of the seraphim in Isaiah 6:3; its preceding Preface speaks of the thankful praises of the worshippers being joined 'with angels and archangels and all the company of the heavenly host'. In the Canon of the Mass Mary, the apostles, and several saints and martyrs are individually named; priest and people are 'united in one communion' with them and with all the saints. In the prayer beginning *Supplices te* the priest prays that the eucharistic gifts may be carried by angelic hands and presented at the heavenly altar in the presence of God, so that all who receive the Sacrament at the earthly altar may be filled with every grace and heavenly blessing.[11]

Two biblical images illustrating the nature of the Church come together in the first reading at the Dedication Festival Mass: 'And I saw the holy city, new Jerusalem, coming down out of heaven from God, prepared as a bride adorned for her husband... (Revelation 21:2).' The Church is the holy city, whose foundation-stones bear the names of the twelve apostles (21:14), and also the Bride of Christ, the 'wife of the Lamb' (21:9).

The idea of the Church as the Bride of Christ is developed in the sequence *Jerusalem et Sion filiae*, one of several alternative sequences provided in the Sarum Use to be sung at a church's Dedication Festival.[12] Gabriel Gillett's translation is at *New English Hymnal* 212; its opening lines reflect the close relationship between earthly and heavenly worship:

> Sion's daughters, sons of Jerusalem,
> All ye hosts of heavenly chivalry,
> Lift your voices, singing right merrily
> Alleluya!
> Christ our Saviour weds on this festival
> Holy Church, the pattern of righteousness ...

At first sight 'Sion' and 'Jerusalem' appear to be synonyms, both referring to the holy city, but the poet was probably following St Augustine in making a distinction between them. In his commentary on Psalm 51:18 (50:20) Augustine interprets 'Jerusalem' (meaning 'vision of peace') as indicating the Church in heaven and 'Sion' ('expectant watching') as signifying the Church on earth.[13] The poet's message is that both parts of the Church unite in celebrating Christ's love for his Bride.

Later in the poem the Bride is described with imagery from Song of Solomon 6:10: 'Who is this that looks forth like the dawn, fair as the moon, bright as the sun ...?' She is also said to have been 'born in a mystery ever wondrous'. The original text makes it clear that this mysterious birth took place on the Cross, when streams of water and blood flowed from the spear-wound in Christ's side (John 19:34). The streams point to the Church's life-giving sacraments of Baptism and Eucharist; they spring from the side of the New Adam just as Eve was created from the opened side of Adam in Genesis 2:21–3. The Church is therefore the New Eve, the 'Mother meet for sinful humanity'.[14]

The twin images of the City and the Bride, derived from Revelation 21:2, also occur in the Dedication Festival Office Hymn *Urbs beata Jerusalem*. J. M. Neale's translation of its two parts is at *New English Hymnal* 204 and 205:

> Blessed City, heavenly Salem,
> Vision dear of peace and love,
> Who, of living stones upbuilded,

Sharing the Worship of Heaven

> Art the joy of heaven above,
> And, with angel cohorts circled,
> As a bride to earth dost move!
> Christ is made the sure foundation,
> And the precious corner-stone,
> Who, the two walls underlying,
> Bound in each, binds both in one,
> Holy Sion's help for ever,
> And her confidence alone.[15]

This poet also follows St Augustine's interpretation of the two names for the holy city: Jerusalem is the heavenly Church, enjoying the eternal vision of peace, and Sion is the Church on earth, finding in Christ her help and her confidence.

The idea that Christians are 'living stones' is found in 1 Peter 2:4:

> Come to him, to that living stone, rejected by men but in God's sight chosen and precious; and like living stones be yourselves built into a spiritual house . . .

The author of 1 Peter goes on to quote Isaiah 28:16, 'Behold, I am laying in Zion a stone, a cornerstone chosen and precious', and Psalm 118 (117):22, 'The very stone which the builders rejected has become the head of the corner'. The same imagery occurs in Ephesians 2:20–1, where Christians are 'built upon the foundation of the apostles and prophets, Christ Jesus himself being the cornerstone, in whom the whole structure is joined together and grows into a holy temple in the Lord'. In *Urbs beata* Christ the cornerstone binds together the earthly and heavenly 'walls' of the Church.

The communion between earth and heaven is portrayed in a different way in the Victorine sequence *Rex Salomon*. This is one of the alternative Dedication sequences in the Sarum Use, and the only one provided in the York Missal. Its depiction of the Church is based on the typology of Solomon's temple, as described in 1 Kings 6:

> Solomon the king instructed
> that a temple be constructed –
> image of the Church's birth.
> Christ Himself caused its creation,
> He its founder and foundation,
> so His grace could reach the earth.
> Set foursquare on their foundation,
> temple walls in due gradation

> rose to soaring heights above;
> now its length and breadth and height,
> when these are perceived aright,
> tell of faith and hope and love.
> Fashioned by the masons' arts,
> lower, middle, upper parts
> formed the temple's threefold state.
> So the Church within her breast
> holds the living, those at rest,
> those who've passed through heaven's gate.[16]

Here the Church is seen as embracing the realm of the dead, as well as Christians on earth and in heaven. Amalarius drew the same doctrinal meaning from the Fraction at Mass, when the Host is broken into three parts (see Chapter 8). The image of the cornerstone is applied to Christ later in *Rex Salomon*, but here he binds Jews and Gentiles into a unity, as prefigured by the blending in Solomon's temple of the work of the king's masons and that of the skilled carpenters sent from Tyre (1 Kings 5:6, 18).

In the sequence *In hoc ortus occidente* the image of the cornerstone has a much wider function, binding earth and heaven into a unity through the saving work of Christ:

> 1a Risen on a world declining,
> and upon its darkness shining,
> from the deep appears the sun.
> He, our human shadows sharing,
> pain and mortal weakness bearing,
> victory over death has won.
>
> 1b Heaven's king shares our condition
> to restore us from perdition,
> gathering the lost and stray.
> Human flesh God's Word encloses
> and His loving care discloses,
> as the Potter moulds our clay.
>
> 2a Overshadowed by God's power
> Mary keeps her virgin flower,
> yet conceives God's only Son.
> Now a creature bears her Maker,
> who, in manhood a partaker,
> deigns on earth His course to run.
>
> 2b He, our Sun, from harm protects us;
> leading onward He directs us,
> as with cloudy pillar bright.

Sharing the Worship of Heaven

> From the law of death He freed us,
> and with strong right hand will lead us
> through life's gateway into light.
>
> 3a Truth and Mercy, gladly meeting,
> now embrace in loving greeting
> as He grants His pardon free.
> Peace her blooms from earth upraises,
> while from heaven upon us gazes
> Justice, bringing liberty.
>
> 3b Mutual kisses add their savour
> and a fresh and novel flavour
> to the closeness these Four own.
> Christ the Rock, whence living water
> flows to every son and daughter,
> is the precious Cornerstone.
>
> 4a Walls that stood in separation
> He unites in close relation
> by the Father's love divine.
> From a dark and tainted sowing
> He creates a fair shoot, growing
> from the rams' unblemished line.
>
> 4b May His robe of mercy ever
> clothe us, when He comes to sever
> goats from sheep, and chaff from grain.
> When the chaff away is driven,
> may we stand, our sins forgiven,
> and within His barn remain.[17]

The poet uses a range of biblical images to illustrate how Christ unites humanity with God and earth with heaven through His Incarnation, Passion, and Resurrection. He begins with an allusion to Malachi 4:2: 'But for you who fear my name the sun of righteousness shall rise, with healing in its wings.' The darkness of the world upon which Christ the Sun rose leads the poet's imagination straight to the Crucifixion, when the sun's light was darkened as Jesus died the death that would overcome death (Mark 15:33). The focus then moves to the Incarnation, when the eternal Word took flesh in Mary's womb. Here the poet refers to the words Jeremiah received from God in 18:6: 'Like the clay in the potter's hand, so are you in my hand, O house of Israel.' The divine Potter takes human nature, formed from earth's clay in Genesis 2:7, and fashions it anew in His likeness.

The Sun appears again in verse 2b, now bringing the new light of Easter, as the Risen Christ opens for humanity the gates of eternal life. The sun's light becomes the shining pillar of fire in Exodus 13:21–2, which was the sign of God's presence with His people as He led them from slavery towards the freedom of the Promised Land. The Exodus story was read at the Easter Vigil, during which the *Exultet* compared the pillar of fire to the Paschal Candle, the symbol of the abiding presence of the Risen Lord.

In verse 3a the poet celebrates Christ's uniting of earth and heaven by using imagery from Psalm 85:10–11 (84:11–12). The Vulgate version of this passage translates as 'Mercy and Truth have met each other; Justice and Peace have kissed. Truth has sprung up from the earth, and Justice looked down from heaven.' In the second half of verse 3b the imagery changes: Christ is compared to the rock struck by Moses in Exodus 17:6. The life-giving streams which poured from this rock were seen as prefiguring those that flowed from Christ's wounded side in John 19:34. This evocation of the Cross, the culmination of Christ's reconciling work, is a preparation for the next shift in imagery, when the Rock becomes the Cornerstone, uniting what had been separated.

The rather obscure imagery in the second half of verse 4a seems to be expressing the effects of Christ's redemption: sinful humanity has been created anew in Him and brought back to God. The reference to rams is probably to be understood in the light of Psalm 29 (28):1–2. The last line of verse 4a is literally 'sons of rams' (*filios arietum*), which is a direct quotation from this psalm. In the Vulgate version it reads

> Bring to the Lord, O sons of God, bring to the Lord the sons of rams. Bring to the Lord glory and honour; bring to the Lord the glory of His name; adore the Lord in His holy court.

In this context the phrase 'sons of rams' represents an offering acceptable to God, the worship of minds and hearts in union with Christ.

The sequence ends with a prayer for mercy at the Last Judgement. This is portrayed with imagery from St Matthew's Gospel, the separation of sheep from goats in 25:31–3, and of grain from chaff in 3:12.

The first part of the poem, as far as the end of verse 3a, appears in four European manuscripts and is thought to be the work of

Walter of Châtillon (d. after 1184). The only complete text is in the manuscript known as 'The Later Cambridge Songs', which dates from the period 1180–1230. Its editor, John Stevens, plausibly suggests that it was compiled by the vicars choral of Leicester Abbey; it is not an official liturgical manuscript but an informally produced song-book.[18]

The worshippers' sense of communion and fellowship with the citizens of heaven was strengthened by the annual cycle of saints' days. As each feast day came round, hymns and sequences reinforced the community's knowledge of the lives and characters of the saints commemorated in the liturgy.

The fourteenth-century missal used by the Benedictine monks of Whitby Abbey contains a sequence for each of the two feast days of their patron, St Hilda. The story of the first part of her life was told on the feast of her Translation, 25 August, in the sequence *Sponso regi castitatis*:

> 1a Now, the Royal Bridegroom praising,
> let our choir sweet songs be raising,
> as our eager hearts are gazing
> on His purity Divine.
>
> 1b On this day of celebration
> Hilda's life with veneration
> we recall, at her translation
> into heavenly light sublime.
>
> 2a Royal Edwin's nephew's daughter,
> at his court the Faith was taught her,
> and the love of learning caught her,
> as Christ's teachings formed her mind.
>
> 2b Saint Paulinus had bestowed
> sacramental grace that showed
> in her faith and love, which glowed
> through her words and actions kind.
>
> 3a Leaving worldly wealth behind her,
> she sought cords of love to bind her
> as a bride to Christ, and find her
> joy in the religious state.
>
> 3b She through prayer and contemplation
> sought Christ's will for her vocation,
> and thought France the best location
> for her own novitiate.
>
> 4a Sister Hereswith did dwell
> in the monastery of Chelles;

'With Angels and Archangels'

      Hilda longed to have her cell
      in a holy exile there.
4b But before she crossed the water
      Bishop Aidan had besought her,
      as his spiritual daughter,
      in his work to have a share.
5a She made sure young nuns were grounded
      in that life where love abounded
      in the house of prayer she founded
      close beside the River Wear.
5b Hartlepool, it was decided,
      should be where they next resided;
      there as abbess she presided,
      giving counsel wise and clear.[19]

The poet has condensed and versified Bede's account of Hilda's life in his *History of the English Church and People*, including his versions of the place-names 'Cale' for Chelles and 'Heruteu' for Hartlepool.[20] Edwin was king of Northumbria; he and his household, including the thirteen-year-old Hilda, were baptized by St Paulinus in his new church of St Peter at York in April 627. Her sister Hereswith was married to the king of the East Angles, and then went to be a nun at Chelles, just east of Paris. Hilda was staying in East Anglia, waiting to go to France, when St Aidan persuaded her to return to Northumbria. He gave her a hide of land, enough to support a family, somewhere on the north bank of the Wear; its exact location is unknown. After her time at Hartlepool she set up a monastery at 'Calcaria', probably Tadcaster, and then founded one at Whitby. The abbey here became famous as a place of holiness and learning; five of its monks became bishops, including St John of Beverley.[21]

It is strange that *Sponso regi*, being a detailed biographical sequence, should end with Hilda's time at Hartlepool. One might expect the story to continue in the sequence for her other feast, but this turns out not to be the case. In the missal this second feast is called the 'Passing (*Transitus*) of St Hilda'; it is the anniversary of her death on 17 November 680. Its sequence is entirely lacking in specific information; there is no mention of Hilda's hosting of the Synod of Whitby, nor of her encouragement of Cædmon's poetic gifts. It is a eulogy written in the older 'classical' sequence-form, and its style is similar to that of the effusive Winchester school:

Sharing the Worship of Heaven

Sponso festivo gratulans

1a The virgin bride, the Church, rejoices in her festal Bridegroom;
1b she solemnly, sweetly, and joyfully sings 'Alleluia'.
2a How beautiful the Bridegroom looks, shining with grace!
2b the choirs of virgins flock round Him with their embrace.
3a Her flesh subdued, Hilda's fervent heart was kindled
3b by the excellence of His surpassing beauty.
4a She gladly consecrates herself to God as a virginal offering;
4b this holy virgin nurtures communities of virgins for Christ the King.
5a Sprung from royal lineage, she is the handmaid of Christ's servants;
5b renouncing this world's joys, she thirsts and sighs for the joys of heaven.
6a With the wisdom of God established in her soul,
6b she gives counsels of peace and words of salvation.
7a Fervent for justice and excelling in knowledge,
7b she governs her sisters with a monastic Rule.
8a When her flesh grows weak and painful, she looks forward to heaven;
8b the royal virgin is glad, for soon she will rejoice in God.
9a The Bridegroom is inviting her, saying 'Come, my beloved,
9b the showers have passed and the rain is over, come, my lovely one'.
10a Freed from her body she gladly ascends to the heavenly realms with the angels;
10b there she is joined to the choirs of the virgins, singing virginal songs to the Lamb.
11a Now, O blessed virgin, be our help and support through your prayers,
11b that with the saints in our native land we may share your glory.[22]

Sponso festivo compensates for its lack of biographical detail by the warmth of its emotional tone. The sequence outlines Hilda's excellence as an abbess in verses 6 and 7, but its main theme is a celebration of her love for Christ. Bridal imagery is prominent, and the influence of the Song of Solomon is especially clear in verse 9, where the Bridegroom's words closely follow the Vulgate text of 2:10–11: 'My Beloved speaks to me: 'Arise, hasten, my beloved, my dove, my lovely one, and come. For now the winter has passed; the rain is over and gone'.'

In their very different ways these two sequences offered a vivid awareness of Hilda's life and character to the monks of Whitby, so that they might experience a deep sense of fellowship with their patron saint as they celebrated her feast-days.

The Communion of Saints and the idea of the church as the gate of heaven could also be portrayed by the symbolism of liturgical colours. There was great variety in the colours of medieval vestments; many smaller churches simply used their best vestments for the major festivals and their less good ones at other times regardless of their colour. There were, however, some symbolic colour-schemes from the twelfth century onwards; before that time the evidence for them is very sparse, and seems to be confined to the basic symbolism of White for joyful occasions and Black for penitential ones.

The earliest surviving reference to colour-symbolism is found in the context of the Gallican Rite: the seventh-century *Expositio liturgiae Gallicanae*, once attributed to Germanus of Paris, says that white vestments are worn for Easter because the angels at the sepulchre were dressed in white.[23] The first evidence from Rome is contained in *Ordo Romanus* 20, which dates from the late eighth century but describes earlier practice. In its account of the Candlemas procession this document says that the Pope puts on black vestments beforehand, and the deacons likewise put on black chasubles (*planitas nigras*). The penitential nature of this procession probably has its roots in pagan Roman religion; by the fourteenth century its colour had lightened to Violet, and this remained the case until 1970.[24] Another penitential procession, the Greater Litanies on 25 April, is described in the ninth-century *Ordo Romanus* 21; here the bishop and deacons wear dark-coloured chasubles (*planitas fuscas*).[25]

The twelfth century saw the appearance of fully developed colour-sequences embracing the whole liturgical year. There may well be a practical reason for this, in that the Crusades opened up trade-routes from the East to Western Europe, thus enabling a much greater quantity and variety of Oriental silks to find their way westwards.[26]

Because of the greater availability of silk in the East, it is perhaps no accident that the earliest colour-sequence should come from the Church of the Holy Sepulchre in Jerusalem. This was the seat of the Latin Patriarch between 1100 and 1187, and was staffed by Augustinian canons. The pattern of colours through the year retains the ancient symbolism of White for Easter and Black for penitential seasons, but it now also includes Red for the fire of Pentecost and for the blood of Christ's Passion and his martyrs. At Christmas the Black of Advent is retained for the Midnight Mass, then the colour lightens to Red for the Dawn Mass and finally to White for the Mass of the Day. White is also used for saints who were not martyrs. A particularly imaginative touch is the use of the colour *celestis* (presumably 'sky-blue') for three feasts which have associations with the sky or the heavens: Epiphany, with its celestial portent of the star, the Ascension, and the feast of the angel-host of heaven at Michaelmas. The variety of the Communion of Saints is expressed by having both white and red vestments worn simultaneously by the three Sacred Ministers on All Saints' Day – the red is the best set with gold embroidery as at the Christmas Dawn Mass – and the idea of variety is developed still further by having an altar-frontal of 'all the colours' (*omnium colorum*). The strangest feature of this colour-sequence is the provision of Black for Marian feasts, which, as far as the evidence goes, is without parallel anywhere else. The likeliest explanation seems to be that it is a reference to the Bride's words in Song of Solomon 1:4 'I am black but comely'.[27]

The colour-scheme used at Rome in the late twelfth century is described by Innocent III in his work *On the Holy Mystery of the Altar*, which was written shortly before his election as Pope in 1198. The scheme is mostly the same as that in use today, with Green as the colour for ordinary Sundays, although Black was still used in Advent and Lent except for *Laetare* (Mid-Lent) Sunday, when Violet was worn.

Innocent gives reasons for the use of the various colours: White represents the purity of Mary, the brightness of angels, the shining Epiphany star, and the glory-cloud at the Ascension. He often relates the colours to biblical texts: Revelation 14:5 ('No lie was found in their mouth, for they are spotless') is quoted to illustrate the use of White for confessors and virgins because of their integrity and innocence. Red is worn for apostles and martyrs because of the shedding of their blood, and for feasts of the Cross because of Christ's blood (Isaiah 63:1 'Who is this that comes from Edom, in crimsoned garments from Bozrah?'). Innocent notes that both Red and White are found in the love-poetry of the Song of Solomon:

'My beloved is white and ruddy' (5:10); 'I am the rose of Sharon and lily of the valley' (2:1). He quotes from the same source when describing the other colours: Black vestments are to be used 'on a day of affliction and abstinence, for sins, and for the dead ('I am black but comely', 1:4). Green is the colour for ordinary days, and is expressed by the phrase 'Cypress with nard, nard and saffron' (*Cypri cum nardo; nardus et crocus*, 4:13). He says that 'some relate roses to martyrs, saffron to confessors, the lily to virgins'.[28]

The colours of the vestments lead Innocent's mind to the trees and flowers of the garden of love in the Song of Solomon, seen as a symbol of Paradise, where the heavenly Church enjoys the love of Christ her Bridegroom. The associations with Paradise would be all the stronger in those churches where carved foliage embellished the arches and columns.

Innocent finds another meditative pathway linking liturgical colours with the life of heaven by way of the symbolism of jewels. He notices that some of the colours of priestly vestments mirror those found in the jewels on Aaron's breast-piece. They were carved with the names of the twelve tribes of Israel, so that Aaron could bear his people on his heart when he ministered in the sanctuary (Exodus 28:15–21, 29). Innocent sees the jewels as representing the virtues which characterize the lives of heaven's citizens: the green stones (emerald, jasper, and beryl) symbolize charity, kindness, and patience; the red ones (garnet and carbuncle) illustrate faith and modesty. He also notes that Ezekiel's lament over the king of Tyre (Ezekiel 28:13) places nine of these Aaronic jewels in the paradisal Garden of Eden: 'You were amidst the delights of the Paradise of God; every precious stone was your covering.'[29]

Twelve jewels appear again in Revelation 21:14, 19–20 as the foundations of the holy city, now bearing the names of the twelve apostles. In Revelation 21:9–10 the new Jerusalem is also the Bride of Christ, and this double image of the heavenly Church is where Innocent's paths of biblical associations have led; they began from the colours of the vestments and took his imagination to the flowers in the bridal garden in the Song of Solomon and to the jewels that form the fabric of the holy city. The same double image of the City and the Bride inspired the poetry sung at a church's Dedication Festival: 'Blessed City' and 'Sion's daughters'.

Poetic images in the Bible and in liturgical poetry combined with paintings, carvings, stained glass, and coloured vestments to give a sense of the close relationship between earthly and heavenly worship within the mystical Body of Christ. This sense was especially strong in the Middle Ages, but all Christian worship takes place 'With angels and archangels and with all the company of heaven'. Every church is a 'gate of heaven' because in it is celebrated the sacred banquet in which, as St Thomas Aquinas put it,

> Christ is received,
> the memory of His Passion is renewed,
> our hearts are filled with grace,
> and a pledge of future glory is given to us.[30]

The strands of Bible, poetry, and worship were interwoven in a glorious variety of ways in the Middle Ages, but all Christians who read the Bible, receive the sacraments, sing hymns, and pray are weaving their individual part of a great tapestry, through which divine grace can work within them to help them grow and flourish as members of Christ's Body. The whole pattern, of course, is known only to God.

NOTES

Notes to Chapter 1

1. F. J. E. Raby, *A History of Christian-Latin Poetry* (Oxford: Clarendon Press, 1953), p. 32.
2. St Augustine, *Confessions*, ix.6.
3. *Confessions*, ix.12.
4. *Deus Creator omnium*, Latin text in F. J. E. Raby, *The Oxford Book of Medieval Latin Verse* (Oxford: Clarendon Press, 1959), p. 11.
5. *English Hymnal*, no. 14.
6. *Intende, qui regis Israel*, Latin text in Raby, *Medieval Latin Verse*, p. 12.
7. A. M. Farrer, *Interpretation and Belief*, ed. Charles Conti (London: SPCK, 1976), pp. 26–7.
8. Raby, *A History of Christian-Latin Poetry*, p. 36.
9. *English Hymnal*, no. 50.
10. *Ibid.*, no. 58.
11. *Ibid.*, no. 59.
12. *Ibid.*, no. 60.
13. *Ibid.*, no. 61.
14. Raby, *A History of Christian-Latin Poetry*, p. 32.

Notes to Chapter 2

1. G. Silagi (ed.), *Liturgische Tropen*, Münchener Beiträge zur Mediävistik und Renaissance-Forschung 36 (Munich: Arbeo-Gesellschaft, 1985), pp. vii–viii; the frontispiece is a facsimile of MS Cod. Guelf. 1062 Helmst. fol. 219^r.
2. Text and music in D. Hiley, *Western Plainchant: A Handbook* (Oxford: Clarendon Press, 1993), p. 212.
3. Laon, Bibliothèque Municipale 263, fol. 26v.
4. *English Hymnal*, no. 154.
5. M. Thornton, *English Spirituality* (London: SPCK, 1963), pp. 76–7.
6. R. Jacobsson (ed.), *Pax et Sapientia: Studies in Text and Music of Liturgical Tropes and Sequences in Memory of Gordon Anderson*, Studia Latina Stockholmiensia 29 (Stockholm: Almqvist & Wiksell, 1986), p. 25.
7. Hiley, *Western Plainchant*, p. 314.
8. *Ibid.*, p. 185.
9. J.-M. Hanssens, *Amalarii Episcopi Opera Liturgica Omnia*, Studi e Testi 13840 (Rome: Biblioteca Apostolica Vaticana, 1948–50), *Liber Officialis*, vol. III, pp. xiii–xiv.
10. G. M. Boone (ed.), *Essays on Medieval Music in Honor of David Hughes* (Harvard: Harvard University Press, 1995), p. 192.

'With Angels and Archangels'

11. Durandus, *Rationale Divinorum Officiorum*, iv.22.
12. Oxford, University College MS 78 B.
13. W. Henderson, *Missale ad Usum Insignis Ecclesiae Eboracensis*, Surtees Society 59–60 (London: Surtees Society, 1874), vol. I, p. 11.
14. Paris: Bibliothèque Nationale MS lat. 1240, dating from about 936.
15. A. Hughes, *Anglo-French Sequelae* (Burnham: The Plainsong and Mediaeval Music Society, 1934; republished Farnborough: Gregg Press, 1966), p. 21, pp. 99–110; R. Crocker, *The Early Medieval Sequence* (Berkeley: University of California Press, 1977), pp. 341–4.
16. Paris, Bibliothèque Nationale, MS lat. 1087.
17. Hughes, *Anglo-French Sequelae*, p. 22; Hiley, *Western Plainchant*, p. 181.
18. Crocker, *The Early Medieval Sequence*, p. 398.
19. Melody: Hughes, *Anglo-French Sequelae*, pp. 70–1; text: Henderson, *Missale Ecclesiae Eboracensis*, vol. I, p. 232.
20. Crocker, *The Early Medieval Sequence*, p. 6; M. Gerbert, *Scriptores Ecclesiastici de Musica Sacra* (St Blasien: Typis Sanblasianis, 1784; republished Hildesheim: Georg Olms Verlag, 1990), vol. I, p. 113.
21. Oxford, Bodleian MS Rawl. liturg. b. 1, fol. 197.
22. T. Bailey and A. Santuosso (eds.), *Music in Medieval Europe* (Aldershot: Ashgate, 2007), p. 313.

Notes to Chapter 3

1. Hughes, *Anglo-French Sequelae*, p. 1.
2. Hiley, *Western Plainchant*, p. 252.
3. A. Kinghorn, *Mediaeval Drama* (London: Evans Brothers. 1968), p. 27.
4. *New English Hymnal*, no. 519.
5. Hiley, *Western Plainchant*, pp. 263–73.
6. A. Cawley (ed.), *Everyman and Medieval Miracle Plays* (London: Dent, 1956), p. xi.
7. Ibid., pp. 171–88.
8. A. Harman, *Man and his Music* (London: Barrie and Jenkins, 1962), vol. I, pp. 40–1. An illustration of a thirteenth-century two-part setting of *Victimae Paschali* is in A. Robertson and D. Stevens, *The Pelican History of Music* (Harmondsworth: Penguin, 1960), vol. I, plate 10.
9. *New English Hymnal*, no. 524.
10. J. Leclercq, *The Love of Learning and the Desire for God* (New York: Fordham University Press, 1961), p. 244.
11. L. Thorpe, *Two Lives of Charlemagne* (Harmondsworth: Penguin Classics, 1969), p. 102.
12. R. McKitterick, *The Frankish Church and the Carolingian Reforms 789–895* (London: Royal Historical Society, 1977), p. 52.
13. E. Bishop, *Liturgica Historica* (Oxford: Oxford University Press, 1918), p. 325.
14. J. Jungmann, *Christian Prayer through the Centuries* (London: SPCK, 2007), pp. 53–4; S. Van Dijk and J. Hazelden Walker, *The Origins of the Modern Roman Liturgy* (London: Darton, Longman & Todd, 1960), p. 20.

Notes to Chapter 3

15 P. Evans, *The Early Trope Repertory of Saint Martial de Limoges* (Princeton, Princeton University Press, 1970), p. 19.
16 W. Arlt and G. Björkvall (eds.), *Recherches nouvelles sur les tropes liturgiques*, Corpus Troporum (Stockholm: Almqvist & Wiksell, 1993), p. 237.
17 C. Hefele and A. Leclercq, *Histoire des Conciles* (Paris: Letouzey & Ane, 1911), vol. IV, p. 14.
18 Hanssens, *Amalarii Episcopi Opera*, vol. III, pp. xiii–xiv.
19 A. Wilson, *The Book of the People* (London: Atlantic Books, 2015), p. 143.
20 G. Dix, *The Shape of the Liturgy* (London: Dacre Press, 1945), p. 744.
21 A. Farrer, *A Celebration of Faith* (London: Hodder & Stoughton, 1970), p. 109.
22 A. Farrer, *The Crown of the Year* (London: Dacre Press, 1952), pp. 71–2.
23 C. Jones *et al.* (eds.), *The Study of Liturgy* (London: SPCK, 1978), pp. 225–8; P. Bradshaw and M. Johnson, *The Eucharistic Liturgies* (London: SPCK, 2012), pp. 193–5.
24 Bradshaw and Johnson, *The Eucharistic Liturgies*, p. 207.
25 *Ibid.*, p. 208.
26 There is a black-and-white photograph in Jones *et al.*, *The Study of Liturgy*, plate 13.
27 J. Lechner and L. Eisenhofer, *The Liturgy of the Roman Rite* (Freiburg: Herder, 1961), p. 317.
28 *De Sacramentis*, iv.27; H. Chadwick (ed.), *St Ambrose on the Sacraments* (London: A. R. Mowbray, 1960), p. 36; Bradshaw and Johnson, *The Eucharistic Liturgies*, p. 106.
29 Bradshaw and Johnson, *The Eucharistic Liturgies*, p. 207; Bishop, *Liturgica Historica*, p. 12.
30 *De Agricultura*, 141.2; C. Mohrmann, *Liturgical Latin* (London: Burns and Oates, 1959), p. 60.
31 Bradshaw and Johnson, *The Eucharistic Liturgies*, p. 199.
32 Text: H. Bannister (ed.), *Missale Gothicum*, vol. I (London: Henry Bradshaw Society, 1917), p. 51; translation: J. Blakesley, *A Garland of Faith* (Leominster: Gracewing, 1998), p. 56.
33 W. Porter, *The Gallican Rite* (London: A. R. Mowbray, 1958), pp. 50–1.
34 P.-M. Gy, 'Les tropes dans l'histoire de la liturgie et de la théologie', in G. Iverson (ed.), *Research on Tropes* (Stockholm: Almqvist & Wiksell, 1983), p. 8.
35 J.-P. Migne (ed.), *Patrologia Latina* (PL), 221 vols. (Paris: 1844–64), vol. 104, col. 330.
36 *Ibid.*, col. 331.
37 *New English Hymnal*, no. 19, verses 4 and 5.
38 PL 104, col. 336.
39 Hefele and Leclercq, *Histoire des Conciles*, vol. IV, p. 91; Hiley, *Western Plainchant*, p. 570.
40 PL 105, col. 1114.
41 PL 119, cols. 71–3.
42 Raby, *A History of Christian-Latin Poetry*, p. 183.
43 G. Cattin, *Music in the Middle Ages* (Cambridge: Cambridge University Press, 1984), vol. I, p. 48.

44 E. Tremp *et al.*, *Eremus und Insula: St Gallen und die Reichenau im Mittelalter* (St Gall: Verlag am Klosterhof, 2002), p. 89.
45 A. Harting-Correâ (ed.), *Walafrid Strabo's Libellus de Exordiis et Incrementis* (Leiden: Brill, 1996), p. 160; PL 114, col. 954.
46 Text in Raby, *Medieval Latin Verse*, p. 102.
47 C. Page, *The Christian West and its Singers* (Yale: Yale University Press, 2010), p. 196.
48 Bede, *Historia Ecclesiastica Gentis Anglorum*, iv.24.
49 L. Sherley-Price (trans.), *Bede, A History of the English Church and People* (Harmondsworth: Penguin Classics, 1955), p. 245.
50 PL 114, col. 932.
51 Jungmann, *Christian Prayer through the Centuries*, p. 54.

Notes to Chapter 4

1 Tremp *et al.*, *Eremus und Insula*, pp. 28–31; a facsimile of the plan is on the front cover.
2 *Ibid.*, pp. 71–2.
3 Raby, *A History of Christian-Latin Poetry*, p. 211.
4 Text of Preface: W. von den Steinen, *Notkeri Poetae Liber Ymnorum* (Bern: Francke Verlag, 1960), p. 6; translation: Crocker, *The Early Medieval Sequence*, p. 1.
5 W. von den Steinen, *Notker der Dichter und seine geistige Welt* (Bern: Francke Verlag, 1948), vol. II, p. 162.
6 von den Steinen, *Notkeri Poetae Liber Ymnorum*, p. 36.
7 A. Farrer, *The Revelation of St John the Divine* (Oxford: Clarendon Press, 1964), p. 43.
8 Percy Dearmer's translation is in *English Hymnal*, no. 95; Raby, *A History of Christian-Latin Poetry*, p. 90.
9 Raby, *A History of Christian-Latin Poetry*, pp. 179 and 211.
10 Crocker, *The Early Medieval Sequence*, p. 29.
11 M. R. James, *The Apocryphal New Testament* (Oxford: Clarendon Press, 1924), pp. 117–23.
12 Crocker, *The Early Medieval Sequence*, p. 40.
13 von den Steinen, *Notker der Dichter*, vol. II, p. 85.
14 D. Norberg, *Manuel pratique de latin médiévale* (Paris: Picard, 1968), p. 60.
15 Henderson, *Missale Ecclesiae Eboracensis*, vol. I, p. 11.
16 Text and music in von den Steinen, *Notkeri Poetae Liber Ymnorum*, p. 93.
17 Crocker, *The Early Medieval Sequence*, p. 345.
18 Hughes, *Anglo-French Sequelae*, p. 52; J. Legg, *The Sarum Missal* (Oxford: Clarendon Press, 1916), p. 203.
19 von den Steinen, *Notker der Dichter*, vol. II, p. 405.
20 von den Steinen, *Notkeri Poetae Liber Ymnorum*, p. 10.
21 Hiley, *Western Plainchant*, p. 528.
22 Lechner and Eisenhofer, *The Liturgy of the Roman Rite*, p. 301.

Notes to Chapter 4

23 A. Farrer, *Lord I Believe* (London: SPCK, 1962), p. 9.
24 Text: von den Steinen, *Notkeri Poetae Liber Ymnorum*, p. 14; melody: Crocker, *The Early Medieval Sequence*, p. 148.
25 James, *The Apocryphal New Testament*, pp. 228–9 and 262–4.
26 Hughes, *Anglo-French Sequelae*, p. 70.
27 Text: von den Steinen, *Notkeri Poetae Liber Ymnorum*, p. 20; melody: Crocker, *The Early Medieval Sequence*, p. 308.
28 Lechner and Eisenhofer, *The Liturgy of the Roman Rite*, p. 226.
29 Text: von den Steinen, *Notkeri Poetae Liber Ymnorum*, p. 22; melody: Crocker, *The Early Medieval Sequence*, p. 228.
30 Text: von den Steinen, *Notkeri Poetae Liber Ymnorum*, p. 24.
31 Text: *Ibid.*, p. 26; melody: Crocker, *The Early Medieval Sequence*, p. 106.
32 Crocker, *The Early Medieval Sequence*, p. 108.
33 *New English Hymnal*, no. 109.
34 L. Gautier, *Histoire de la poésie liturgique au moyen âge* (Paris: Palmé & Picard, 1886; republished Ridgewood, New Jersey: Gregg Press, 1966), pp. 28 and 200.
35 Hughes, *Anglo-French Sequelae*, p. 130.
36 Cattin, *Music in the Middle Ages*, vol. I, p. 104.
37 Text: von den Steinen, *Notkeri Poetae Liber Ymnorum*, p. 32.
38 *New English Hymnal*, no. 101, verse 7.
39 *Ibid.*, verse 1.
40 von den Steinen, *Notkeri Poetae Liber Ymnorum*, p. 32.
41 Farrer, *The Revelation of St John the Divine*, p. 105.
42 E. Yarnold, *The Awe-inspiring Rites of Initiation* (Slough: St Paul Publications, 1971), p. 124.
43 von den Steinen, *Notkeri Poetae Liber Ymnorum*, p. 38.
44 *Ibid.*, p. 44.
45 *New English Hymnal*, no. 291.
46 von den Steinen, *Notkeri Poetae Liber Ymnorum*, p. 46.
47 *Ibid.*, p. 50.
48 Text and melody: *ibid.*, p. 90.
49 Hughes, *Anglo-French Sequelae*, p. 32.
50 Crocker, *The Early Medieval Sequence*, pp. 189–203.
51 Text: Raby, *Medieval Latin Verse*, p. 10; translation: *English Hymnal*, no. 52.
52 Text: Raby, *Medieval Latin Verse*, p. 116; verse translation: *English Hymnal*, no. 154.
53 Raby, *Medieval Latin Verse*, p. 468.
54 E. Stommel, *Studien zur Epiklese der römischen Taufwasserweihe*, Theophaneia 5 (Bonn: Peter Hanstein Verlag, 1950), pp. 13 and 108.
55 J. Tolhurst (ed.), *The Ordinale and Customary of Barking Abbey*, Henry Bradshaw Society 65 (London: Henry Bradshaw Society, 1927), p. 135.
56 von den Steinen, *Notkeri Poetae Liber Ymnorum*, p. 58.
57 R. Davies, *Medieval English Lyrics* (London: Faber, 1963), p. 157.

58 W. Ryan (trans.), *Jacobus de Voragine: The Golden Legend* (Princeton: Princeton University Press, 1993), vol. II, p. 67.
59 Text: von den Steinen, *Notkeri Poetae Liber Ymnorum*, p. 62.
60 *Ibid.*, p. 88.
61 P. Dronke, *The Medieval Lyric* (London: Hutchinson, 1968), pp. 43–4.
62 *Ibid.*, p. 41.

Notes to Chapter 5

1 Raby, *A History of Christian-Latin Poetry*, p. 151.
2 Hiley, *Western Plainchant*, p. 581.
3 W. Frere (ed.), *The Winchester Troper* (London: Henry Bradshaw Society, 1894).
4 Henderson, *Missale Ecclesiae Eboracensis*, vol. II, pp. 283–318.
5 Text: *ibid.*, p. 291; the melody is in Hughes, *Anglo-French Sequelae*, p. 31.
6 von den Steinen, *Notker der Dichter*, vol. II, p. 85; J. Szörvérffy, *Annalen der lateinischen Hymnendichtung* (Berlin: Erich Schmidt Verlag, 1964), vol. I, pp. 324–6.
7 Text: Henderson, *Missale Ecclesiae Eboracensis*, vol. II, p. 291; melody: Hughes, *Anglo-French Sequelae*, p. 48.
8 Text: *ibid.*, vol. II, p. 300; melody: *Ibid.*, pp. 53–4.
9 *New English Hymnal*, no. 1, verse 3.
10 *Ibid.*, no. 503.
11 Thornton, *English Spirituality*, p. 103.
12 Henderson, *Missale Ecclesiae Eboracensis*, vol. II, p. 309.
13 *Ibid.*, p. 306.
14 *English Hymnal*, no. 125, verse 2.
15 Text and melody: Hughes, *Anglo-French Sequelae*, pp. 80–91.
16 *Ibid.*, pp. 77–121.
17 Frere, *The Winchester Troper*, p. 28.
18 *Ibid.*, p. 24.
19 Hiley, *Western Plainchant*, pp. 581–2.
20 Text: Raby, *Medieval Latin Verse*, p. 184; translation: *New English Hymnal*, no. 519.

Notes to Chapter 6

1 G. Evans (ed.), *The Medieval Theologians* (Oxford: Blackwell, 2001), pp. 104–14.
2 *Ibid.*, pp. 129–46.
3 Thornton, *English Spirituality*, pp. 106–18.
4 Hiley, *Western Plainchant*, p. 611.
5 Raby, *A History of Christian-Latin Poetry*, p. 321; PL 178, col. 379.
6 *New English Hymnal*, no. 432.
7 Texts: Raby, *A History of Christian-Latin Poetry*, pp. 321–6; PL 178, cols 1771–1816.

Notes to Chapter 6

8   J. Kehrein, *Lateinische Sequenzen des Mittelalters* (Mainz: Florian Kupferberg, 1873; republished Hildesheim: Georg Olms Verlag, 1969), p. 158; Legg, *The Sarum Missal*, p. 527; Henderson, *Missale Ecclesiae Eboracensis*, vol. II, p. 206; Arlt and Björkvall, *Recherches nouvelles*, p. 417.
9   M. Fassler, *Gothic Song* (Cambridge: Cambridge University Press, 1993), p. 89; A. Robertson, *The Service Books of the Royal Abbey of Saint-Denis* (Oxford: Clarendon Press, 1991), pp. 176–8.
10 Text: Raby, *Medieval Latin Verse*, pp. 204–8.
11 *New English Hymnal*, no. 517.
12 Raby, *A History of Christian-Latin Poetry*, pp. 88–95.
13 E. Lillie and N. Petersen (eds.), *Liturgy and the Arts in the Middle Ages* (Copenhagen: Museum Tusculanum Press, 1996), p. 119.
14 A. Wilmart, *Auteurs spirituels et textes dévots du moyen âge latin* (Paris: Bloud & Gay, 1932), p. 166.
15 E. Duffy, *The Stripping of the Altars* (New Haven: Yale University Press, 1992), pp. 266–76; B. Nichols and A. Macgregor, *Deliver Us from Evil* (Durham: Ushaw College, 2003), vol. II, p. 51.
16 E. Dewick, 'Consecration crosses and the ritual connected with them', *Archaeological Journal* 65 (1908).
17 Fassler, *Gothic Song*, p. 235.
18 J. Kelly, *Early Christian Doctrines* (London: Adam and Charles Black, Fourth Edition, 1968), p. 69; J. Barton, *A History of the Bible* (London: Allen Lane, 2019), pp. 363–70.
19 *New English Hymnal*, no. 521.
20 Fassler, *Gothic Song*, pp. 310 and 431.
21 H. White (ed.), *Ancrene Wisse: Guide for Anchoresses* (Harmondsworth: Penguin Classics, 1993), pp. 10–11 and 18.
22 Legg, *The Sarum Missal*, pp. 265 and 321.
23 Text: Raby, *Medieval Latin Verse*, pp. 234–7.
24 Evans, *The Medieval Theologians*, pp. 142–4; Raby, *A History of Christian-Latin Poetry*, pp. 355–63.
25 R. Barber, *Bestiary* (Woodbridge: Boydell Press, 1999), pp. 24–5.
26 The best-known version of 'Ye choirs of New Jerusalem' is that of Robert Campbell in *New English Hymnal*, no. 124; J. M. Neale's more literal translation is in *English Hymnal*, no. 122, and the Latin text is in Raby, *A History of Christian-Latin Poetry*, p. 263.
27 *New English Hymnal*, no. 519.
28 Legg, *The Sarum Missal*, p. 138, n. 6; Henderson, *Missale Ecclesiae Eboracensis*, vol. I, p. 133.
29 Text: Kehrein, *Lateinische Sequenzen des Mittelalters*, p. 110.
30 Legg, *The Sarum Missal*, p. 162.
31 *Ibid.*, pp. 125 and 129; Henderson, *Missale Ecclesiae Eboracensis*, vol. I, p. 122.
32 Fassler, *Gothic Song*, p. 158; Hughes, *Anglo-French Sequelae*, p. 131; Henderson, *Missale Ecclesiae Eboracensis*, pp. 157 and 159.
33 Text: Kehrein, *Lateinische Sequenzen des Mittelalters*, p. 112.
34 Fassler, *Gothic Song*, pp. 277–8.

35 Robertson, *The Service Books of the Royal Abbey of Saint-Denis*, p. 247; Leclercq, *The Love of Learning and the Desire for God*, p. 249.
36 Fassler, *Gothic Song*, p. 158; Kehrein, *Lateinische Sequenzen des Mittelalters*, p. 112.
37 Text: Kehrein, *Lateinische Sequenzen des Mittelalters*, p. 305.
38 Paris, Arsenal 135.
39 Fassler, *Gothic Song*, p. 159; Legg, *The Sarum Missal*, p. 337, n. 1; Henderson, *Missale Ecclesiae Eboracensis*, vol. II, p. 116.
40 C. Kirchberger, *Richard of St Victor, Selected Writings on Contemplation* (London: Faber, 1957), p. 50, n.1 and pp. 198–9.

Notes to Chapter 7

1 W. Berschin and H. Schipperges, *Hildegard von Bingen, Symphonia* (Gerlingen: Verlag Lambert Schneider, 1995), p. 16, plate II.
2 *Ibid.*, p. 218; L. Menzies, *Mirrors of the Holy* (London: Mowbrays, 1928), p. 6.
3 Dronke, *The Medieval Lyric*, pp. 233–5.
4 Text: Berschin and Schipperges, *Hildegard von Bingen, Symphonia*, p. 134.
5 *Ibid.*, p. 230.
6 Text: *ibid.*, p. 150.
7 Text: *ibid.*, p. 180.
8 *New English Hymnal*, no. 79.
9 *Ibid.*, no. 204.
10 Text: Berschin and Schipperges, *Hildegard von Bingen, Symphonia*, p. 186.
11 *Ibid.*, pp. 222–3.
12 Dronke, *The Medieval Lyric*, p. 78.
13 Berschin and Schipperges, *Hildegard von Bingen, Symphonia*, p. 221.
14 A. Clark, *Elisabeth of Schönau* (New York: Paulist Press, 2000), p. 2.
15 *Ibid.*, pp. 111 and 289; P. Schmitz, *Histoire de l'Ordre de St Bénoît* (Maredsous: Éditions de Maredsous, 1956), vol. VII, p. 287.
16 Clark, *Elisabeth of Schönau*, p. 201.
17 Text: F. Roth, *Die Visionen und Briefe der heiligen Elisabeth* (Brünn: Hutter, 1886), p. 7.
18 C. Wolters (ed.), *Revelations of Divine Love* (Harmondsworth: Penguin Classics, 1966), p. 65.
19 Clark, *Elisabeth of Schönau*, p. 280 n. 57; R. Stroppel, *Liturgie und geistliche Dichtung zwischen 1050 und 1300* (Frankfurt: 1927; republished Hildesheim: Georg Olms Verlag, 1973), pp. 136–7; the text of the sequence is in Kehrein, *Lateinische Sequenzen des Mittelalters*), p. 196.
20 Text: Roth, *Die Visionen und Briefe der heiligen Elisabeth*, p. 9.
21 Clark, *Elisabeth of Schönau*, p. 76.
22 Text: Roth, *Die Visionen und Briefe der heiligen Elisabeth*, p. 26.
23 *Ibid.*, p. 12.
24 *Ibid.*, p. 15.
25 Text: *Ibid.*, p. 23.

Notes to Chapter 8

26 Text: *Ibid.*, p. 19.
27 Clark, *Elisabeth of Schönau*, pp. 21–2.
28 Roth, *Die Visionen und Briefe der heiligen Elisabeth*, p. xv.
29 Text: Kehrein, *Lateinische Sequenzen des Mittelalters*, p. 536.

Notes to Chapter 8

1 See the chapter on 'The Vernacular' in McKitterick, *The Frankish Church and the Carolingian Reforms 789–895*.
2 Duffy, *The Stripping of the Altars*, p. 124.
3 J. Bryant and V. Hunter, *How Thow Schalt Thy Paresche Preche* (Barton-on-Humber: Workers' Educational Association, 1999), p. 58, line 290; Duffy, *The Stripping of the Altars*, p. 117.
4 N. Orme, *Going to Church in Medieval England* (New Haven: Yale University Press, 2021), p. 259.
5 Legg, *The Sarum Missal*, p. 248.
6 Ryan, *Jacobus de Voragine: The Golden Legend*, vol. I, p. 150.
7 It is illustrated in Duffy, *The Stripping of the Altars*, Plate 1.
8 W. Butler-Bowden (ed.), *The Book of Margery Kempe* (Oxford: Oxford University Press, 1954), pp. 260–1.
9 Duffy, *The Stripping of the Altars*, p. 20.
10 Legg, *The Sarum Missal*, p. 51.
11 J. Dalton (ed.), *Ordinale Exoniense* (London: Henry Bradshaw Society, 1909), vol. I, p. 116; L. McClachlan (ed.), *The Ordinale of St Mary's Abbey, York* (London: Henry Bradshaw Society, 1934), vol. II, p. 245.
12 Text: Legg, *The Sarum Missal*, p. 93.
13 D. Knowles (ed.), *The Monastic Constitutions of Lanfranc* (London: Nelson, 1951), p. 152.
14 Text: Legg, *The Sarum Missal*, p. 95.
15 *New English Hymnal*, no. 509.
16 Raby, *A History of Christian-Latin Poetry*, pp. 174–5; Knowles, *The Monastic Constitutions of Lanfranc*, p. 25; P. Baxter, *Sarum Use* (Reading: Spire Books Ltd., 2008), pp. 72–3.
17 Text: Legg, *The Sarum Missal*, p. 96.
18 Tolhurst, *The Ordinale and Customary of Barking Abbey*, p. 90; R. Pfaff, *Liturgical Calendars, Saints, and Services in Medieval England* (Aldershot: Routledge, 1998), V, p. 88.
19 R. Woolley, *The Gilbertine Rite* (London: Henry Bradshaw Society, 1921), p. 30; Legg, *The Sarum Missal*, p. 101 n.6.
20 McClachlan, *The Ordinale of St Mary's Abbey, York*, vol. II, p. 270; Knowles, *The Monastic Constitutions of Lanfranc*, p. 27.
21 Text: Legg, *The Sarum Missal*, p. 105. Richard Rutt's fine paraphrase of this hymn is at *New English Hymnal*, no. 512.
22 Henderson, *Missale Ecclesiae Eboracensis*, vol. I, p. 101.
23 Text: Raby, *Medieval Latin Verse*, p. 102. More translated verses are in Blakesley, *A Garland of Faith*, p. 199.

24. Woolley, *The Gilbertine Rite*, pp. 33 and 35.
25. Legg, *The Sarum Missal*, p. 110 n. 1.
26. *New English Hymnal*, nos. 516 and 517.
27. Butler-Bowden, *The Book of Margery Kempe*, p. 183.
28. McClachlan, *The Ordinale of St Mary's Abbey, York*, vol. II, p. 292.
29. Legg, *The Sarum Missal*, p. 117.
30. A. Macgregor, *Fire and Light in the Western Triduum* (Collegeville: Alcuin Club, 1992), p. 260.
31. Woolley, *The Gilbertine Rite*, p. 39.
32. R. Austin, *The Rites of Durham* (Durham: no date), p. 8; Macgregor, *Fire and Light*, p. 265; McClachlan, *The Ordinale of St Mary's Abbey, York*, vol. II, p. 293.
33. Text: Legg, *The Sarum Missal*, p. 129.
34. Stommel, *Studien zur Epiklese*, p. 13.
35. Baxter, *Sarum Use*, p. 68; Legg, *The Sarum Missal*, p. 129.
36. Stommel, *Studien zur Epiklese*, p. 45.
37. Henderson, *Missale Ecclesiae Eboracensis*, vol. I, p. 122.
38. McClachlan, *The Ordinale of St Mary's Abbey, York*, vol. II, p. 294.
39. *Ibid.*, p. 298.
40. Tolhurst, *The Ordinale and Customary of Barking Abbey*, p. 107.
41. *New English Hymnal*, no. 109.
42. McClachlan, *The Ordinale of St Mary's Abbey, York*, vol. II, p. 300.
43. Legg, *The Sarum Missal*, p. 11; Baxter, *Sarum Use*, pp. 69–73.
44. McClachlan, *The Ordinale of St Mary's Abbey, York*, vol. II, p. 318.
45. *New English Hymnal*, no. 124; Legg, *The Sarum Missal*, pp. 150 and 153 n. 1; Dalton, *Ordinale Exoniense*, vol. I, pp. 327–8.
46. Woolley, *The Gilbertine Rite*, p. 50; McClachlan, *The Ordinale of St Mary's Abbey, York*, vol. II, p. 319.
47. Woolley, *The Gilbertine Rite*, p. 54.
48. *English Hymnal*, no. 154.
49. McClachlan, *The Ordinale of St Mary's Abbey, York*, vol. II, p. 332.
50. Tolhurst (ed.), *The Ordinale and Customary of Barking Abbey*, p. 135.
51. Yarnold, *The Awe-Inspiring Rites of Initiation*, pp. 227–8 and 245.
52. E. Ratcliffe (ed.), *Expositio Antiquae Liturgiae Gallicanae* (London: Henry Bradshaw Society, 1971).
53. J. Jungmann, *The Mass of the Roman Rite* (New York: Benzinger, 1951), vol. I, p. 89.
54. J. Stevens, *Words and Music in the Middle Ages* (Cambridge: Cambridge University Press, 1986), p. 316.
55. J. Braun, *Die liturgische Gewandung im Occident und Orient* (Freiburg: Herder, 1907), p. 711.
56. PL 217, col. 834.
57. Dix, *The Shape of the Liturgy*, p. 605; J. Legg, *Tracts on the Mass* (London: Henry Bradshaw Society, 1904), p. 19.
58. Braun, *Die liturgische Gewandung im Occident und Orient*, p. 727.

Notes to Chapter 9

1. MS Barlow 1.
2. London, BL Add. 24198.
3. Text: G. Dreves et al., *Analecta Hymnica Medii Aevi* (Leipzig: 55 vols., 1886–1922), vol. XL, pp. 33–4.
4. *New English Hymnal*, no. 291.
5. R. Pfaff, *New Liturgical Feasts in Later Medieval England* (Oxford: Clarendon Press, 1970), p. 84.
6. *New English Hymnal*, no. 521; the parallels between the Latin texts are set out in J. Blakesley, 'La sequence Plangat Syon', *Questions Liturgiques* 4 (Louvain: Abbaye du Mont César, 1973), pp. 295–300.
7. Raby, *A History of Christian-Latin Poetry*, p. 299; Davies, *Medieval English Lyrics*, p. 376.
8. Dronke, *The Medieval Lyric*, p. 65; H. Allen, *Richard Rolle, English Writings* (Oxford: Clarendon Press, 1931), pp. 68 and 148.
9. Song of Solomon 6:2 (Vulgate 6:1).
10. *English Hymnal*, no. 192.
11. A. Quiller-Couch, *The Oxford Book of English Verse* (Oxford: Clarendon Press, 1939), p. 39.
12. Text: Kehrein, *Lateinische Sequenzen des Mittelalters*, p. 180, verses 5–11.
13. Pfaff, *New Liturgical Feasts*, p. 98.
14. Text: Kehrein, *Lateinische Sequenzen des Mittelalters*, p. 181, verses 17–23.
15. Text: *ibid.*, pp. 181–2, verses 30–4.
16. Text: *ibid.*, p. 177.
17. *Ibid.*, p. 21, source 15.
18. Text: *ibid.*, p. 72, verses 3–4a.
19. Text: *ibid.*, p. 72, verse 2.
20. Oxford, Bodleian Library, MS Laud misc. 302; Pfaff, *New Liturgical Feasts*, p. 86.
21. Text: Kehrein, *Lateinische Sequenzen des Mittelalters*, p. 64, verses 13–15.
22. Text: Raby, *Medieval Latin Verse*, p. 245.
23. Legg, *The Sarum Missal*, p. 113.
24. St Gall, Codex Sangallensis 546.
25. *New English Hymnal*, no. 519, verses 4–7.
26. Text: Kehrein, *Lateinische Sequenzen des Mittelalters*, pp. 178–9.
27. Text: Raby, *Medieval Latin Verse*, p. 380; a translation by Laurence Housman is in *New English Hymnal*, no. 174.
28. Duffy, *The Stripping of the Altars*, p. 31.

Notes to Chapter 10

1. Henderson, *Missale Ecclesiae Eboracensis*, vol. II, p. 245.
2. *Missa Rex Splendens* (London: The Plainsong and Medieval Music Society, 1908), p. 3.

3 Hiley, *Western Plainchant*, p. 581.
4 Gerbert, *Scriptores Ecclesiastici de Musica Sacra*, vol. I, p. 234.
5 Leclercq, *The Love of Learning and the Desire for God*, p. 245.
6 Text: Legg, *The Sarum Missal*, p. 462.
7 PL 195, col. 109.
8 It dates from about 1225; there is a translation in P. Matarasso, *The Quest of the Holy Grail* (London: Penguin Books, 1969).
9 T. Heffernan and E. Matter (eds.), *The Liturgy of the Medieval Church* (Kalamazoo: Western Michigan University, 2001), p. 579.
10 R. Wood, *Romanesque Yorkshire* (Leeds: Yorkshire Archaeological Society, Occasional Paper No. 9, 2012), pp. 13–14.
11 See Chapter 3; the translated text is in Bradshaw and Johnson, *The Eucharistic Liturgies*, pp. 206–9.
12 Legg, *The Sarum Missal*, pp. 203 and 473.
13 Raby, *Medieval Latin Verse*, p. 462 n. 63.
14 Kehrein, *Lateinische Sequenzen des Mittelalters*, p. 582, verses 5–7.
15 Text: Raby, *Medieval Latin Verse*, p. 83.
16 Text: Henderson, *Missale Ecclesiae Eboracensis*, vol. I, pp. 257–8.
17 Text: J. Stevens, *The Later Cambridge Songs* (Oxford: Oxford University Press, 2005), pp. 84–5.
18 *Ibid.*, pp. 32, 35, and 85.
19 Oxford, Bodleian Library, MS Rawl. liturg. b. 1, fol. 195.v
20 Bede, iv.23; Sherley-Price, *Bede, A History of the English Church and People*, p. 241.
21 B. Ward, *High King of Heaven* (London: Mowbray, 1999), pp. 20–1.
22 Text: Oxford: Bodleian Library, MS Rawl. liturg. b. 1, fol. 198.v
23 Braun, *Die liturgische Gewandung im Occident und Orient*, p. 732.
24 A. Macgregor, 'Candlemas – A Roman Festival? II, Rome', *Ushaw Library Bulletin and Liturgical Review* 8, April 1999 (Durham: Ushaw College, 1999), p. 3.
25 M. Andrieu, *Les Ordines Romani du haut moyen âge* (Louvain: Spicilegium Sacrum Lovaniense, 1951), vol. III, pp. 236 and 247.
26 P. Johnstone, *High Fashion in the Church* (Leeds: Maney, 2002), p. 21.
27 J. Legg, *Essays Liturgical and Historical* (London: SPCK, 1917), p. 157; W. Hope and E. Atchley, *English Liturgical Colours* (London: SPCK, 1918), p. 147.
28 PL 217, cols. 799–802.
29 *Ibid.*, col. 783; J. Blakesley, 'Colours of Day(s)', *In illo tempore* 16, June 2001 (Durham: Ushaw College, 2001), pp. 16 and 30.
30 Magnificat antiphon at Second Vespers of Corpus Christi.

BIBLIOGRAPHY

Allen, H. E., *Richard Rolle, English Writings* (Oxford: Clarendon Press,1931)
Andrieu, M., *Les 'Ordines Romani' du Haut Moyen Âge* (Louvain: Spicilegium Sacrum Lovaniense, 1951)
Arlt, W., and G. Björkvall (eds.), *Recherches nouvelles sur les tropes liturgiques*. Corpus Troporum (Stockholm: Almqvist & Wiksell, 1993)
Austin, R. W., *The Rites of Durham* (Durham, no date)
Bailey, T., and A. Santosuosso (eds.), *Music in Medieval Europe* (Aldershot: Ashgate, 2007)
Bannister, H. M. (ed.), *Missale Gothicum*, vol. I (London: Henry Bradshaw Society, 1917)
Barber, R., *Bestiary* (Woodbridge: Boydell Press, 1999)
Barton, J., *A History of the Bible* (London: Allen Lane, 2019)
Baxter, P., *Sarum Use* (Reading: Spire Books Ltd., 2008)
Berschin, W., and H. Schipperges, *Hildegard von Bingen, Symphonia* (Gerlingen: Verlag Lambert Schneider, 1995)
Bishop, E., *Liturgica Historica* (Oxford: Oxford University Press, 1918)
Blakesley, J., *A Garland of Faith* (Leominster: Gracewing, 1998)
Blakesley, J., 'La sequence *Plangat Syon*', *Questions liturgiques* 4 (Louvain: Abbaye du Mont César, 1973)
Blakesley, J., 'Colours of day(s)', *In illo tempore* 16, June 2001 (Durham: Ushaw College, 2001)
Boone, G. M. (ed.), *Essays on Medieval Music in Honor of David Hughes* (Cambridge, Mass.: Harvard University Department of Music, 1995)
Bradshaw, P. F., and M. E. Johnson, *The Eucharistic Liturgies* (London: SPCK, 2012)
Braun, J., *Die liturgische Gewandung im Occident und Orient* (Freiburg-im-Breisgau: Herder, 1907)
Bryant, G. F., and V. M. Hunter, *'How Thow Schalt Thy Paresche Preche'* (Barton-on-Humber: Workers' Educational Association, 1999)
Butler-Bowden, W. (ed.), *The Book of Margery Kempe* (Oxford: Oxford University Press, 1954)
Cattin, G., *Music of the Middle Ages*, vol. I (Cambridge: Cambridge University Press, 1984)
Cawley, A. C. (ed.), *Everyman and Medieval Miracle Plays* (London: J. M. Dent, 1956)
Chadwick, H. (ed.), *St Ambrose on the Sacraments* (London: A. R. Mowbray, 1960)
Clark, A. L., *Elisabeth of Schönau* (New York: Paulist Press, 2000)
Crocker, R. L., *The Early Medieval Sequence* (Berkeley: University of California Press, 1977)

Dalton, J. N. (ed.), *Ordinale Exoniense* (London: Henry Bradshaw Society, 1909)
Davies, R. T., *Medieval English Lyrics* (London: Faber, 1963; new edition, 1968)
Dewick, E. S., 'Consecration crosses and the ritual connected with them', *Archaeological Journal* 65 (1908)
Dickinson, F. H. (ed.), *Missale ad Usum Insignis et Praeclarae Ecclesiae Sarum* (Burntisland: E prelo de Pitsligo,1861–83)
Dix, G. *The Shape of the Liturgy* (London: Dacre Press, 1945; new edition, 2005)
Dreves, G. M., C. Blume, and H. M. Bannister (eds.), *Analecta Hymnica Medii Aevi*, 55 vols. (Leipzig: 1886–1922)
Dronke, C. P. M., *The Medieval Lyric* (London: Hutchinson, 1968;)
Duffy, E., *The Stripping of the Altars* (New Haven: Yale University Press, 1992)
Evans, G. R. (ed.), *The Medieval Theologians* (Oxford: Blackwell, 2001)
Evans, P., *The Early Trope Repertory of Saint Martial de Limoges* (Princeton: Princeton University Press, 1970)
Farrer, A. M., *The Glass of Vision* (London: Dacre Press, 1948)
Farrer, A. M., *The Crown of the Year* (London: Dacre Press, 1952)
Farrer, A. M., *Lord I Believe* (London: SPCK, 1962)
Farrer, A. M., *The Revelation of St John the Divine* (Oxford: Oxford University Press, 1964)
Farrer, A. M., *A Celebration of Faith* (ed. Leslie Houlden, London: Hodder & Stoughton, 1970)
Farrer, A. M., *Interpretation and Belief* (ed. Charles Conti, London: SPCK, 1976)
Fassler, M., *Gothic Song* (Cambridge: Cambridge University Press, 1993)
Frere, W. H., *The Winchester Troper* (London: Henry Bradshaw Society, 1894)
Gautier, L., *Histoire de la poésie liturgique au moyen âge: les tropes* (Paris: Palmé & Picard, 1886; republished Ridgewood, New Jersey: Gregg Press, 1966)
Gerbert, M., *Scriptores Ecclesiastici de Musica Sacra* (St Blasien: Typis Sanblasianis, 1784; republished Hildesheim: Georg Olms Verlag, 1990)
Hanssens, J.-M., *Amalarii Episcopi Opera Liturgica Omnia* (Rome: Studi e testi 13840, 1948–50)
Harman, A., *Man and his Music. Part 1: Mediaeval and Early Renaissance Music* (London: Barrie & Jenkins, 1962)
Harting-Correâ, A. (ed.), *Walafrid Strabo's Libellus de Exordiis et Incrementis* (Leiden: Brill, 1996)
Hefele, C. J., and H. Leclercq, *Histoire des Conciles* (Paris: Letouzey & Ane, vol. III, 1909; vol. IV, 1911)
Heffernan, T. J., and E. A. Matter (eds.), *The Liturgy of the Medieval Church* (Kalamazoo: Western Michigan University, 2001)
Henderson, W. G., *Missale ad Usum Insignis Ecclesiae Eboracensis*. Surtees Society 59–60 (London, 1874)
Hiley, D., *Western Plainchant: A Handbook* (Oxford: Clarendon Press, 1993)

Bibliography

Hope, W., and E. Atchley, *English Liturgical Colours* (London: SPCK, 1918)
Hughes, A., *Anglo-French Sequelae* (Burnham: Plainsong and Mediaeval Music Society, 1934; republished Farnborough: Gregg Press, 1966)
Iversen, G. (ed.), *Research on Tropes* (Stockholm: Almqvist & Wiksell, 1983)
Jacobsson, R. (ed.), *Pax et Sapientia: Studies in Text and Music of Liturgical Tropes and Sequences in Memory of Gordon Anderson.* Studia Latina Stockholmiensia 29 (Stockholm: Almqvist & Wiksell, 1986)
James, M. R., *The Apocryphal New Testament* (Oxford: Clarendon Press, 1924)
Johnstone, P., *High Fashion in the Church* (Leeds: Maney, 2002)
Jones, C., G. Wainwright, and E. Yarnold (eds.), *The Study of Liturgy* (London: SPCK, 1978; new edition 1992)
Jungmann, J. A., *The Mass of the Roman Rite* (New York: Benzinger, 1951)
Jungmann, J. A., *Christian Prayer through the Centuries.* Alcuin Club Collections 83, ed. Christopher Irvine (London: SPCK, 2007)
Kehrein, J., *Lateinische Sequenzen des Mittelalters* (Mainz: Florian Kupferberg, 1873; republished Hildesheim: Georg Olms Verlag, 1969)
Kelly, J. N. D., *Early Christian Doctrines*, 4th edn (London: Adam & Charles Black, 1968)
Kinghorn, A. M., *Mediaeval Drama* (London: Evans, 1968)
Kirchberger, C., *Richard of St Victor, Selected Writings on Contemplation* (London: Faber, 1957)
Knowles, D. (ed.), *The Monastic Constitutions of Lanfranc* (London: Nelson, 1951)
Lechner, J., and L. Eisenhofer, *The Liturgy of the Roman Rite* (Freiburg: Herder, 1961)
Leclercq, J., *The Love of Learning and the Desire for God* (New York: Fordham University Press, 1961)
Legg, J. W., *Tracts on the Mass* (London: Henry Bradshaw Society, 1904)
Legg, J. W., *The Sarum Missal* (Oxford: Clarendon Press, 1916)
Legg, J. W., *Essays Liturgical and Historical* (London: SPCK, 1917)
Lillie, E. L., and N. H. Petersen (eds.), *Liturgy and the Arts in the Middle Ages* (Copenhagen: Museum Tusculanum Press, 1996)
Macgregor, A., *Fire and Light in the Western Triduum* (Collegeville: Alcuin Club, 1992)
Macgregor, A., 'Candlemas – A Roman Festival? II Rome', *Ushaw Library Bulletin and Liturgical Review* 8, April 1999 (Durham: Ushaw College, 1999)
Matarasso, P., *The Quest of the Holy Grail* (London: Penguin Books, 1969)
McClachlan, L., Abbess of Stanbrook (ed.), *The Ordinale of St Mary's Abbey, York* (London: Henry Bradshaw Society, 1934)
McKitterick, R., *The Frankish Church and the Carolingian Reforms 789–895* (London: Royal Historical Society, 1977)
Menzies, L., *Mirrors of the Holy* (London: Mowbrays, 1928)
Migne, J.-P. (ed.), *Patrologiae Cursus Completus, Series Latina* (PL), 221 vols. (Paris: 1844–64)
Mohrmann, C., *Liturgical Latin* (London: Burns and Oates, 1959)

Nichols, B., and A. Macgregor, *Deliver Us from Evil* (Durham: Ushaw College, 2003)
Norberg, D., *Manuel pratique de latin médiévale* (Paris: Picard, 1968)
Orme, N., *Going to Church in Medieval England* (Newhaven and London: Yale University Press, 2021)
Page, C., *The Christian West and its Singers* (Yale: Yale University Press, 2010)
Pfaff, R. W., *New Liturgical Feasts in Later Medieval England* (Oxford: Clarendon Press, 1970)
Pfaff, R. W., *Liturgical Calendars, Saints, and Services in Medieval England* (Aldershot: Routledge, 1998)
Pfaff, R. W., *The Liturgy in Medieval England – A History* (Cambridge: Cambridge University Press, 2009)
Porter, W. S., *The Gallican Rite* (London: Mowbrays, 1958)
Quiller-Couch, A., *The Oxford Book of English Verse* (Oxford: Clarendon Press, new edition 1939)
Raby, F. J. E., *A History of Christian-Latin Poetry from the Beginnings to the Close of the Middle Ages* (Oxford: Clarendon Press, 1927; 2nd edn 1953)
Raby, F. J. E., *The Oxford Book of Medieval Latin Verse* (Oxford: Clarendon Press, 1959)
Ratcliffe, E. C. (ed.), *Expositio Antiquae Liturgiae Gallicanae* (London: Henry Bradshaw Society 98, 1971)
Robertson, A., and D. Stevens, *The Pelican History of Music. Volume 1: Ancient Forms to Polyphony* (Harmondsworth: Penguin Books, 1960)
Robertson, A. W., *The Service Books of the Royal Abbey of Saint-Denis* (Oxford: Clarendon Press, 1991)
Roth, F. W. E., *Die Visionen und Briefe der heiligen Elisabeth* (Brünn: Hutter, 1886)
Ryan, W. G. (trans.), *Jacobus de Voragine: The Golden Legend* (Princeton: Princeton University Press, 1993)
Schmitz, P., *Histoire de l'Ordre de St Bénoît* (Maredsous: Editions de Maredsous, 1956)
Sherley-Price, L. (trans.), *Bede, A History of the English Church and People* (Harmondsworth: Penguin Books, 1955)
Silagi, G. (ed.), *Liturgische Tropen* Münchener Beiträge zur Mediävistik und Renaissance-Forschung 36 (Munich: Arbeo-Gesellschaft 1985)
Steinen, W. von den, *Notker der Dichter und seine geistige Welt* (Bern: Francke Verlag, 1948)
Steinen, W. von den, *Notkeri Poetae Liber Ymnorum* (Bern: Francke Verlag, 1960)
Stevens, J., *Words and Music in the Middle Ages* (Cambridge: Cambridge University Press, 1986)
Stevens, J., *The Later Cambridge Songs* (Oxford: Oxford University Press, 2005)
Stommel, E., *Studien zur Epiklese der römischen Taufwasserweihe*. Theophaneia 5 (Bonn: Peter Hanstein Verlag, 1950)

Bibliography

Stroppel, R., *Liturgie und geistliche Dichtung zwischen 1050 und 1300* (Frankfurt: 1927; republished Hildesheim: Georg Olms Verlag, 1973)
Szörvérffy, J., *Annalen der lateinischen Hymnendichtung* (Berlin: Erich Schmidt Verlag, 1964–5)
Thornton, M., *English Spirituality* (London: SPCK, 1963)
Thorpe, L. (trans.), *Einhard and Notker the Stammerer: Two Lives of Charlemagne* (London: Penguin Books, 1969)
Tolhurst, J. (ed.), *The Ordinale and Customary of Barking Abbey.* Henry Bradshaw Society 65 (London: 1927)
Tremp, E., K. Schmuki, and T. Flury, *Eremus und Insula, St Gallen und die Reichenau im Mittelalter* (St Gall: Verlag am Klosterhof St Gallen, 2002)
Van Dijk, S., and J. Hazelden Walker, *The Origins of the Modern Roman Liturgy* (London: Darton, Longman & Todd, 1960)
Ward, B., *High King of Heaven* (London: Mowbray, 1999)
White, H. (ed.), *Ancrene Wisse: Guide for Anchoresses* (Harmondsworth: Penguin Books, 1993)
Wilmart, A., *Auteurs spirituels et textes dévots du moyen âge latin* (Paris: Bloud & Gay, 1932)
Wilson, A. N., *The Book of the People* (London: Atlantic Books, 2015)
Wolters, C. (ed.), *Julian of Norwich: Revelations of Divine Love* (Harmondsworth: Penguin Books, 1966)
Wood, R., *Romanesque Yorkshire*, Yorkshire Archaeological Society, Occasional Paper 9 (Leeds: Yorkshire Archaeological Society, 2012)
Woolley, R. M. (ed.), *The Gilbertine Rite*, Henry Bradshaw Society 59 (London, 1921)
Yarnold, E., *The Awe-Inspiring Rites of Initiation* (Slough: St Paul Publications, 1971)

www.ingramcontent.com/pod-product-compliance
Lightning Source LLC
Chambersburg PA
CBHW032255150426
43195CB00008BA/458